I0800498

IMAGES
of America

PAULSBORO

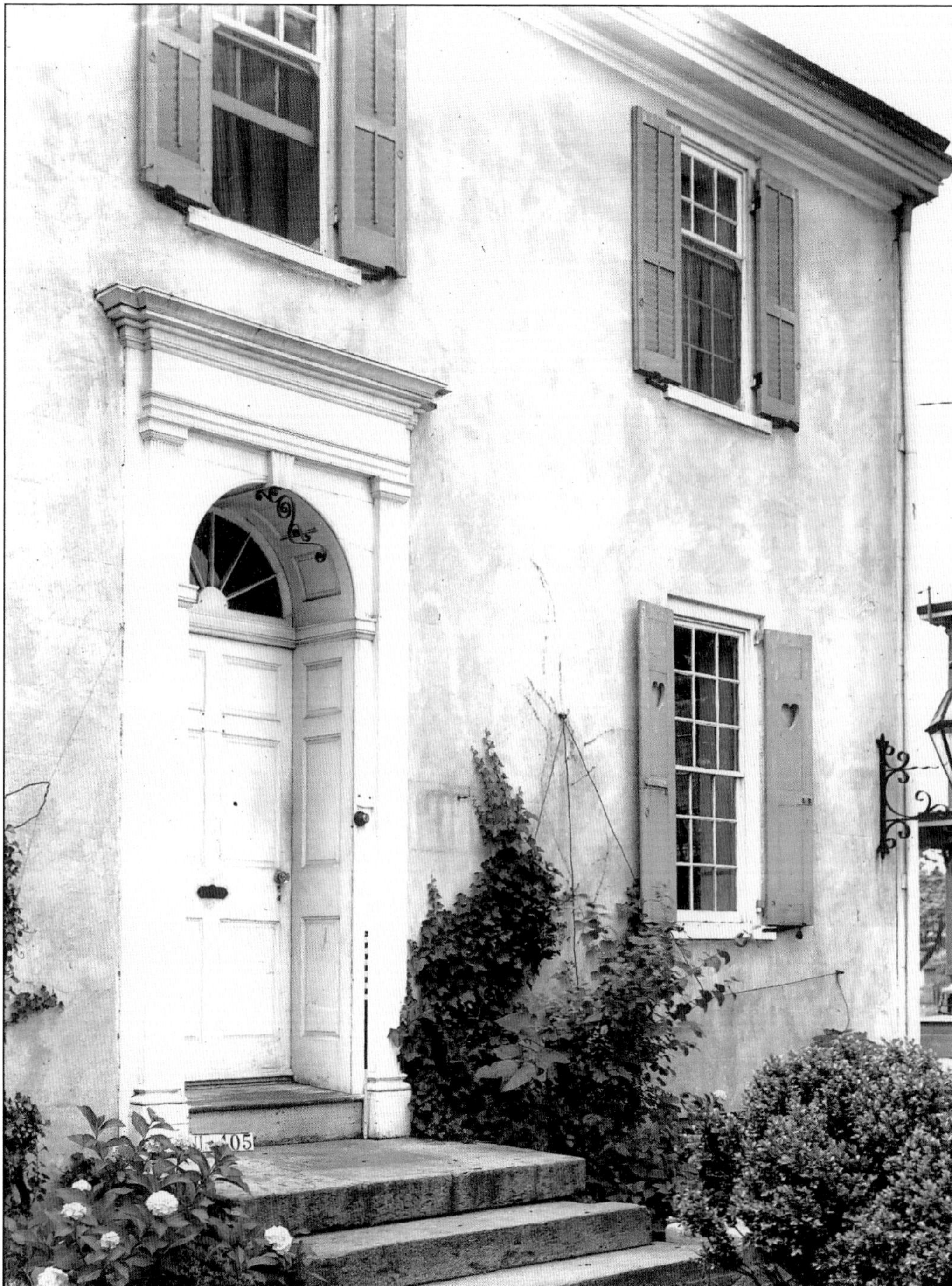

This is a front view of the Paul House, which was built in 1804 by architect John Clark. In 1806, Clark built the Matthew Gill House, which now houses the Gill Memorial Library. The Matthew Gill House and the Paul House are the two oldest buildings in Paulsboro.

IMAGES
of America

PAULSBORO

James R. Pratz and Violet J. Valentin

ARCADIA
PUBLISHING

ISBN 978-0-7385-3612-5

Published by Arcadia Publishing
Charleston, South Carolina

Printed in the United States of America

Library of Congress Catalog Card Number: 2004103890

For all general information, contact Arcadia Publishing:
Telephone 843-853-2070
Fax 843-853-0044
E-mail sales@arcadiapublishing.com
For customer service and orders:
Toll-free 1-888-313-2665

Visit us on the Internet at www.arcadiapublishing.com

On the cover: Buck Street School students pose for this photograph in the late 1800s.

Contents

ACKNOWLEDGMENTS

We want to thank the board of trustees of the Gill Memorial Library for its support of this endeavor. James Pratz would like to thank his wife, Mary, who helped organize and type the history in this book and also his daughter Michelle for her photography. Violet Valentin would like to thank her husband, Mike, for his many donations of postcards and memorabilia and her children, Christina, Lauren, and Anthony, and granddaughter Sierra for their support. We both want to thank our families for their understanding and patience with us for the time we spent away from them to dedicate hours on the research for this project. We both have a love of history and would like to dedicate this book to Jennie English, Theda Ashton, Clara Wilkerson Jones, Elizabeth Fish, and all the citizens from our community who shared our passion for history and helped collect the photographs in Gill Memorial Library collection that were used in this book. They all helped save Paulsboro's past for the generations to come.

INTRODUCTION

The borough of Paulsboro was officially incorporated in 1904, although the history of the area goes back to the Lenni Lenape Indians, who inhabited the area they called Crown Point. Paulsboro is named in honor of Philip Paul, one of the 250 colonists who came to America from England in 1685 and settled along the Mantua Creek.

Located on the Delaware River, the area now known as Paulsboro played an important role in the nation's fight during the Revolutionary War. George Washington was looking for locations to defend the Delaware River and prevent the British fleet from reaching Philadelphia. The council of safety of Philadelphia bought 96 acres from Margaret Paul on July 5, 1776, only one day after the adoption of the Declaration of Independence. The land was charged to the newly formed Congress, giving this land the distinction of being the first federal land purchase. Fort Billings was erected on this site in 1777 as part of the defense system in the Revolutionary War. Fort Billings was again briefly occupied by American troops during the War of 1812. In 1834, the land was passed back into private hands to John Ford and Joseph Gill.

The first schoolhouse was built in 1820 with Benjamin Lodge as the schoolmaster. By 1858, another school was built on Buck Street. Paulsboro High School opened in 1916 with only 17 rooms. In 1924, Billingsport School was built. Loudenslager School followed in 1926, replacing the old Buck Street School.

In 1825, the first religious meeting was held in the schoolhouse, and the Methodist church was built in 1838. This started the growth of many denominations that became a vital part of the community. Some of the early churches built in Paulsboro were the Presbyterian church in 1868, St. James Episcopal Church in 1873, the Methodist Episcopal church in 1892, the Taylor Memorial Baptist Church in 1898, St. John the Evangelist Roman Catholic Church in 1903, Second Baptist Church in 1906, and the Billingsport Methodist Church in 1925.

The first post office in town was opened in 1844, with Jacob Price serving as the first postmaster. The current post office was dedicated on November 24, 1939.

By the 1850s, the town had about 450 residents, most of whom were farmers and fisherman. The area was well known for its shad fishing, which thrived until waste from industry polluted the river.

The railroad came to town in 1876 and eventually became part of the Pennsylvania Railroad. The railroad spurred business and settlement, and the town grew.

The federal government decided *c.* 1880 that Billingsport would be a good location for a lighthouse. The town eventually had three lighthouses. All three are still used today, but they do not have houses or keepers.

Lincoln Park, situated on 28 acres along the river, formally opened on June 14, 1890. Built by Robert Patterson, it was an amusement park famous for its merry-go-round with brass ring. It also had a waterslide, stone observation tower, and musical shell that held a 60-piece orchestra and daily fireworks. It attracted a large crowd from Philadelphia who came to enjoy the swimming, picnics, and amusements. At the height of the park's popularity, 16 trains brought in passengers daily, along with two ferries and five steamboats. After 10 years of success, the franchise for dispensing liquor and beer was taken away, and the park closed shortly thereafter.

The Paulsboro Volunteer Fire Company was formed in 1899. The fire department moved into its current building in 1962. The Billingsport Volunteer Fire Company was formed in 1904 following a devastating blaze at the Billingsport Ferry Company. Both of these fire companies have served the community for over 100 years.

The public library was founded in 1901 and was housed at 26 West Broad Street, a private residence of Elizabeth Nolen. It moved to the borough hall on 28 East Broad Street in 1932 and moved to its existing home at Broad and Commerce Streets in 1954. The present-day library building was donated to the borough by Mary England Fish as a memorial to her mother, Sallie Jessup Gill, and her grandparents Matthew and Mary Jessup Gill.

In 1935, the current drawbridge over the Mantua Creek was built to handle the increased traffic. It replaced the original single-lane wooden bridge over the creek.

Also around this time, the famous All-Thompson Brothers baseball team was gaining fame. The team consisted of brothers, all of whom lived in town. They played teams all over the area and even played exhibition games at the Chicago World's Fair of 1933–1934.

The development of industry along the Delaware River helped to change Paulsboro from a fishing and agricultural community into an industrial town. Today, Paulsboro has a population of about 6,500 people. After a period of declining business and population in the 1970s and 1980s, the town is committed to revitalization. Many owners of businesses along Delaware and Broad Streets have upgraded their facades, and new businesses are being opened. There are numerous medical and dental offices, restaurants, fast-food places, and even a production theater. The Tinicum Rear Lighthouse has been restored and offers an open house and tours from April through October. This lighthouse has become is a major stop on the yearly tour of New Jersey lighthouses.

In the 21st century, Paulsboro anticipates the continued growth of business and industry, as well as the development of recreational facilities along the Delaware River. This growth will ultimately lead to an increase in demand for housing as Paulsboro once again becomes the sought-after location that the Paul family first inhabited.

This book is a journey through Paulsboro's long history, showing that although Paulsboro may not be a large town, its people make it a big community filled with Paulsboro pride.

One

Paulsboro's Golden Jubilee Celebration

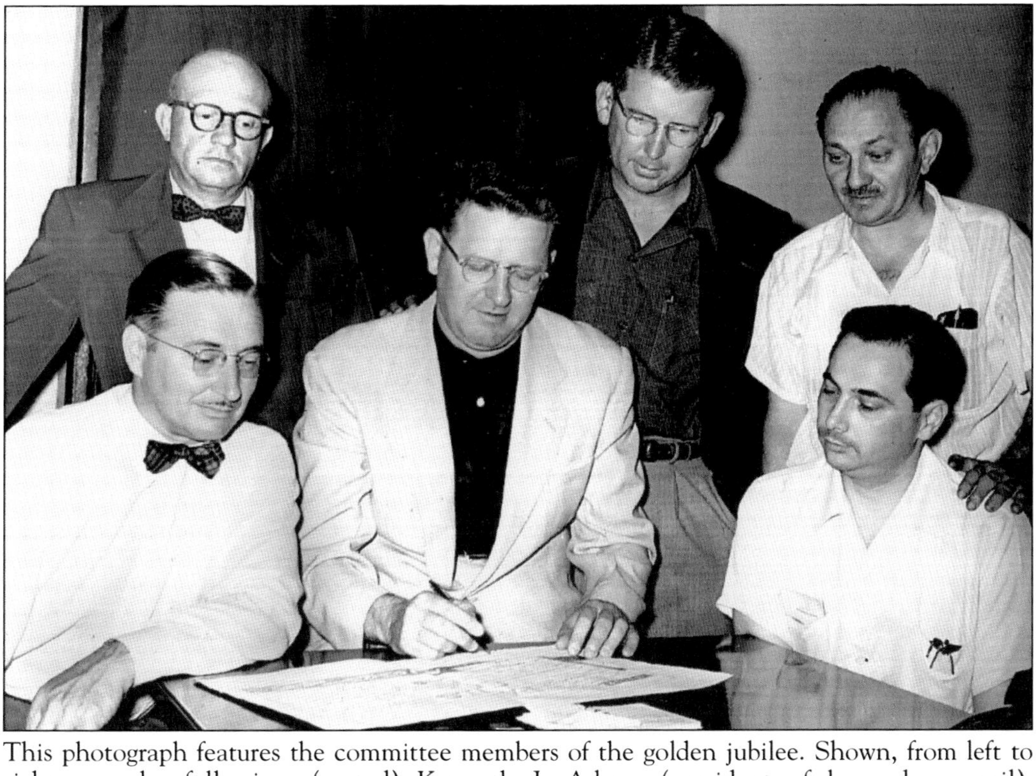

This photograph features the committee members of the golden jubilee. Shown, from left to right, are the following: (seated) Kenneth J. Adams (president of borough council), Samuel W. McCall (chairman of the committee), and Dave Rosen (representing the chamber of commerce); (standing) Russ Irwin Sr., Marvin Bonner, and Nick Isaac.

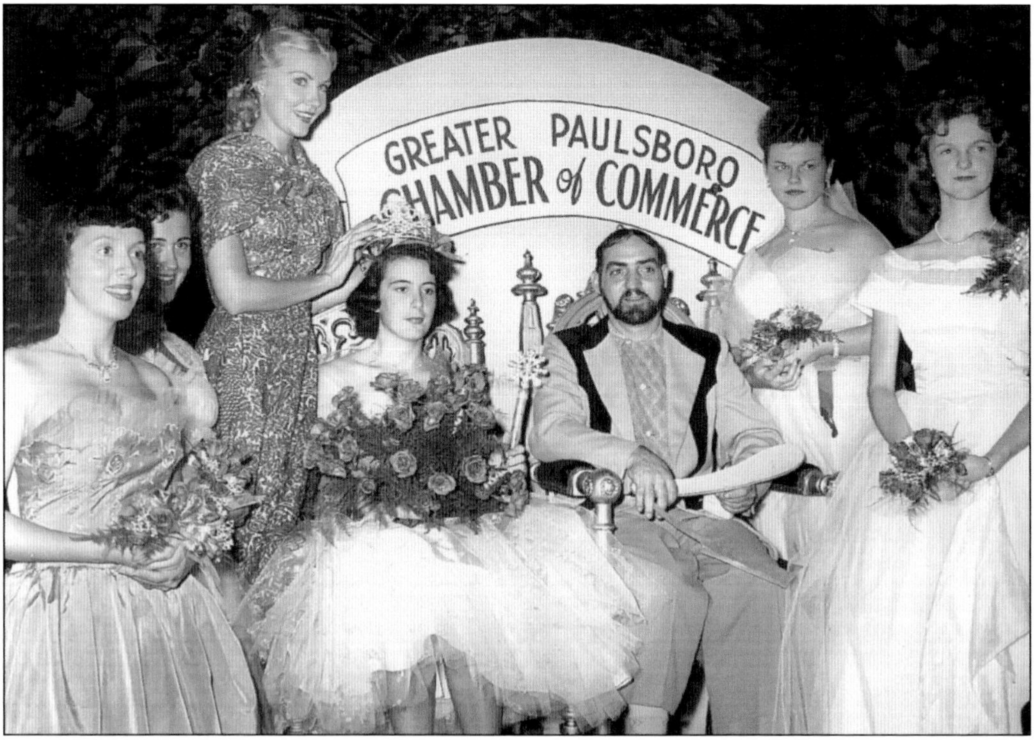

The crowning of the king and queen of the golden jubilee is captured in this photograph. Shown, from left to right, are Dolores Salvatore and Margaret Taylor (members of the court of honor), Jessica Paz (a John Robert Powers model of New York), Louise Oswald (the queen), Jack Fleming (the king), and Leane Hughes and Miriam Rickert (members of the court of honor).

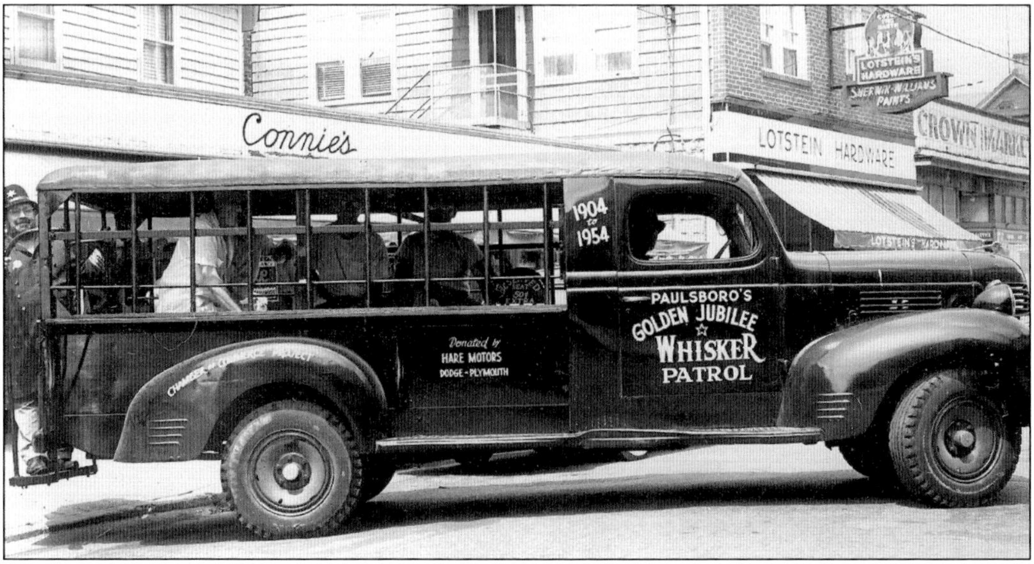

During the week of the golden jubilee celebration, any man who did not have whiskers was picked up and taken away in the Whisker Patrol paddy wagon to face the mock judge and pay a $1 fine.

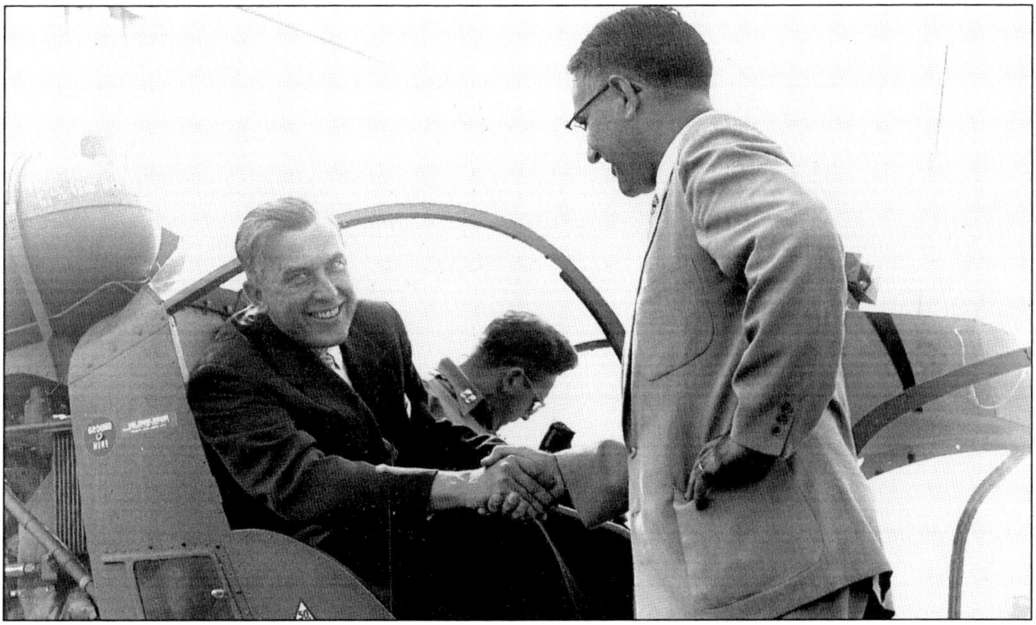

Governor Meyner arrived in a helicopter for Governor's Day and was greeted by acting mayor Joseph Mennite.

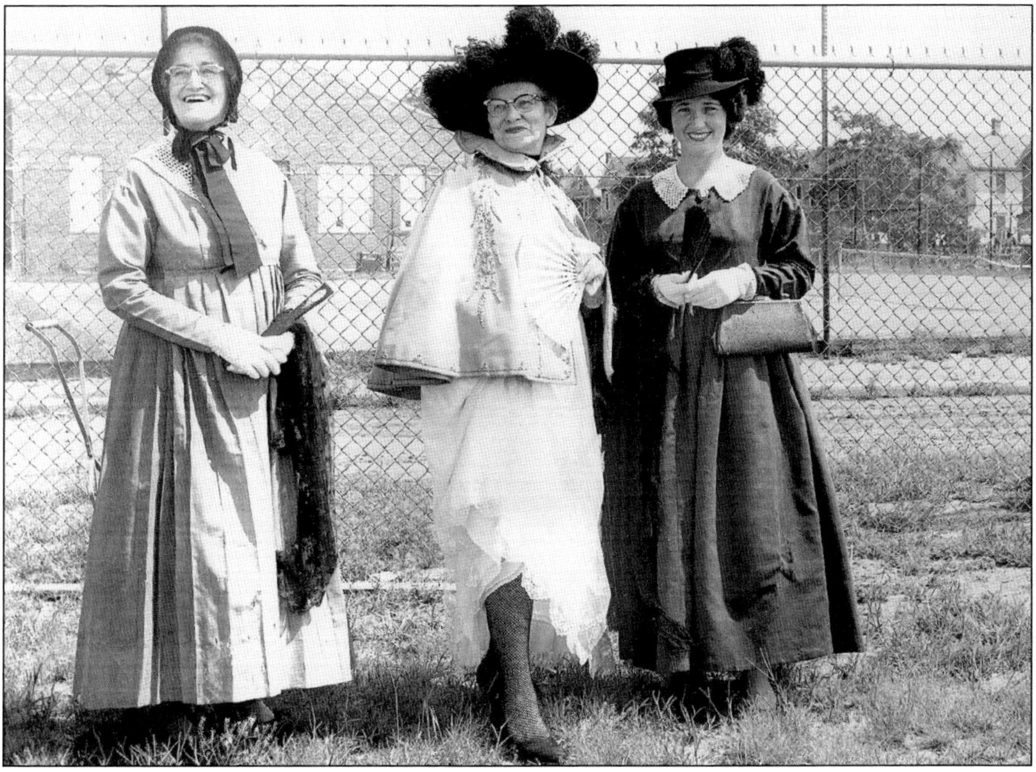

Edna Titus, Frances Vanneman, and Martha Gardner are dressed in period costumes during the golden jubilee. The costume worn by Frances Vanneman is now part of the historical collection at the Gill Memorial Library.

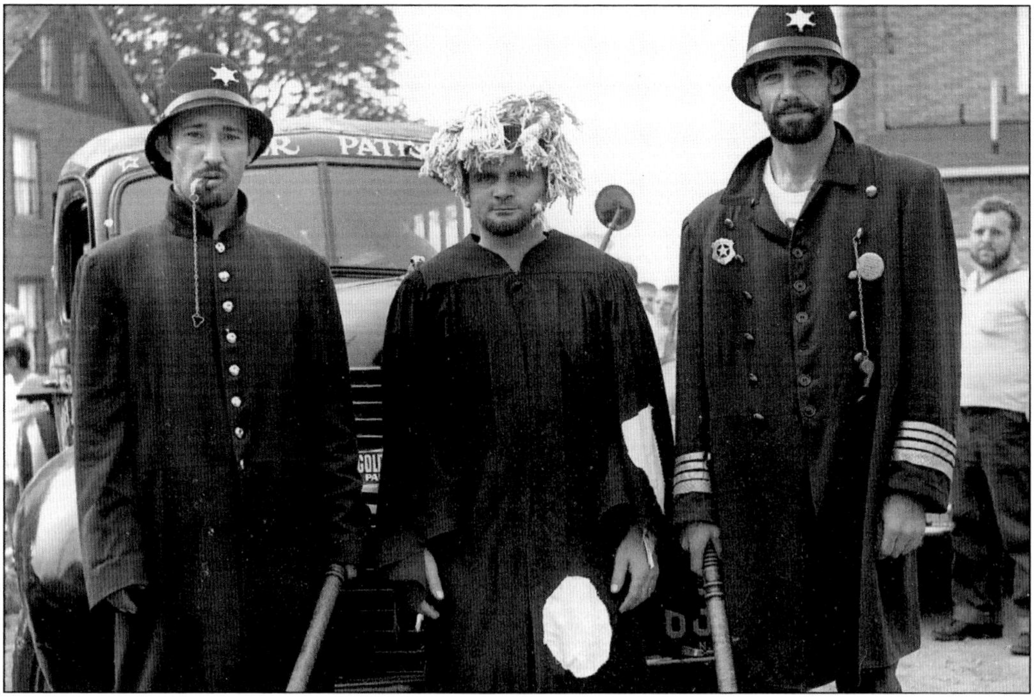

Two of the golden jubilee Whisker Patrol Keystone Kops are pictured here with the mock judge in the middle. The last cop on the right is Bob Miller.

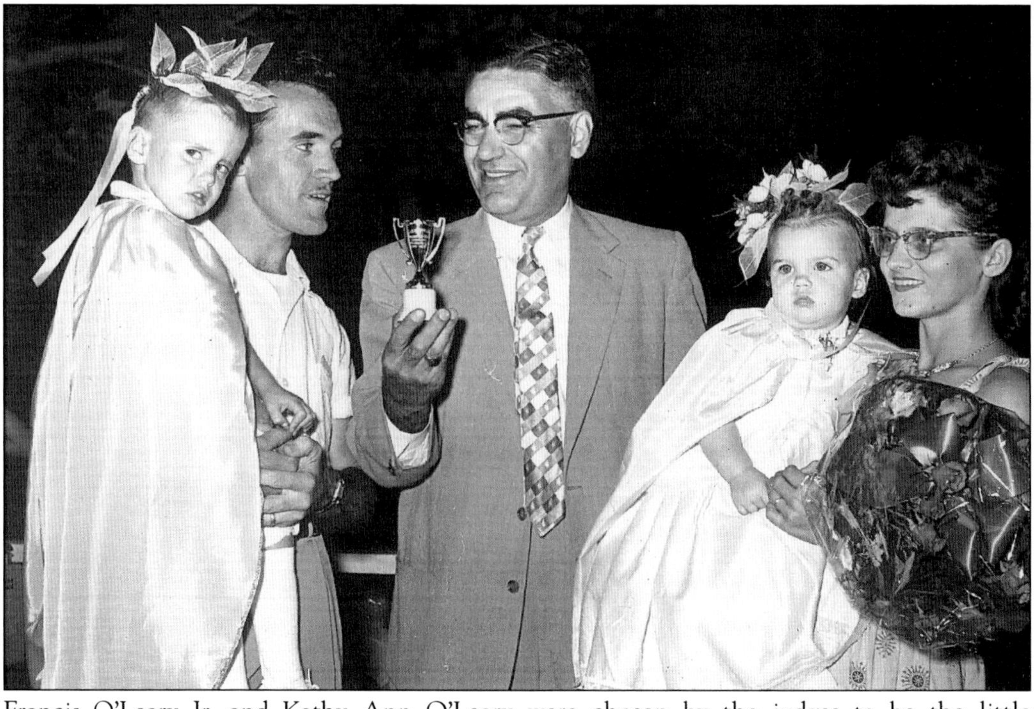

Francis O'Leary Jr. and Kathy Ann O'Leary were chosen by the judges to be the little king and queen.

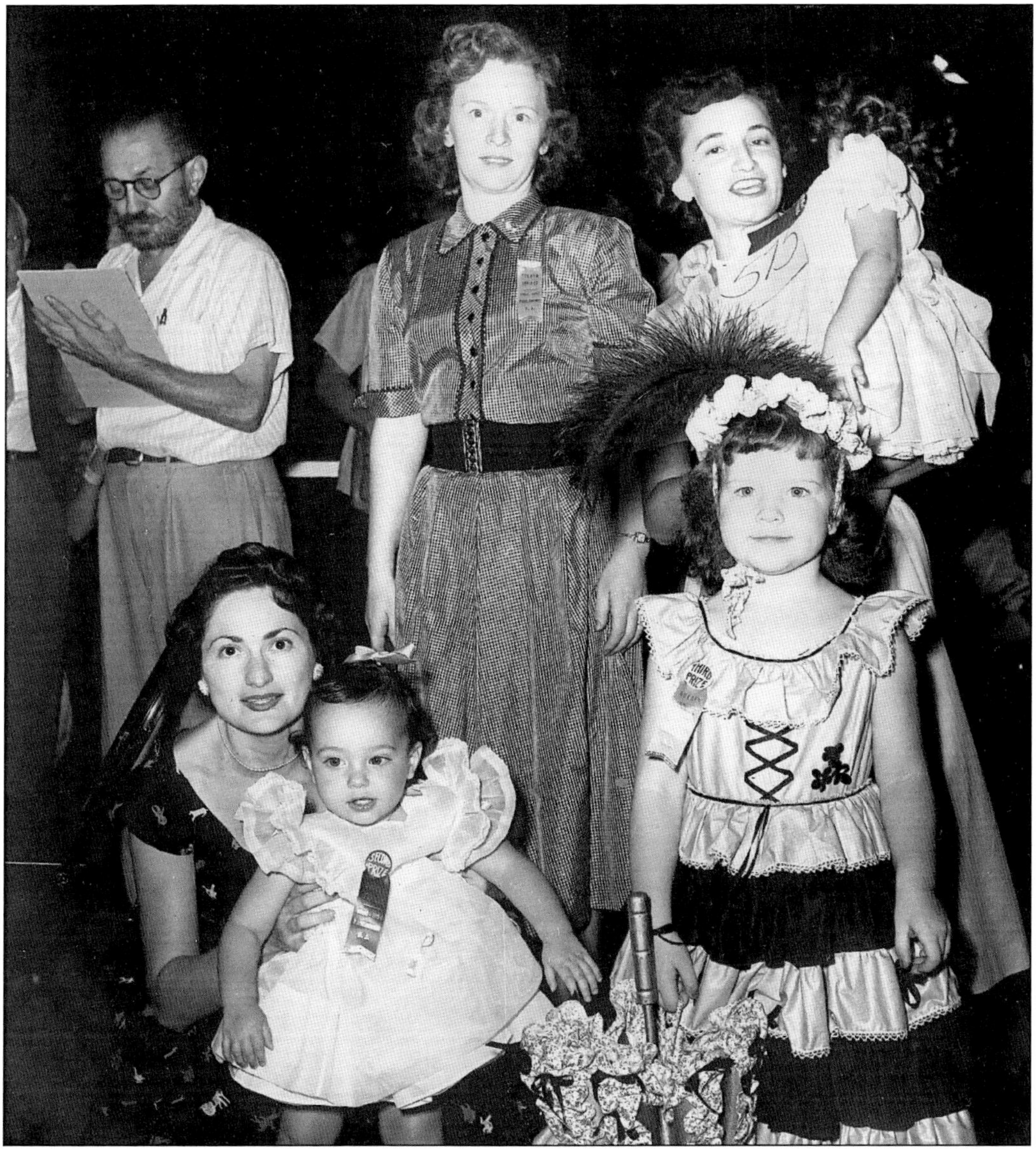

More prizewinners of the children contests are shown here.

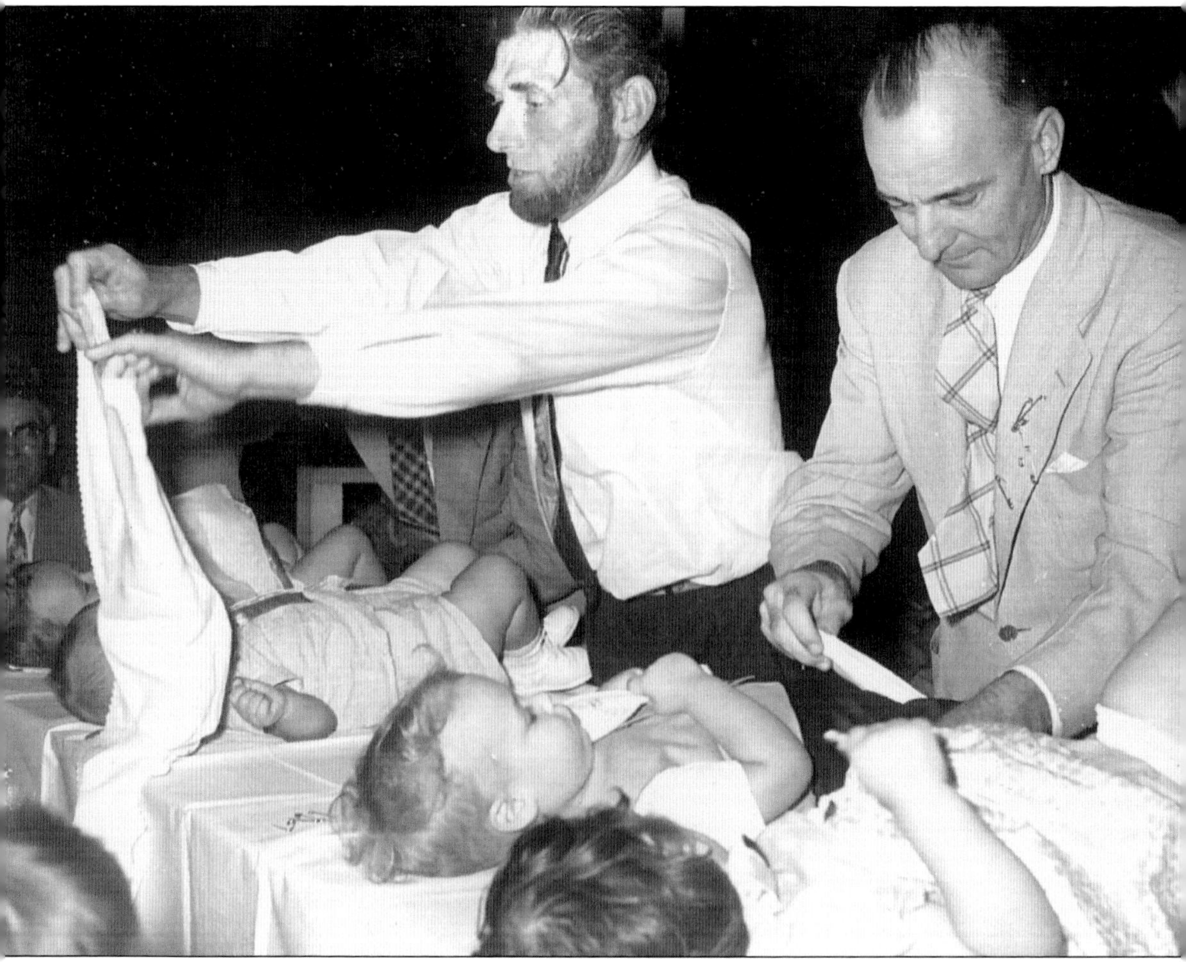

The baby changing contest was another amusing activity offered at the golden jubilee.

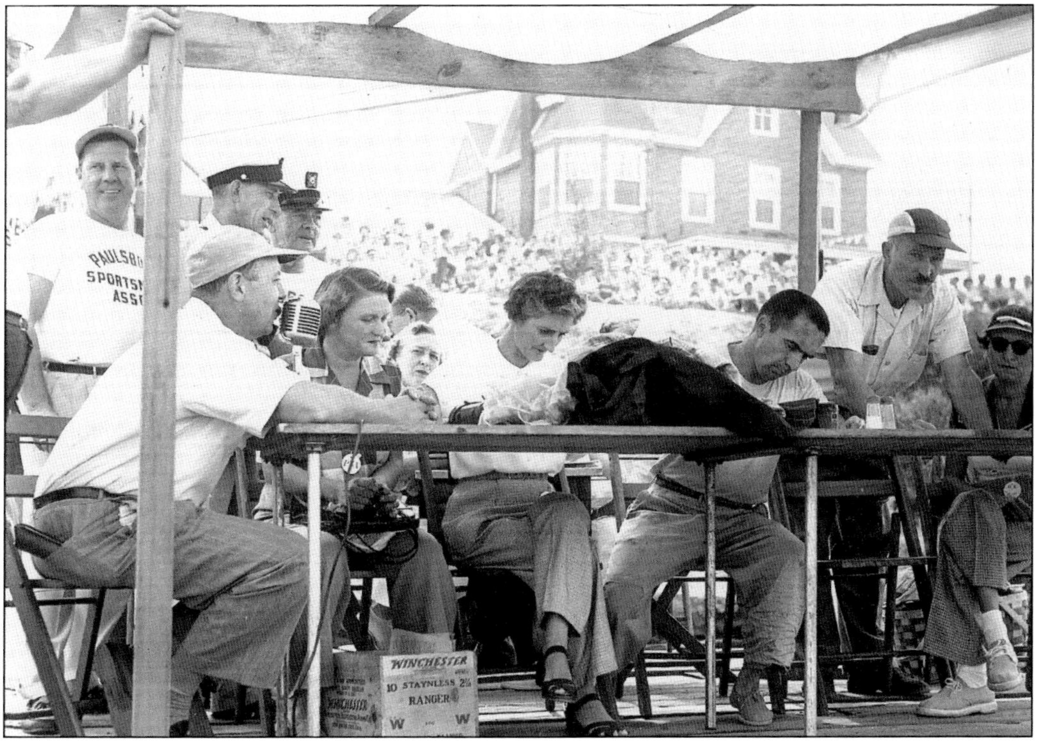

The Paulsboro Sportsman Association provided the announcement booth for the boat races during the golden jubilee.

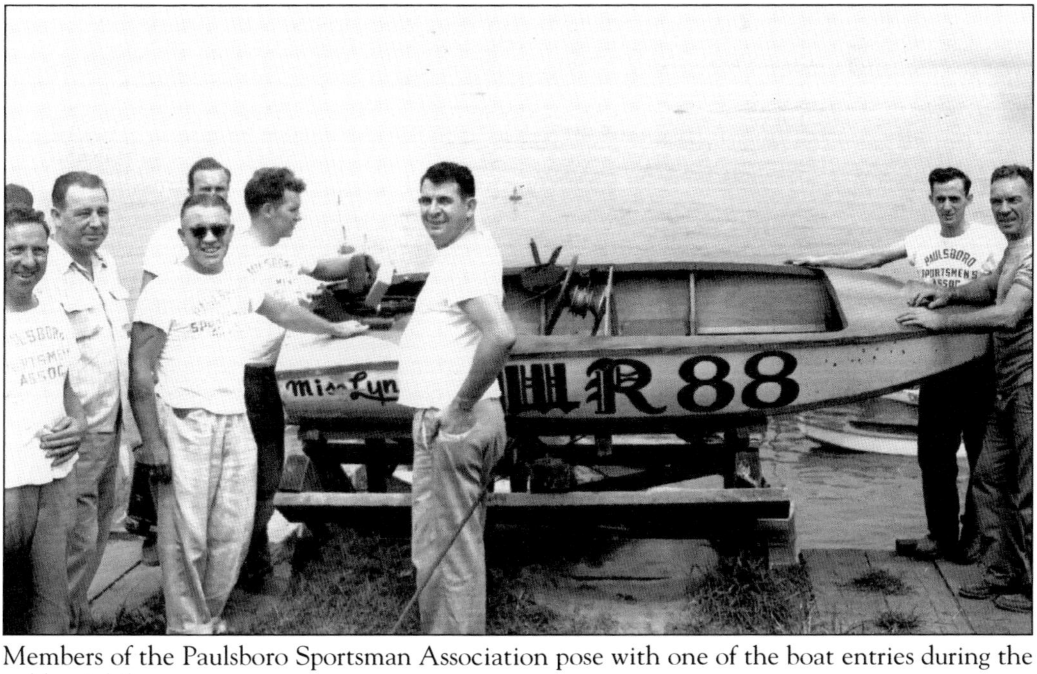

Members of the Paulsboro Sportsman Association pose with one of the boat entries during the golden jubilee races.

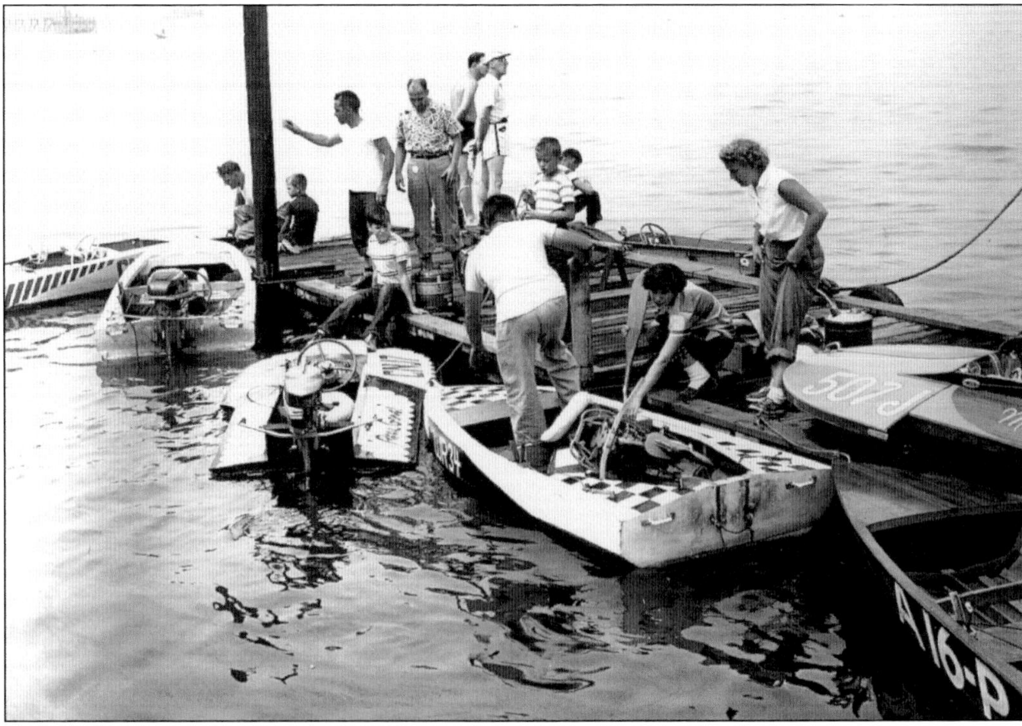

Hank Gill, standing in his boat, is shown with other boat entries preparing for the races.

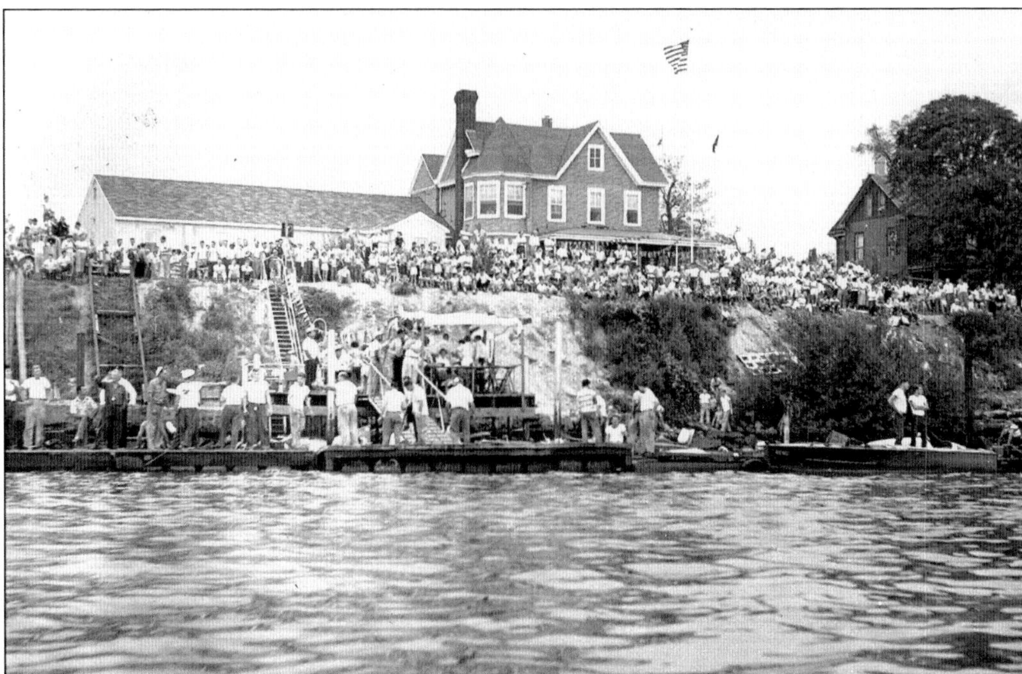

Volumes of spectators line the banks of the river to get a great view of the races during the golden jubilee.

Two

THE GILL MEMORIAL LIBRARY

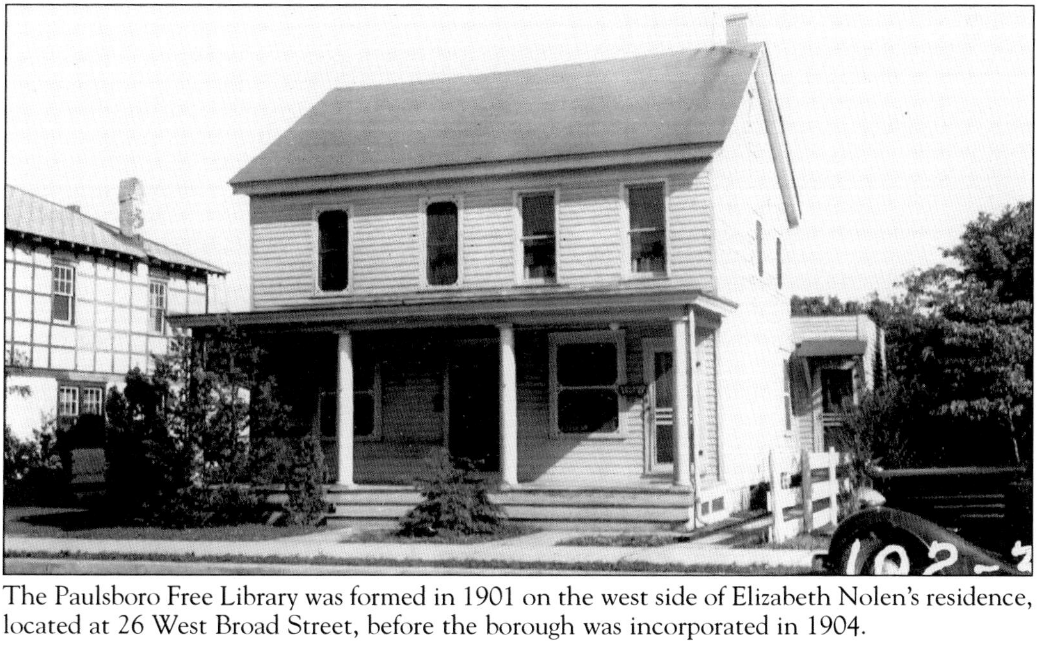

The Paulsboro Free Library was formed in 1901 on the west side of Elizabeth Nolen's residence, located at 26 West Broad Street, before the borough was incorporated in 1904.

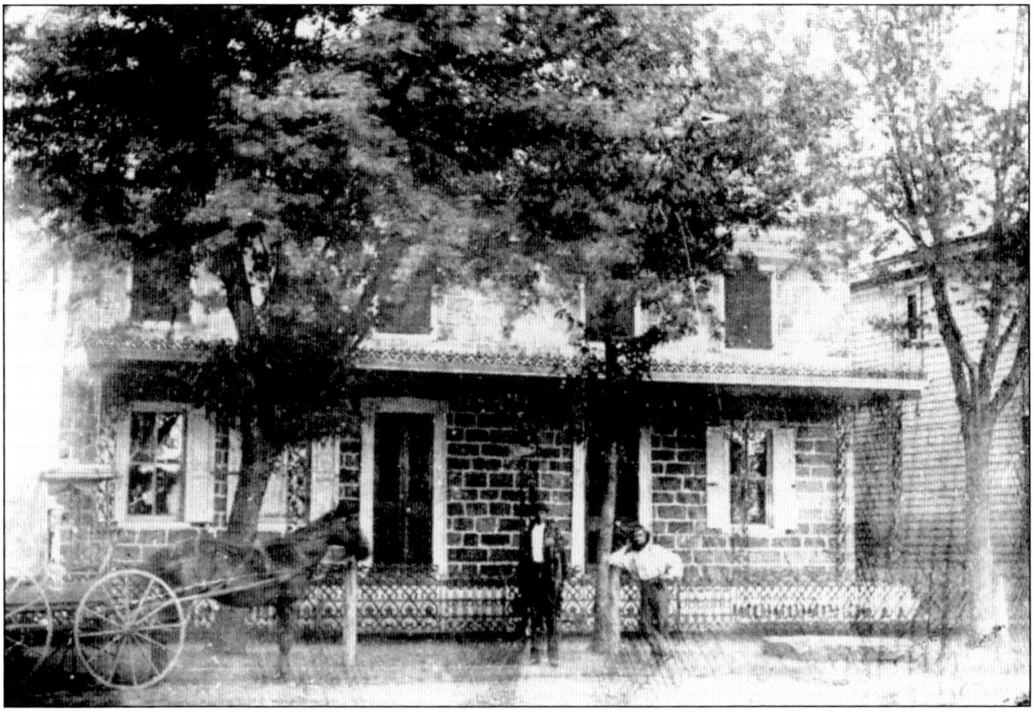

This *c.* 1900 photograph is the earliest known picture of the Matthew Gill residence. Now the Gill Memorial Library, the building was built in 1806 by architect John C. Clark.

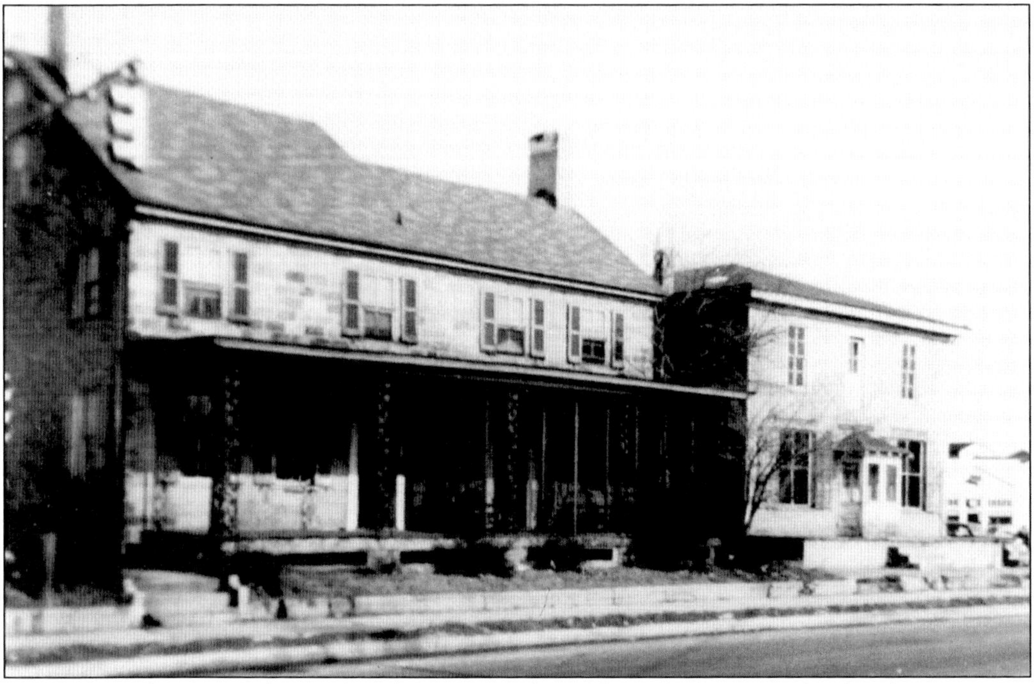

The Gill residence was donated to the borough for a library by Mary England Fish in memory of her grandparents Matthew Gill and Sally Jessup Gill and her mother, Sallie Jessup England. This *c.* 1950 photograph shows the building before the front porch was removed.

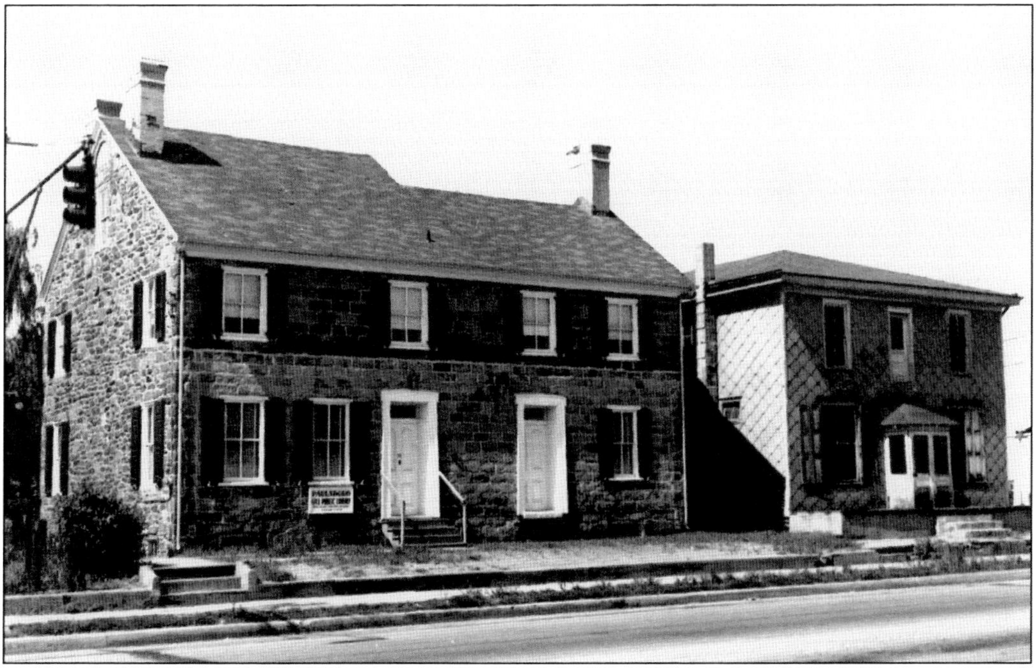

Once the porch was removed, inside renovations completed the transformation of the building from a private home to a public library. The Paulsboro Free Library changed its name to Gill Memorial Library with its dedication on July 7, 1951.

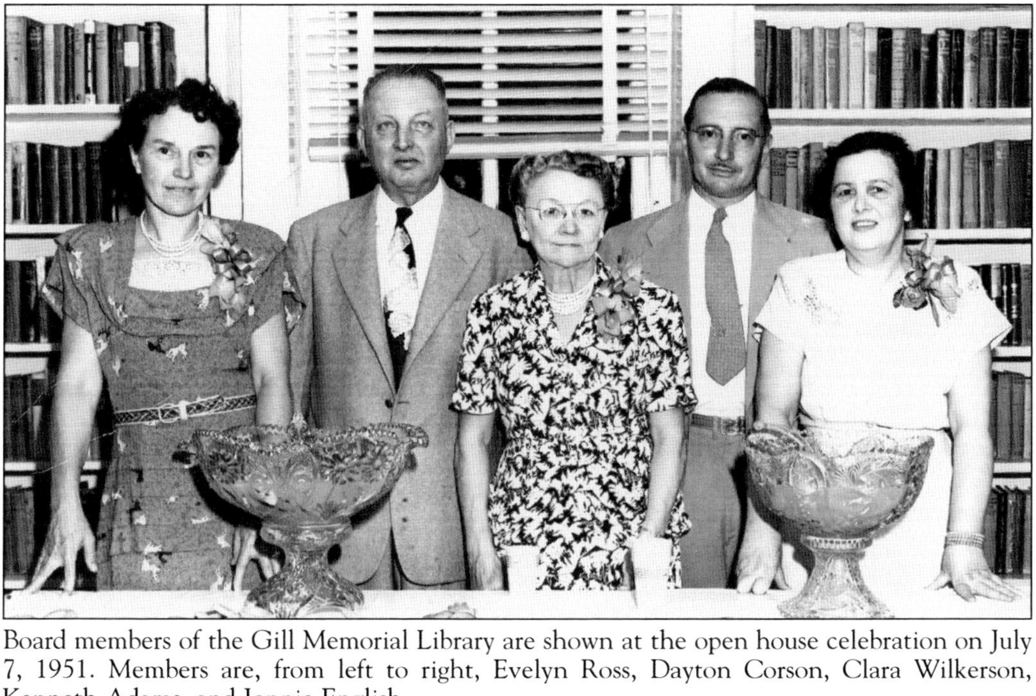

Board members of the Gill Memorial Library are shown at the open house celebration on July 7, 1951. Members are, from left to right, Evelyn Ross, Dayton Corson, Clara Wilkerson, Kenneth Adams, and Jennie English.

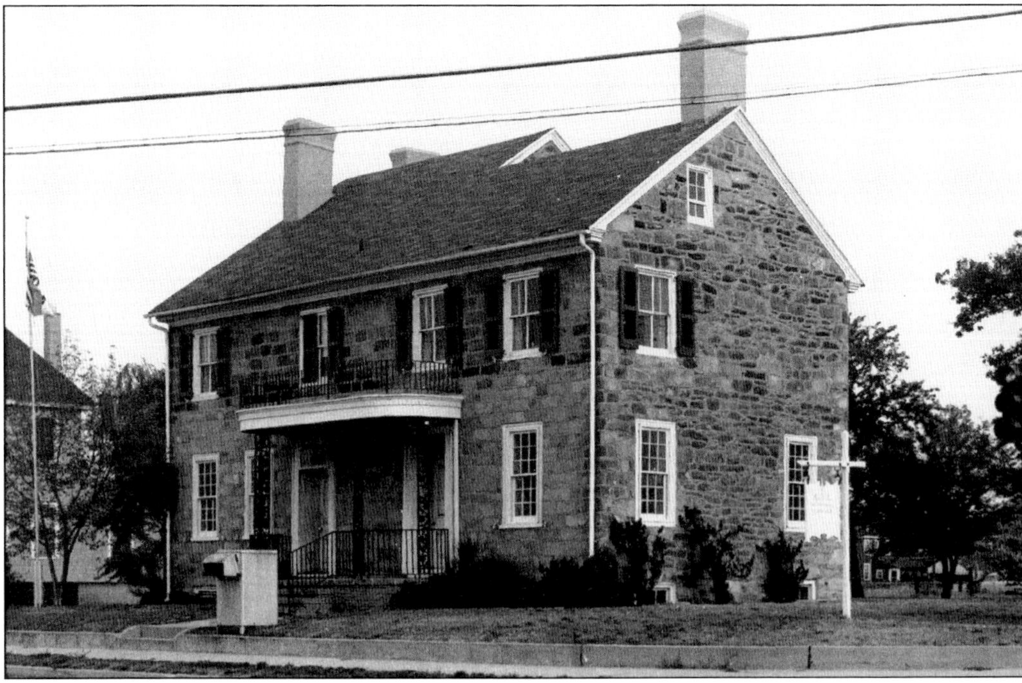

By 1959, the library had gained the addition of a new porch, and the window-replacement project was under way.

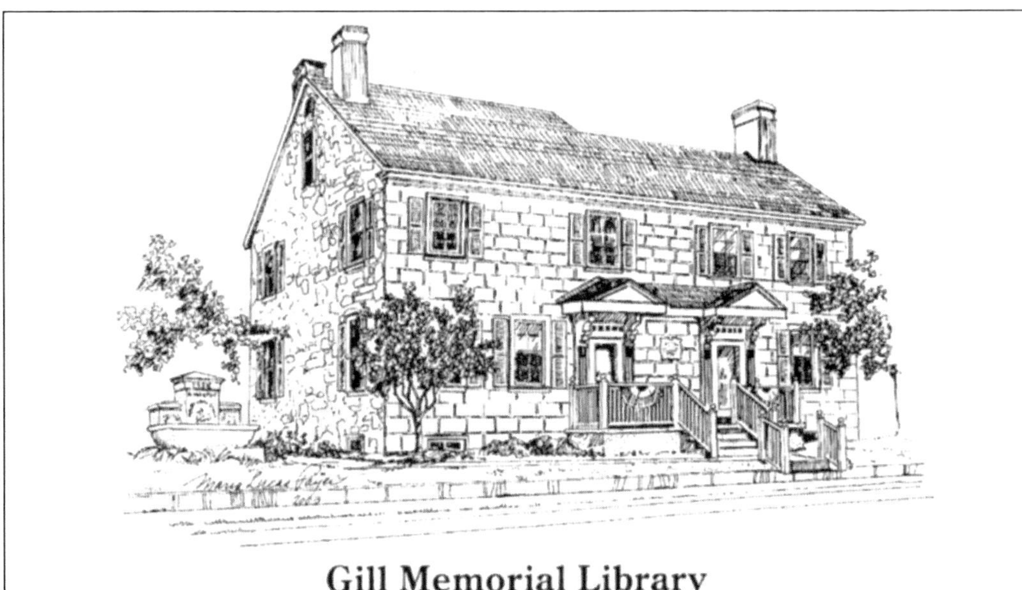

This drawing by Maria Lucas Payer is now available in a postcard and an 8- by 10-inch print at the Gill Memorial Library.

Three

CHURCHES

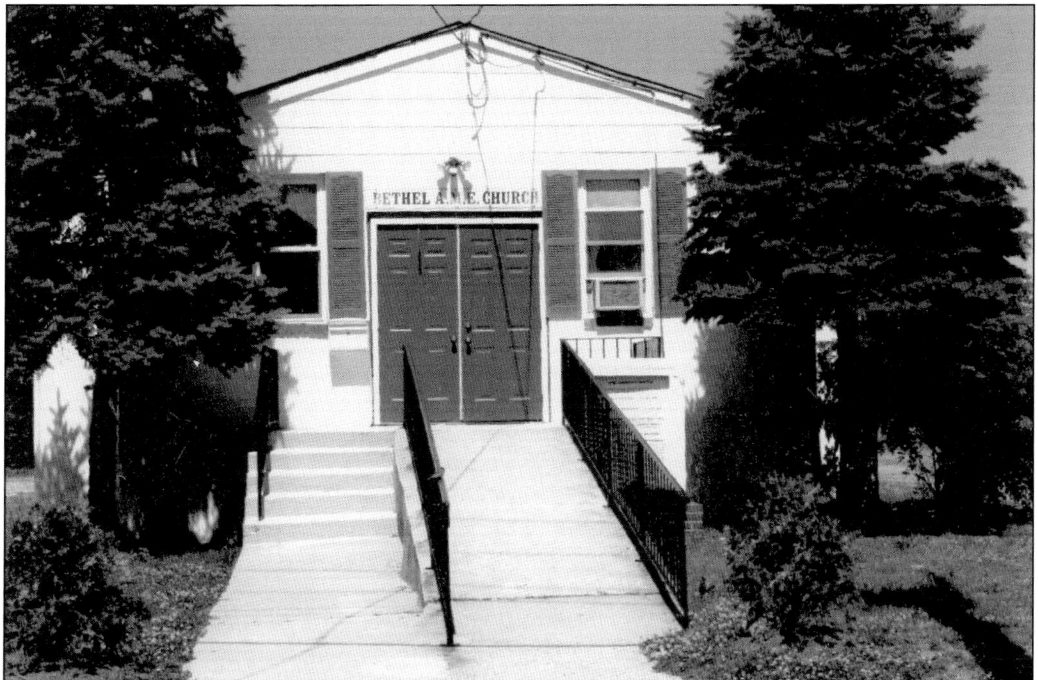

The front of the Bethel African Methodist Episcopal Church is shown in this photograph.

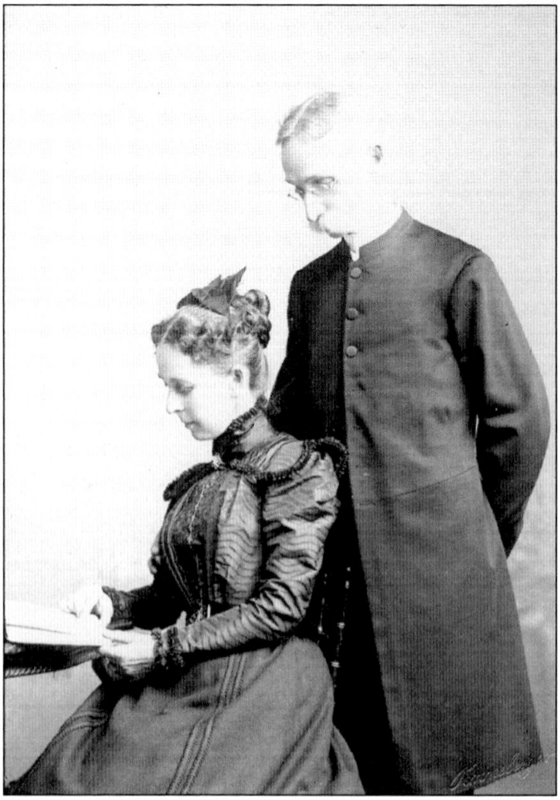

Rev. Robert King, Billingsport Congregational Methodist Church's first pastor, is shown here with his wife.

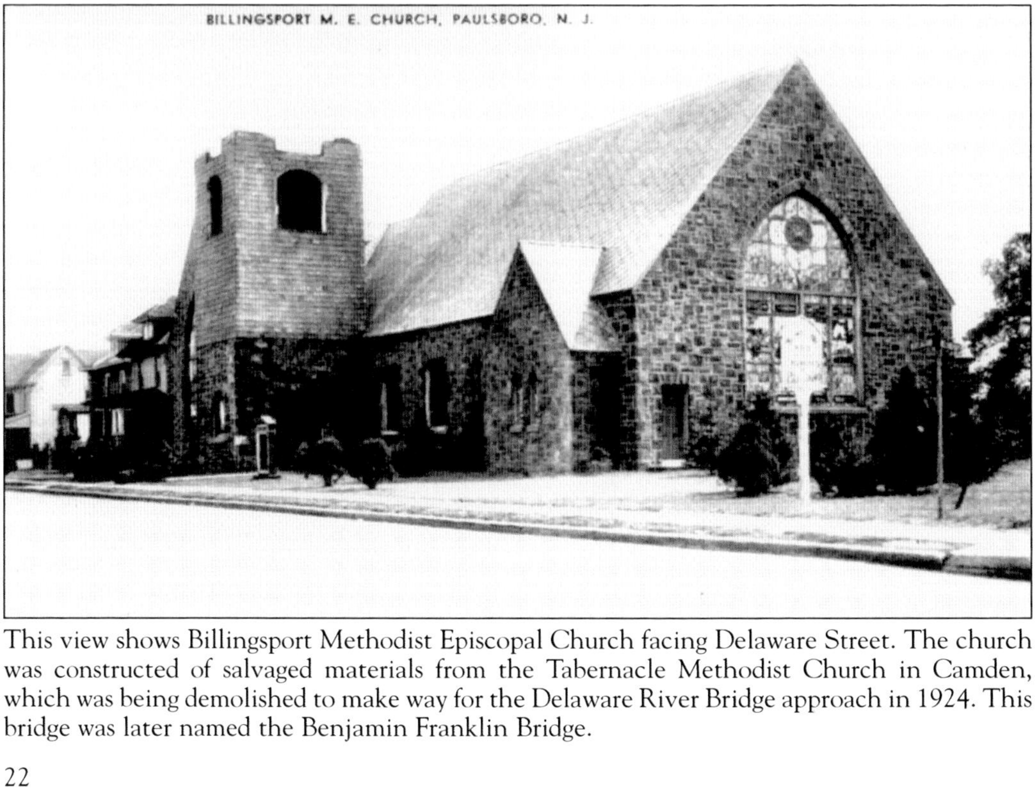

This view shows Billingsport Methodist Episcopal Church facing Delaware Street. The church was constructed of salvaged materials from the Tabernacle Methodist Church in Camden, which was being demolished to make way for the Delaware River Bridge approach in 1924. This bridge was later named the Benjamin Franklin Bridge.

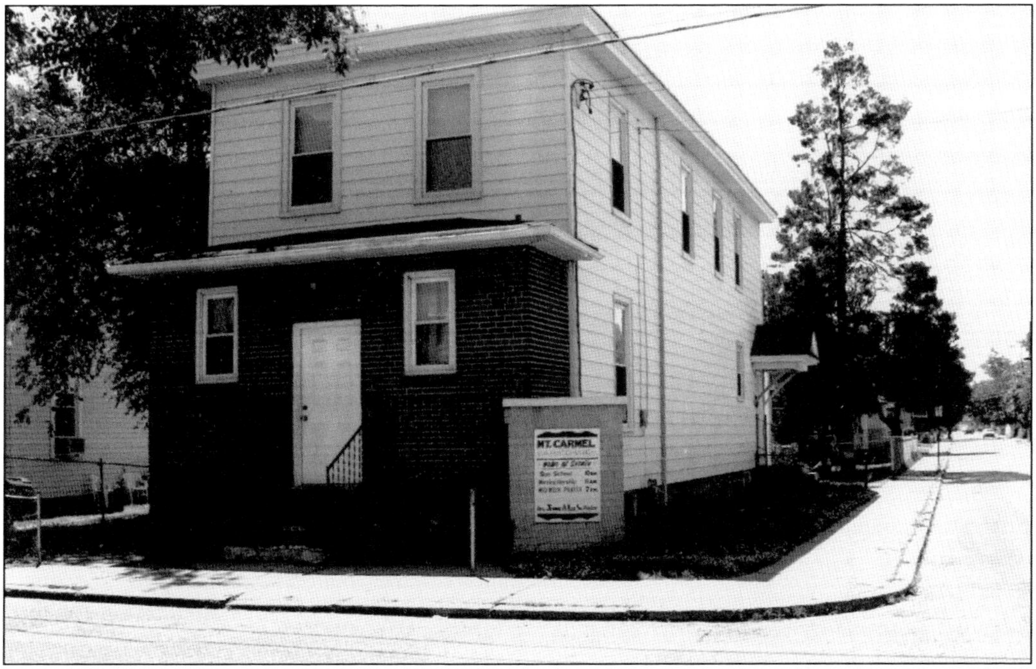

This is a corner view of the Mount Carmel United African Methodist Episcopal Church.

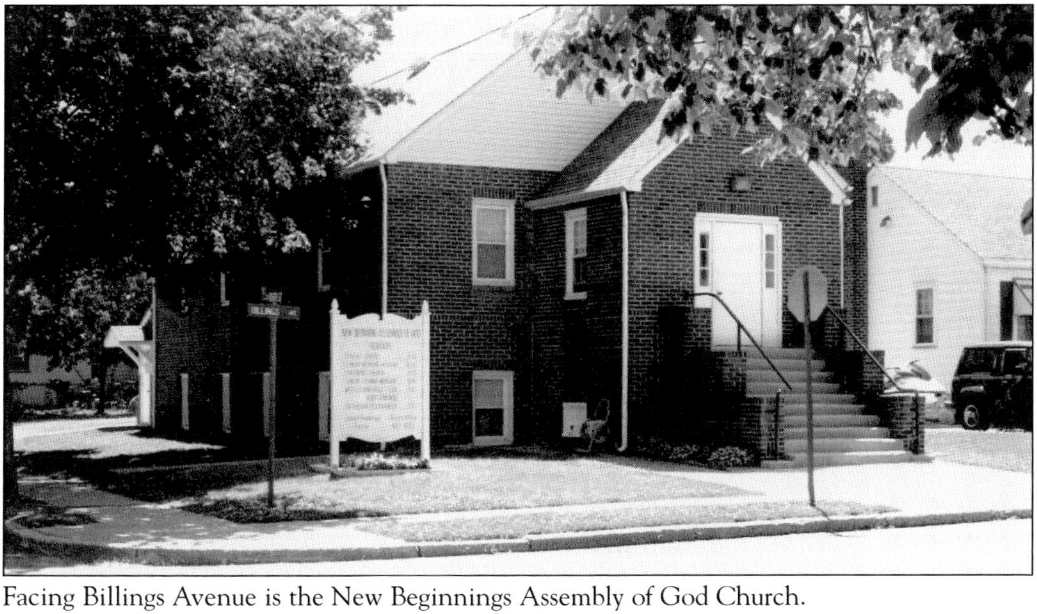

Facing Billings Avenue is the New Beginnings Assembly of God Church.

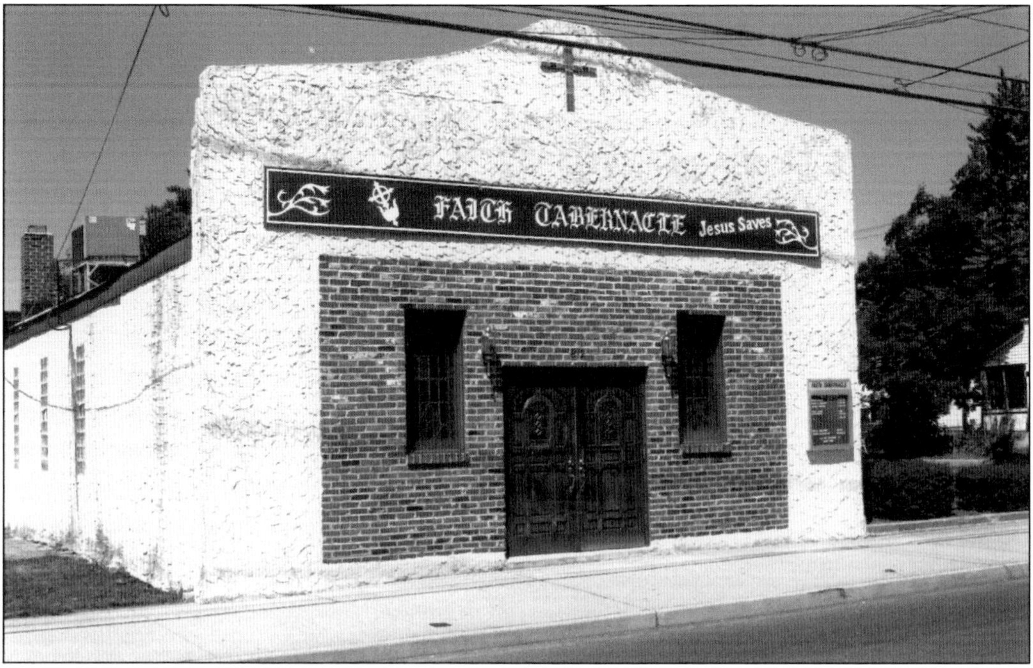

Here is a front view of Pentecostal Faith Tabernacle Church, facing North Delaware Street.

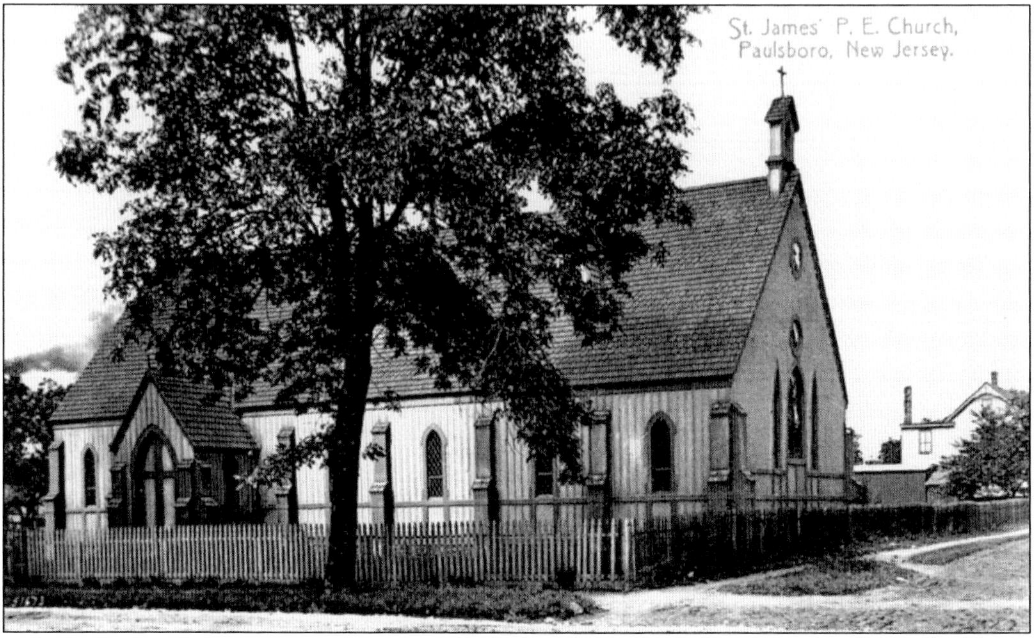

Built in 1873, St. James Episcopal Church burned to the ground in 1909. (Postcard by E. W. Humphreys.)

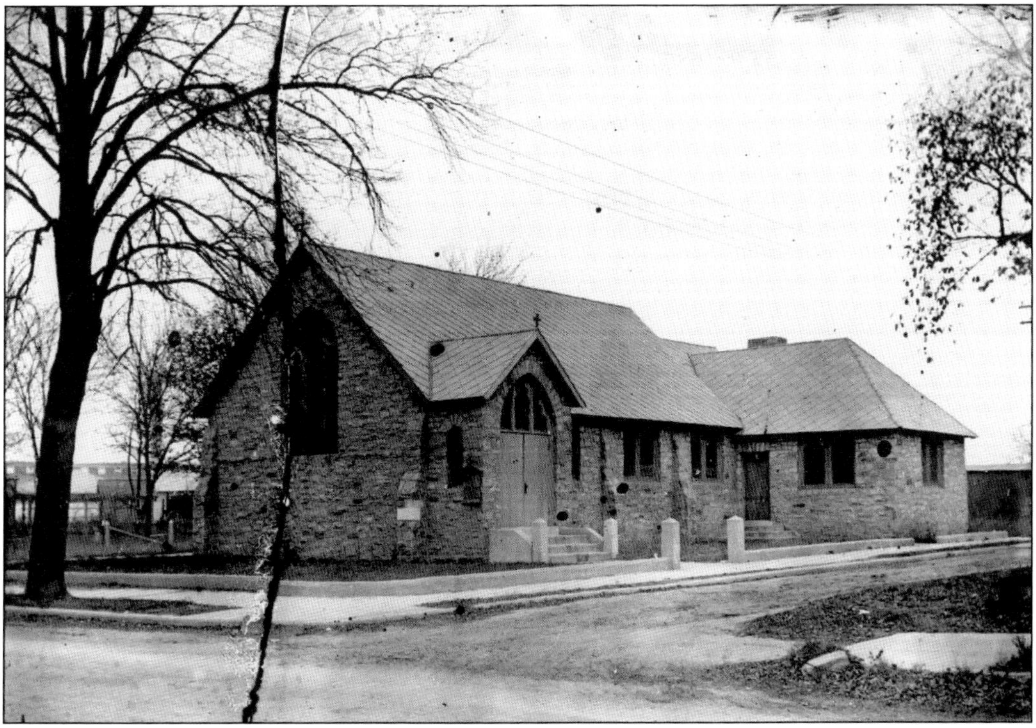

Made from a glass-plate negative, this photograph of St. James Episcopal Church shows the unpaved roads of Paulsboro.

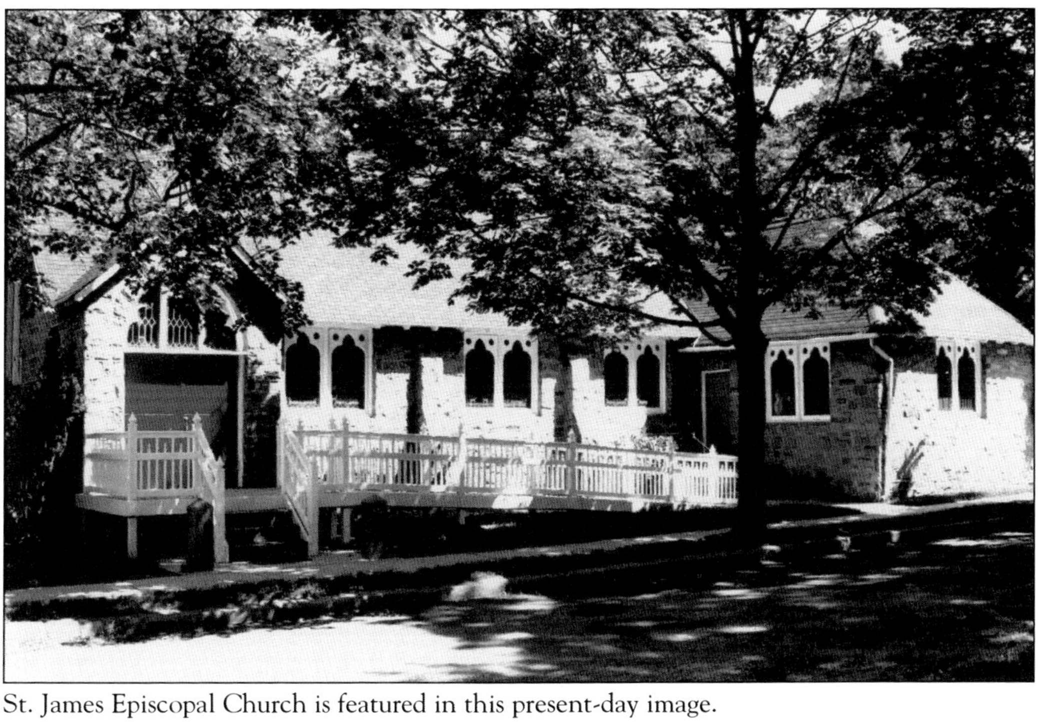

St. James Episcopal Church is featured in this present-day image.

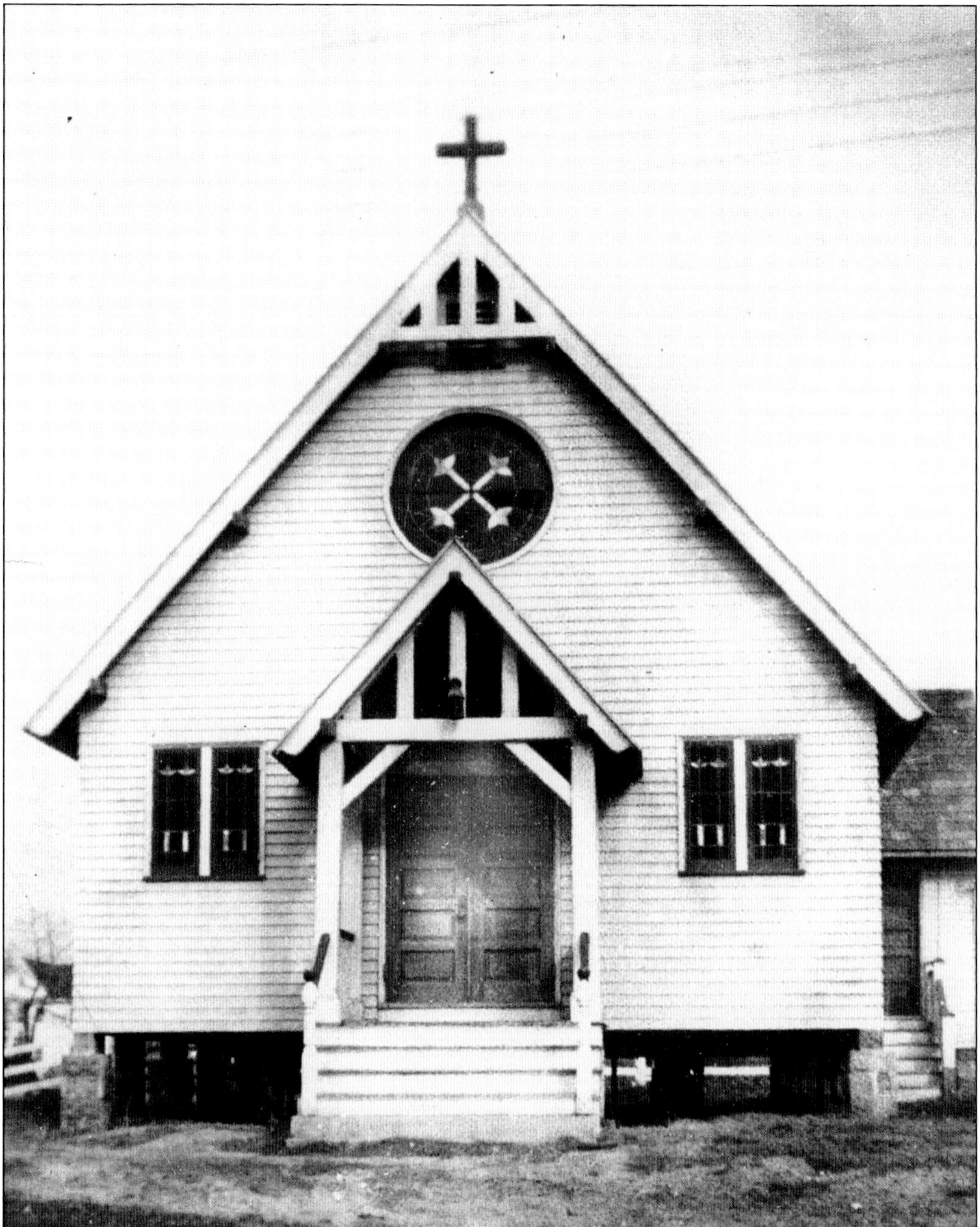

The front entrance of St. John the Evangelist Roman Catholic Church is captured in this early-1900s photograph.

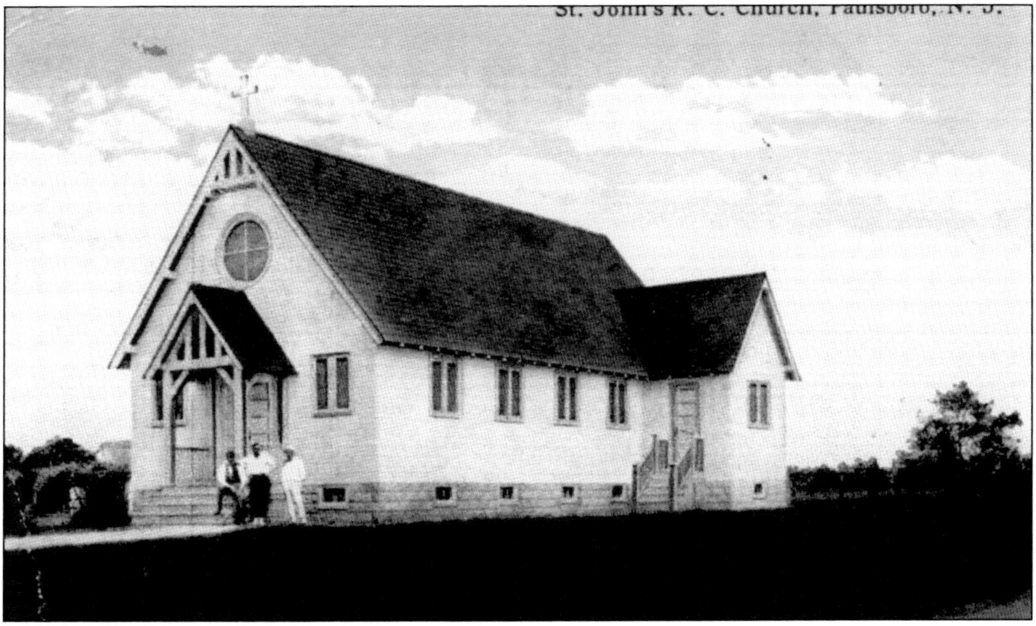

People stand by the front steps of St. John the Evangelist Roman Catholic Church *c.* 1917. This view shows the undeveloped area surrounding the church.

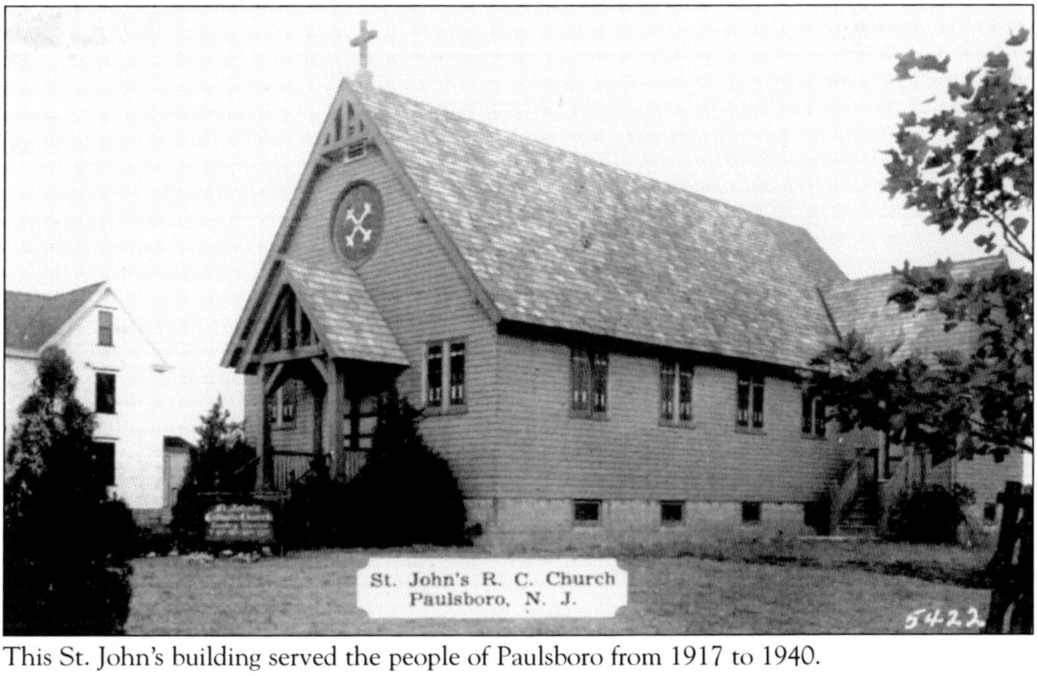

This St. John's building served the people of Paulsboro from 1917 to 1940.

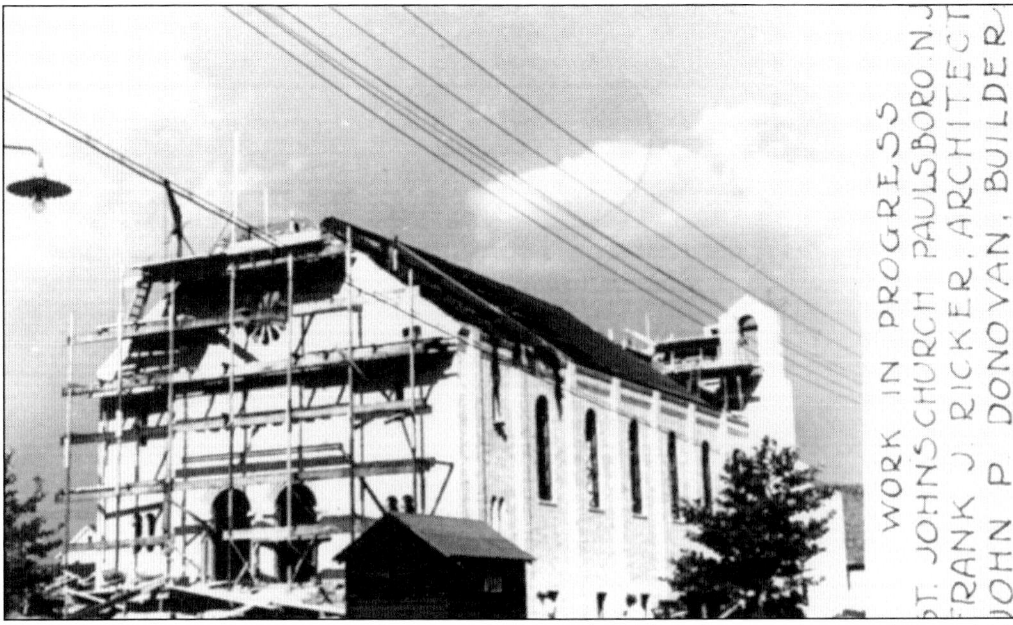

Work on the new St. John's church was under way when this photograph was taken in 1940. The final cost of the church was $75,000. During construction of the new church, the old church was moved to the corner of Seventh and Mantua Avenues and then later to St. Mary's Nursing Home, in Cherry Hill.

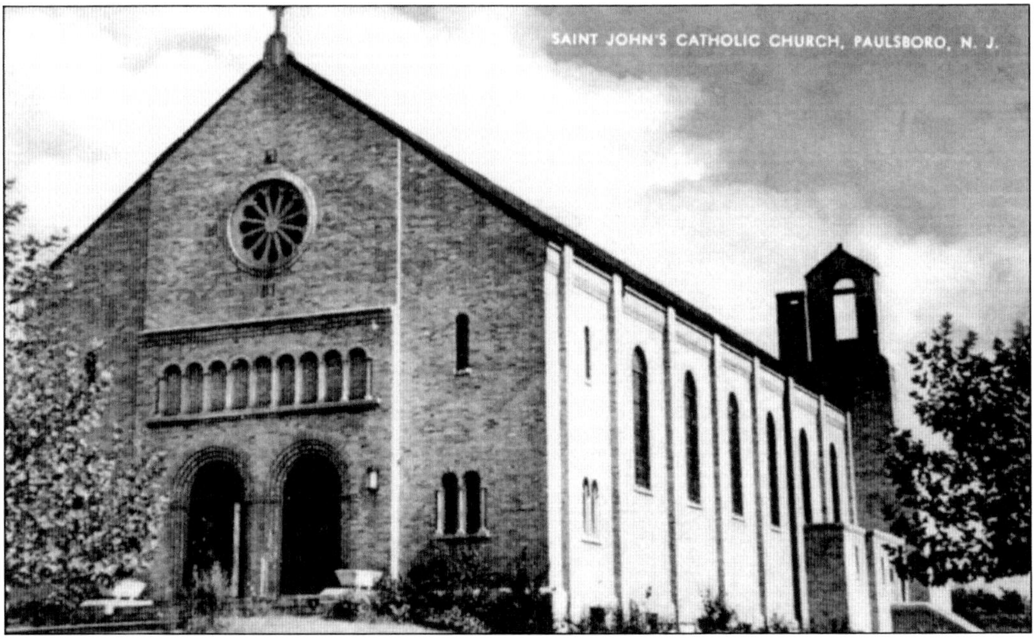

In this view, construction is finally complete on the new St. John's.

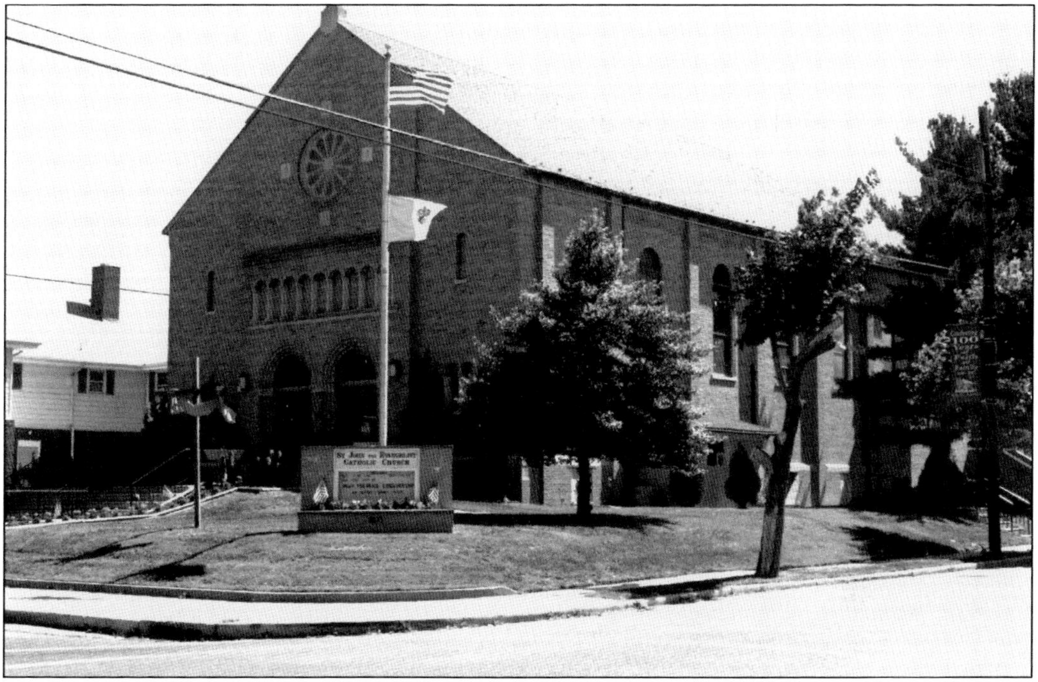

St. John the Evangelist Roman Catholic Church celebrated its 100th anniversary in 2003.

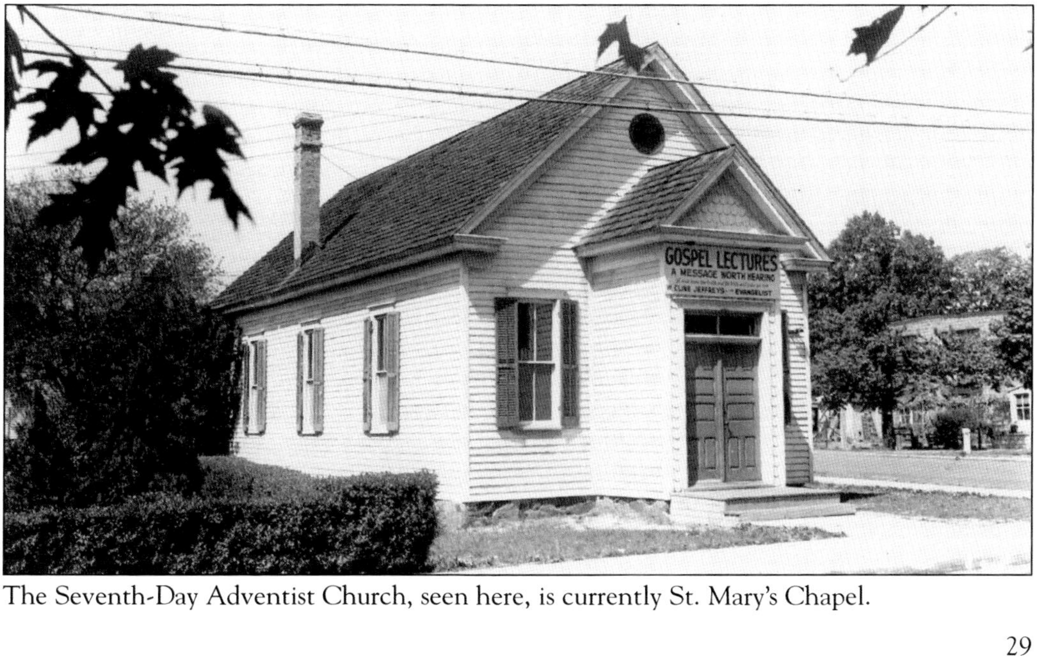

The Seventh-Day Adventist Church, seen here, is currently St. Mary's Chapel.

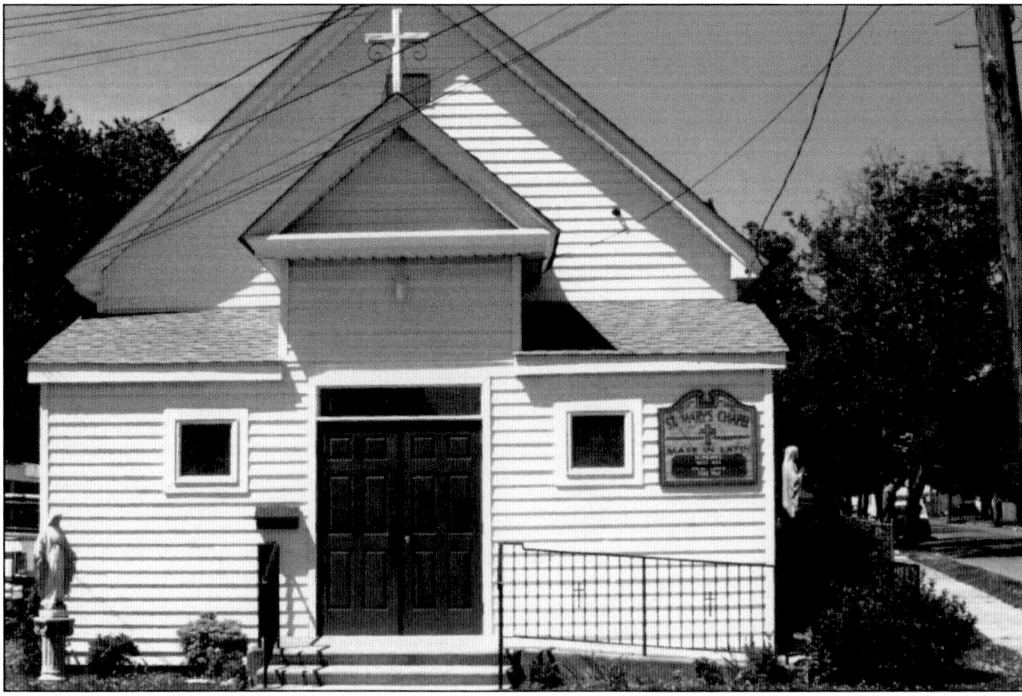

Facing South Delaware Street in this photograph is St. Mary's Chapel, where masses are given in Latin.

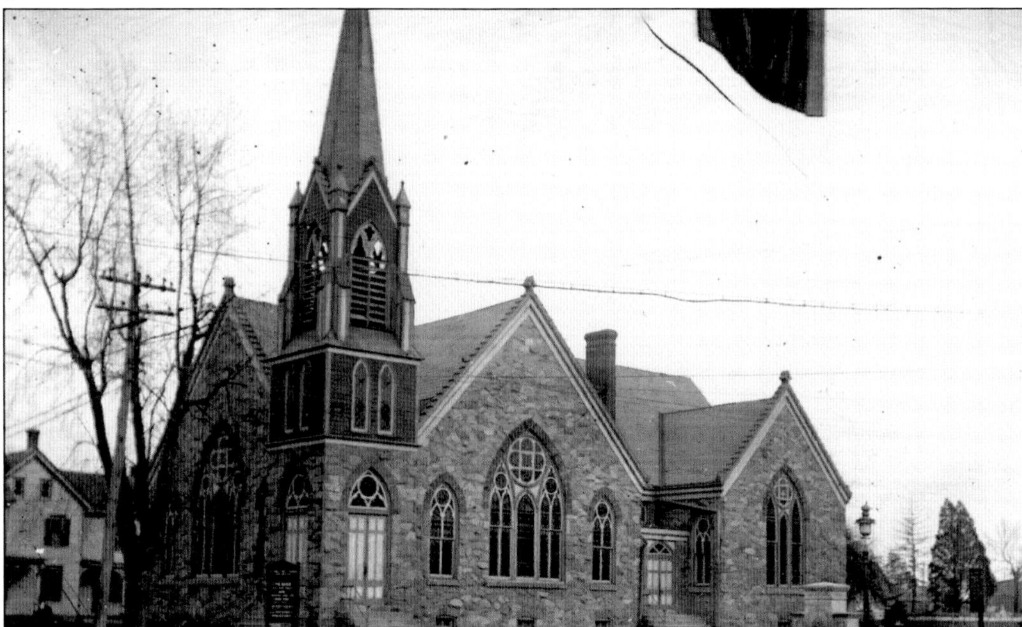

A fire in 1853 destroyed the original St. Paul's United Methodist Church at this location, and church services were held in the Buck Street School until a new brick church was built in 1855. The building was later replaced with a stone structure, and the new St. Paul's building was dedicated in 1893.

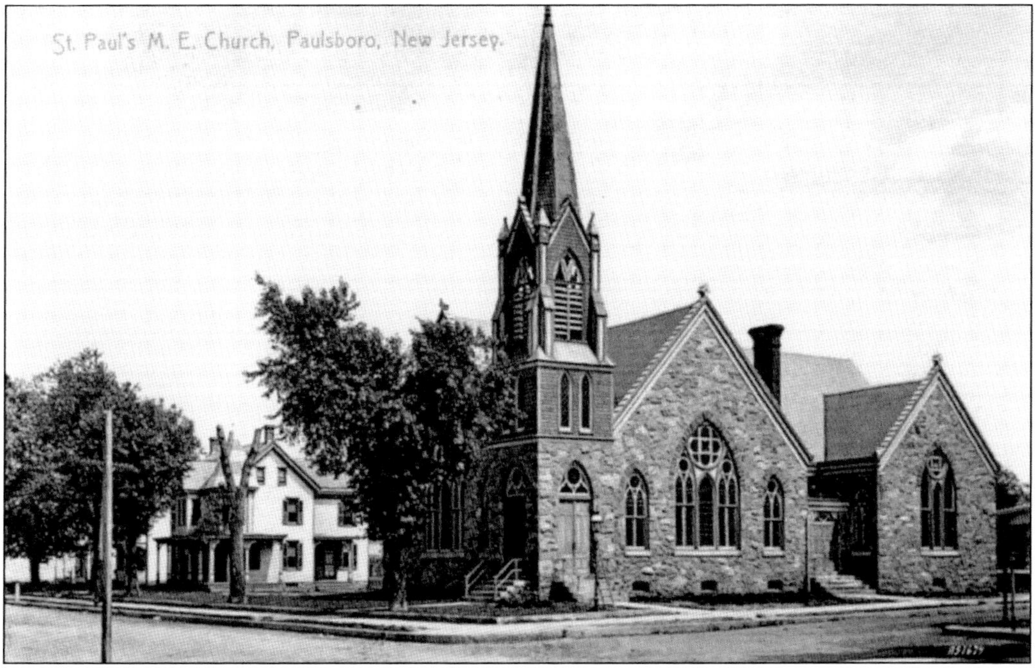

The parsonage of St. Paul's United Methodist Church can be seen on the left of this postcard. The steeple was destroyed by a tornado in 1917 and was later replaced with the present-day bell tower. (Postcard by E. W. Humphreys.)

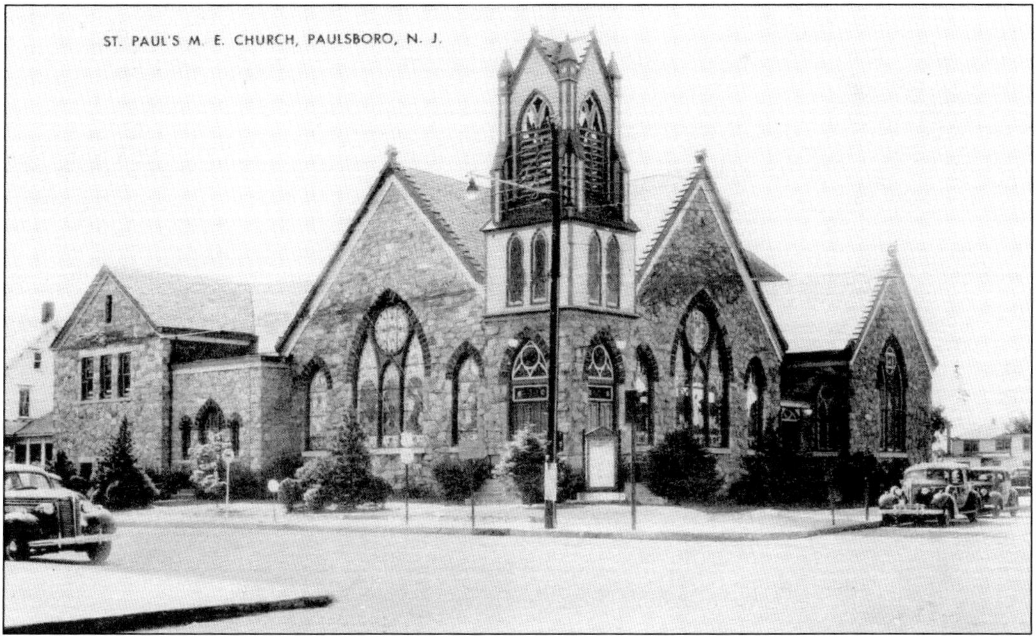

St. Paul's United Methodist Church is seen in the 1940s with its new bell tower and the addition of the building to the left. The side view facing South Delaware Street shows old cars parked along the street.

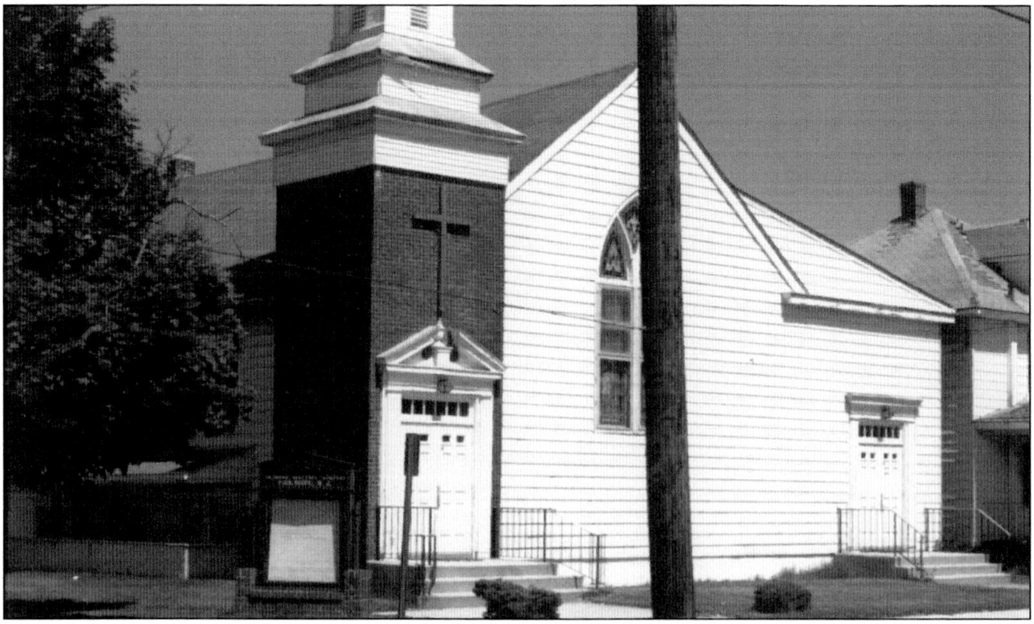

The original Second Baptist Church, which was constructed in 1905, was destroyed by fire. The second building is seen in this present-day photograph.

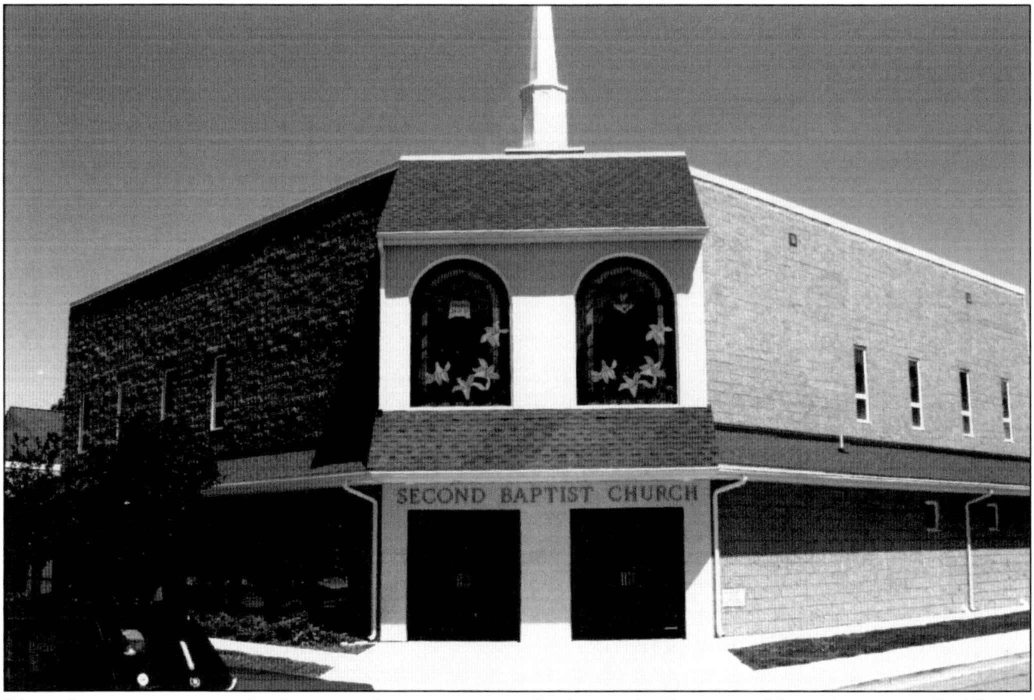

The first services of the newly constructed Second Baptist Church were held on November 26, 2001.

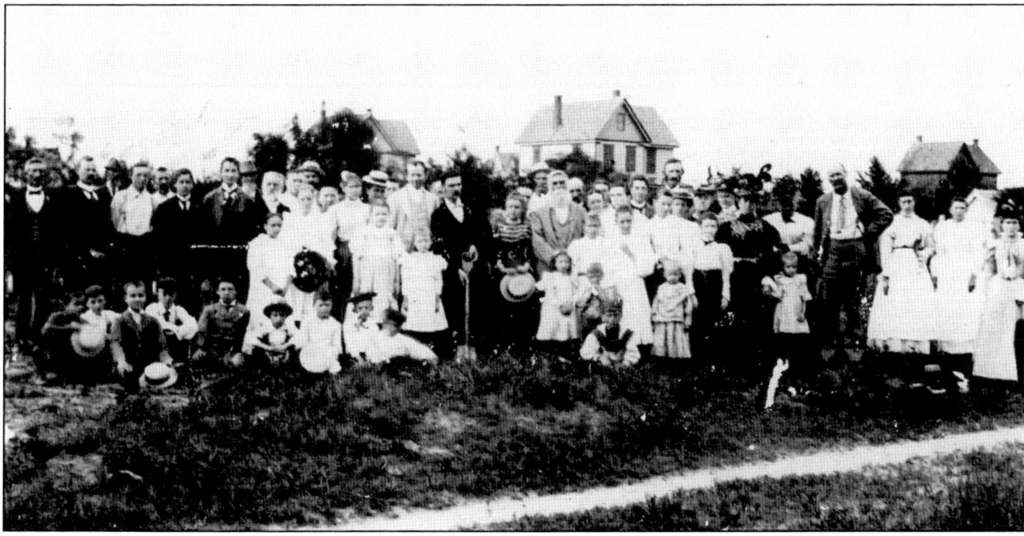

The groundbreaking ceremony for Memorial Baptist Church was held on July 23, 1898. The church's name was later changed to Taylor Memorial Baptist Church.

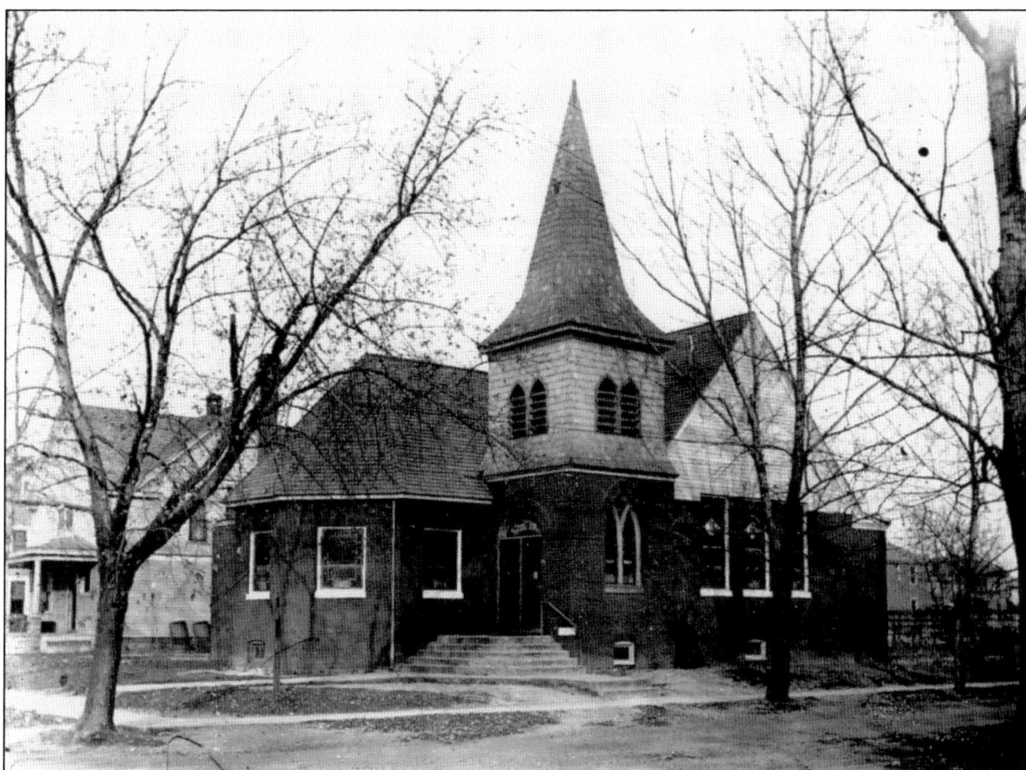

The steeple of the Taylor Memorial Baptist Church can be seen in this photograph, which was made from a glass-plate negative.

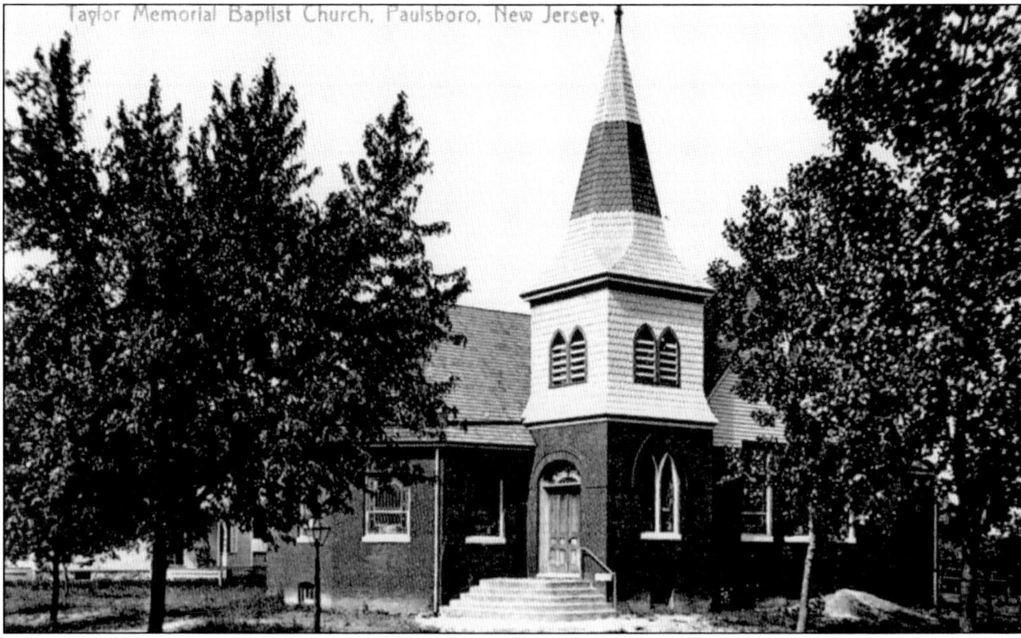

The cornerstone of the Taylor Memorial Baptist Church was set on September 18, 1898. (Postcard by E. W. Humphreys.)

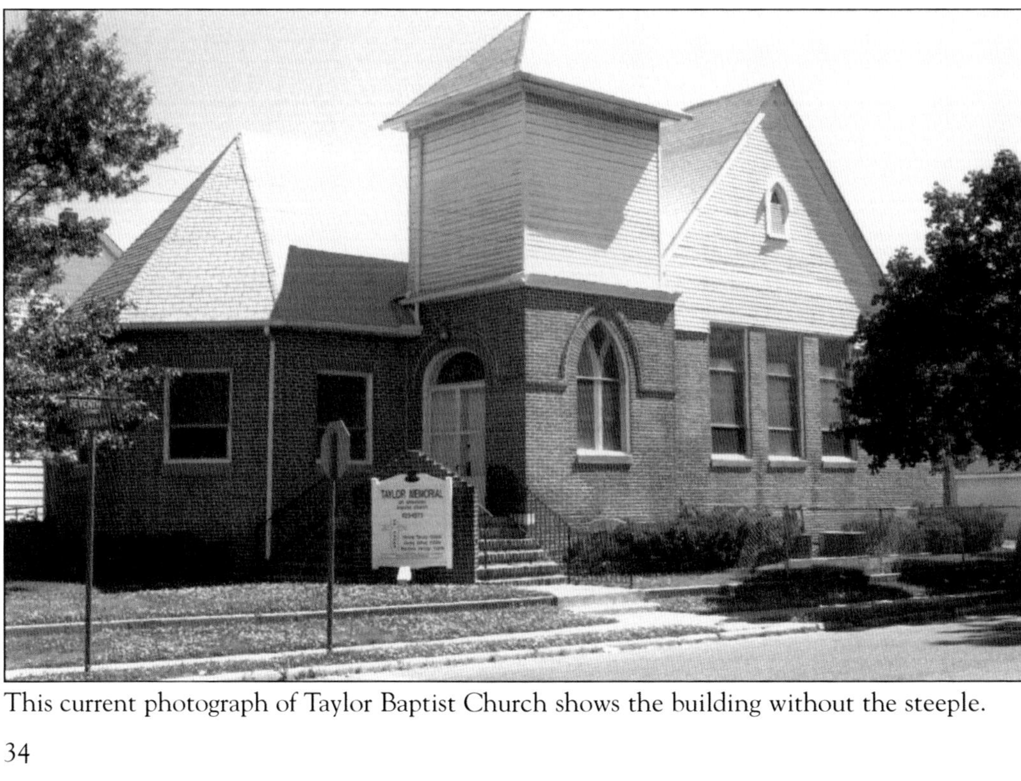

This current photograph of Taylor Baptist Church shows the building without the steeple.

Four

Schools

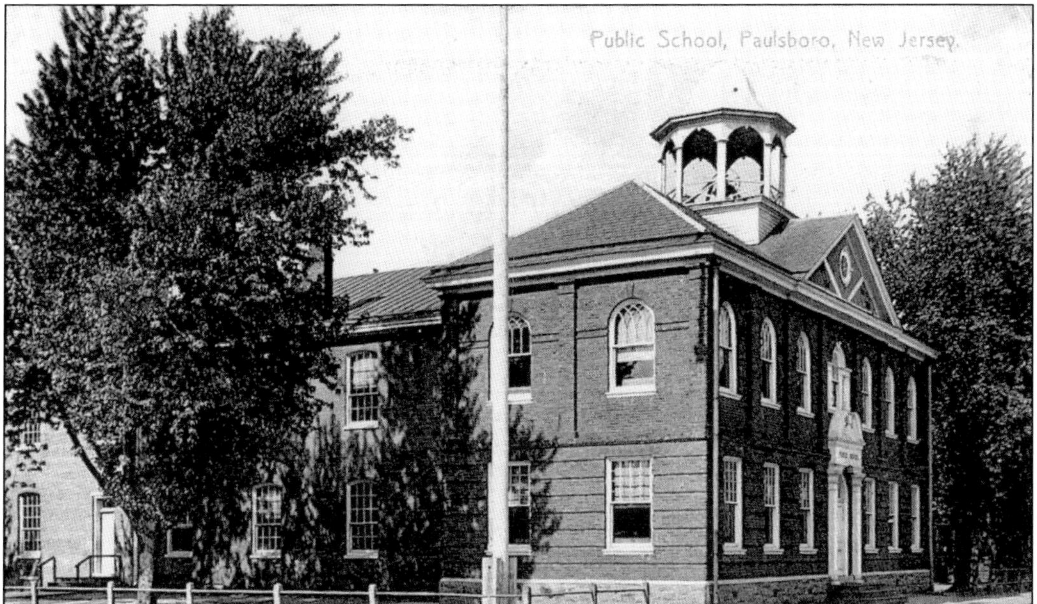

Buck Street School was built in 1861 and closed its doors to students on June 7, 1957. It was demolished in 1959 and is the present site of the borough of Paulsboro's municipal building. The municipal building now faces Delaware Street instead of Buck Street. (Postcard by E. W. Humphreys.)

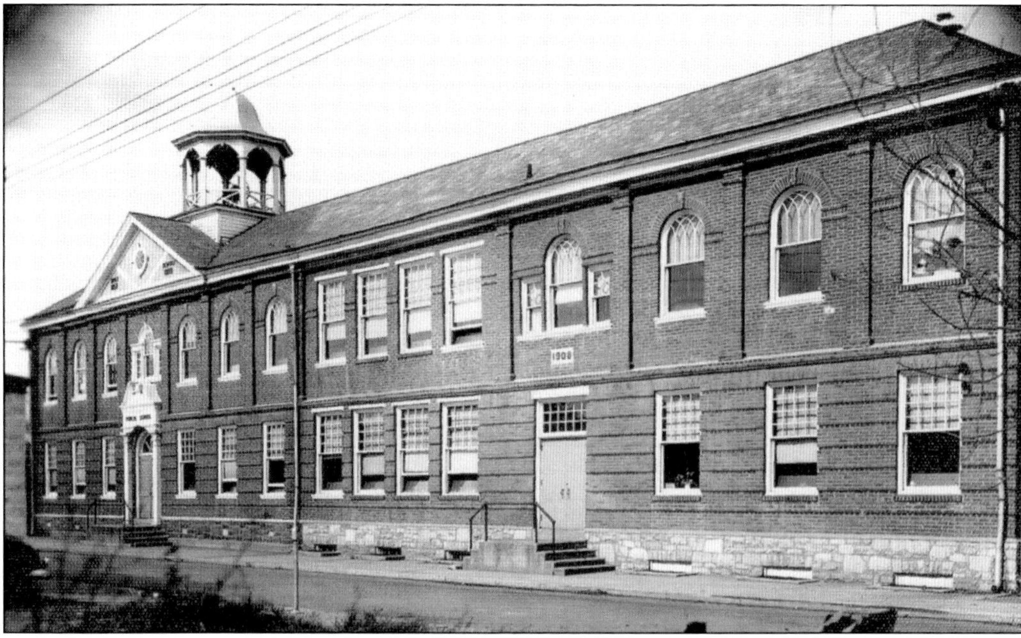

The second addition of Buck Street School can be seen in this photograph dated July 3, 1950. The addition was built in 1908 by Walter Titus (contractor), Wilbert R. Titus (foreman), and Edward Miller (architect), son of Edward G. Miller of the Paulsboro Lumber Company.

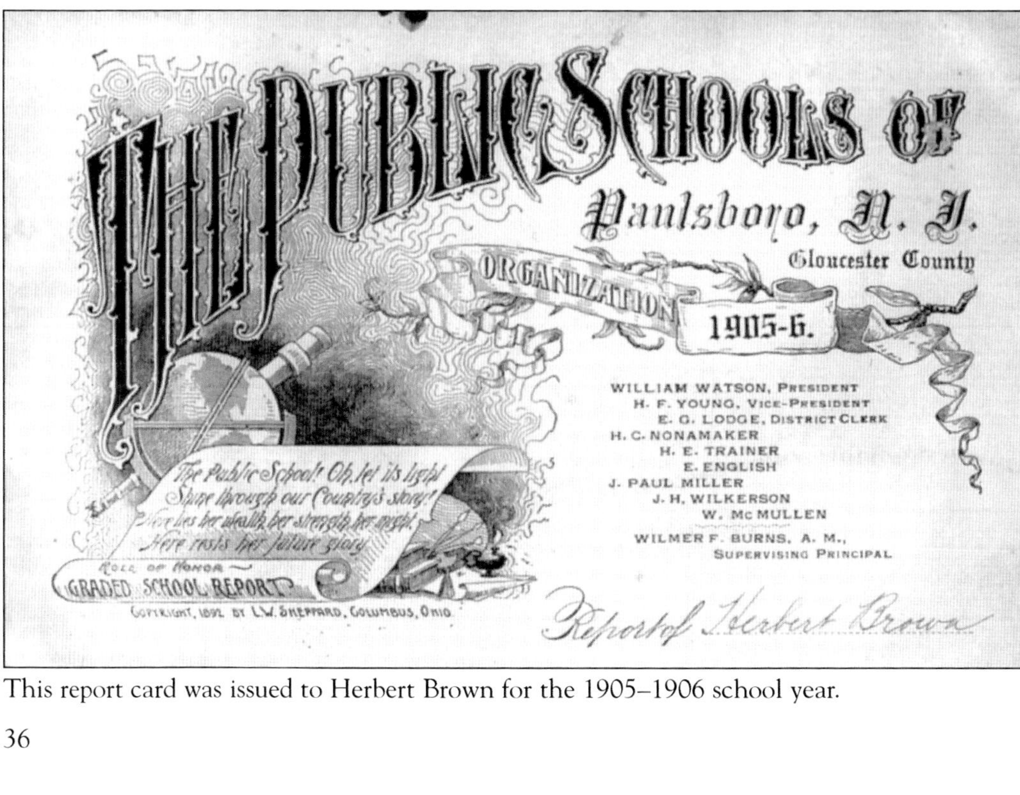

This report card was issued to Herbert Brown for the 1905–1906 school year.

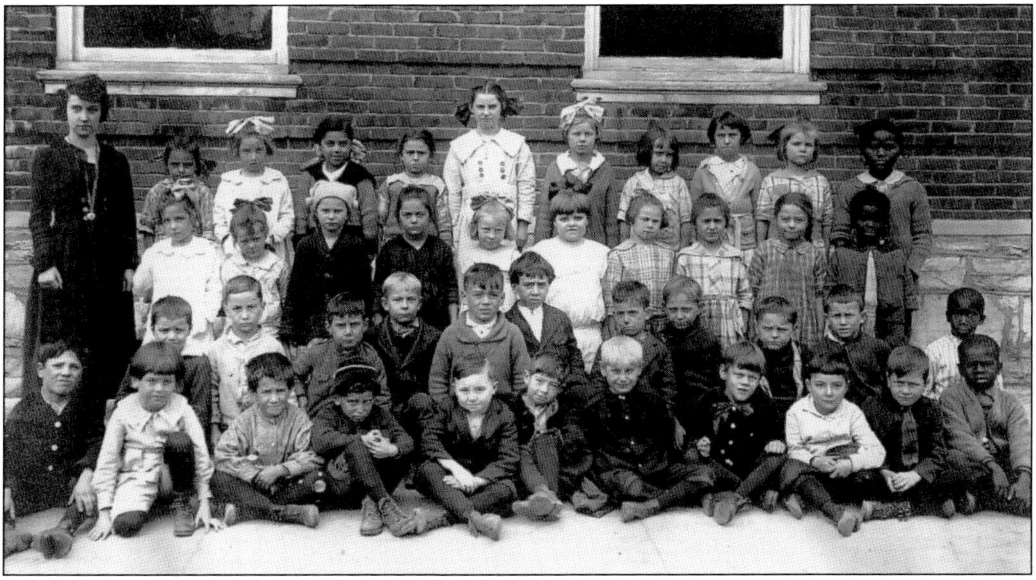

Buck Street Elementary School students and their teacher pose for a class picture.

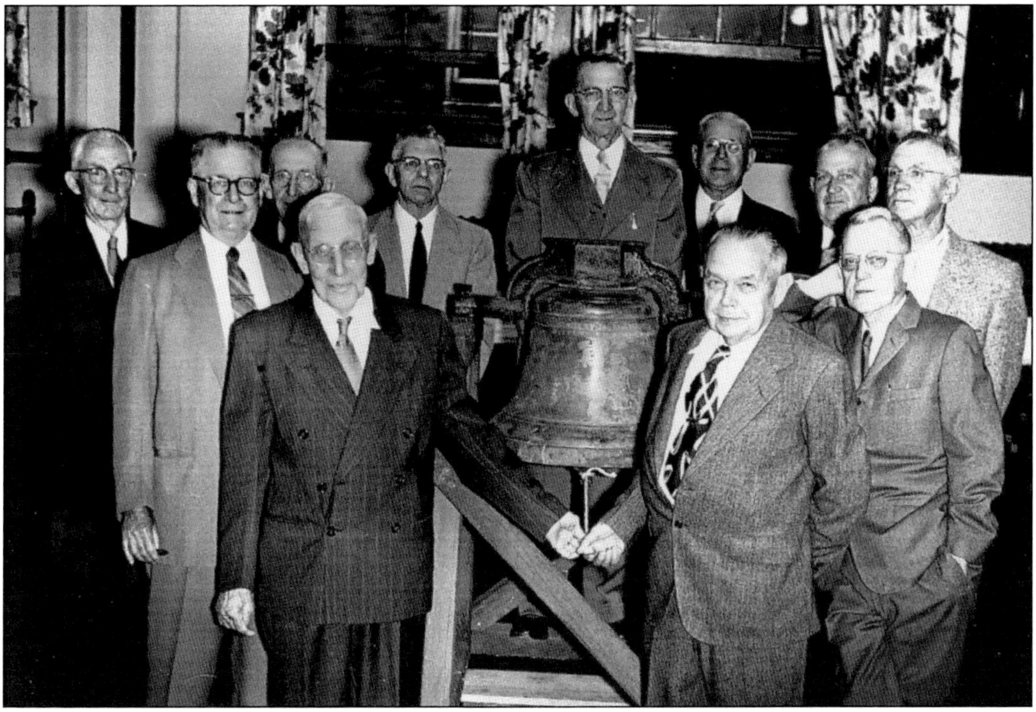

As a part of the celebration of the 34th annual reunion of the William Bennett School Boys Club, members ring the bell of the Old Buck Street School in memory of departed members of the club. In the foreground are the club's oldest member, 84-year-old Charles P. Wingate, and the club's youngest member, 63-year-old Warren Gudbranson. Standing behind them are, from left to right, John Craig (treasurer), Walter C. Thomson, Herbert Clark, John P. Reed (president), Alexander Bonsack (master of ceremonies), Isaac Vanneman, J. B. McCorkell, Tyler Miller, and W. W. Wingate (secretary).

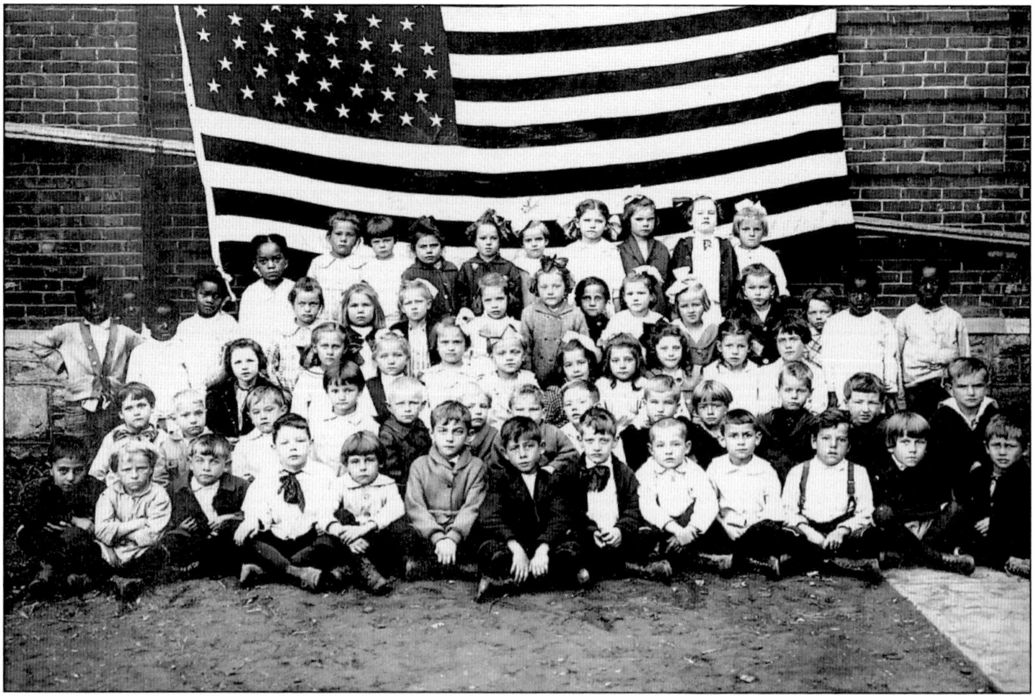

Old Glory can be seen in the background of these c. 1860s photographs of Buck Street School classes.

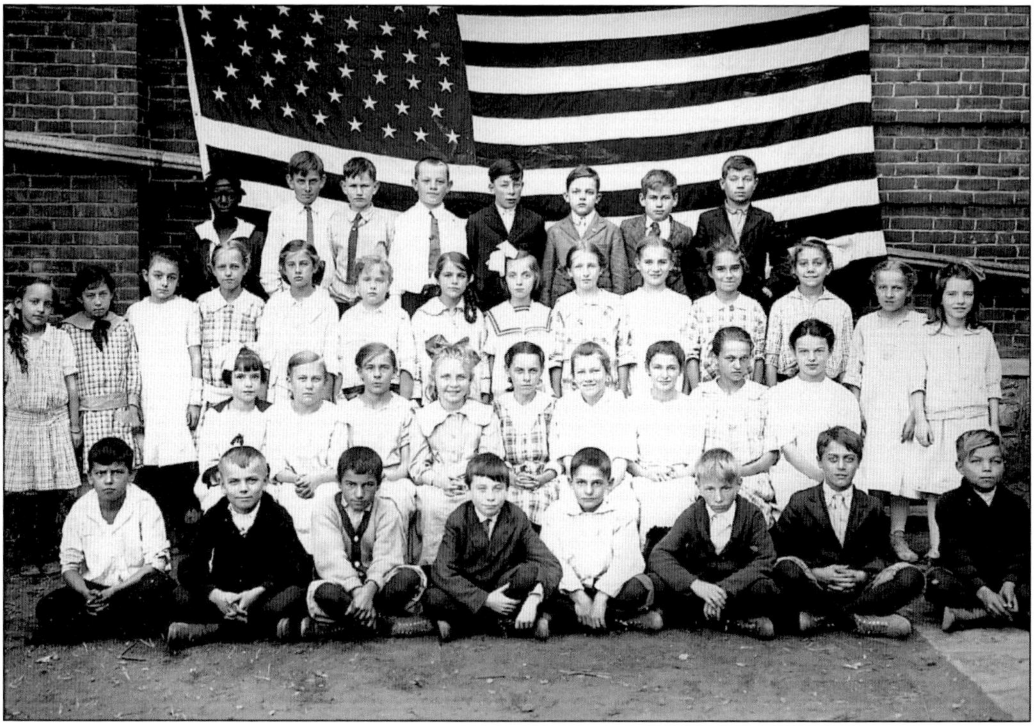

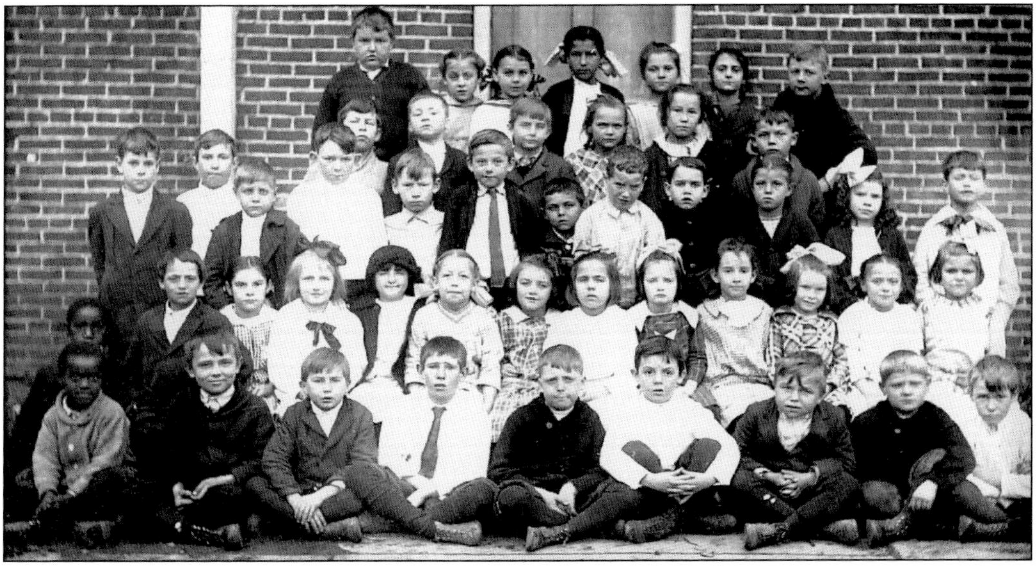

Students pose for this *c.* 1860s class picture at Buck Street School.

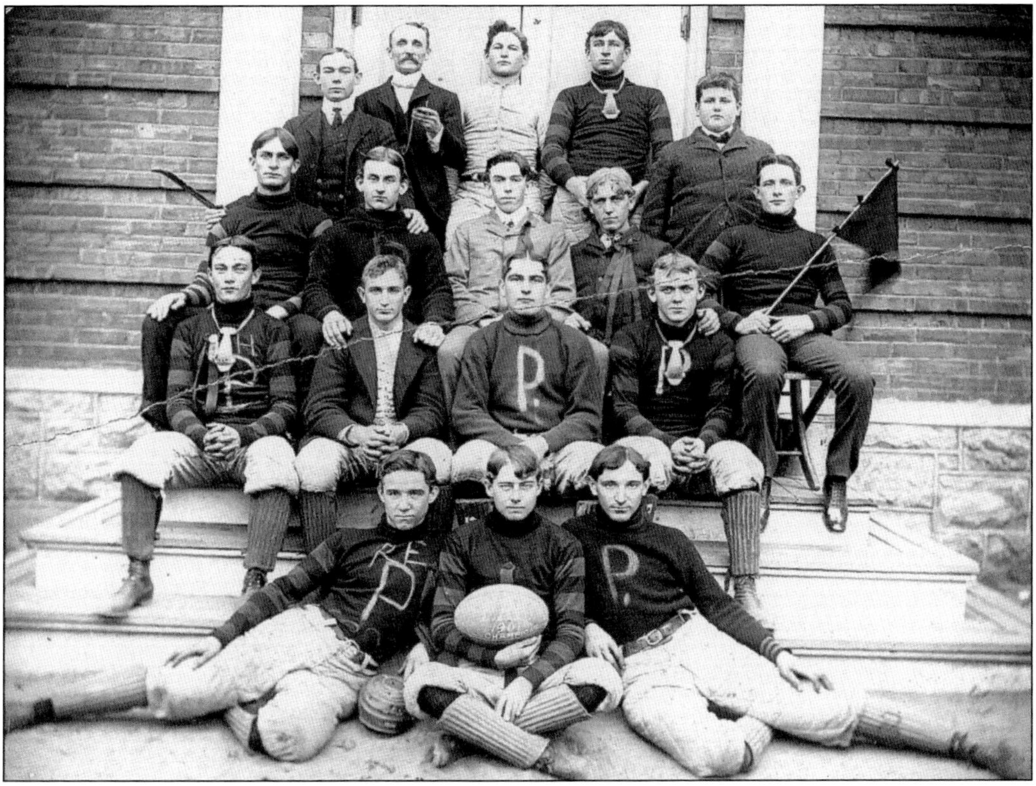

Members of the Paulsboro football team of 1901 are, from left to right, as follows: (first row) Charles Haussman, Walter "Bing" Thomson, and Edward Clark; (second row) Walter DeVault, Elwood Clark, Will DuBrink, and Joe Lock; (third row) Joe Thompson, Ed Miller, Harry Adamson, George Brown, and William Snyder; (fourth row) Frank Bonsack, Ambler Stetser (manager), Charles Burr, Jim Thompson, and Walter Stratton.

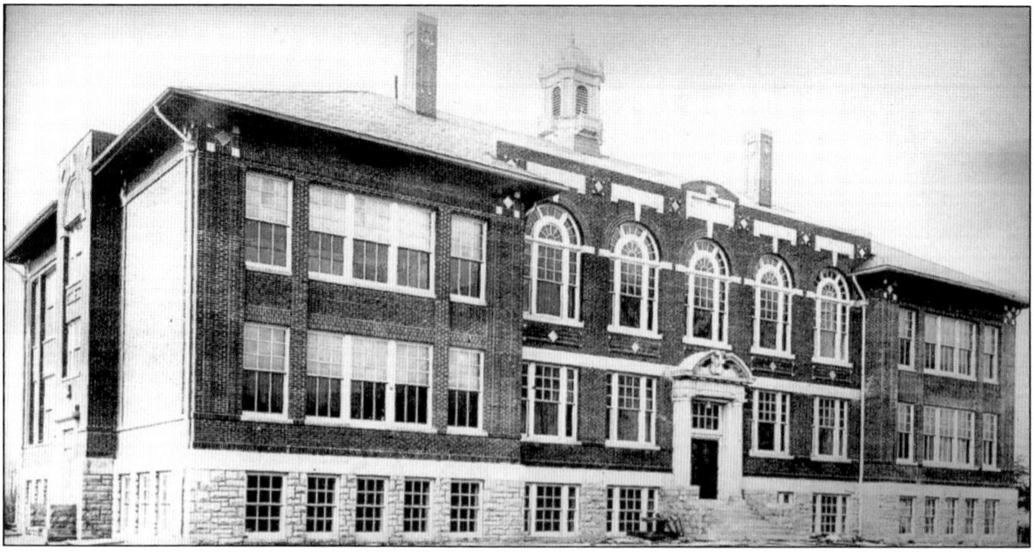

Paulsboro High School is seen under construction in 1917.

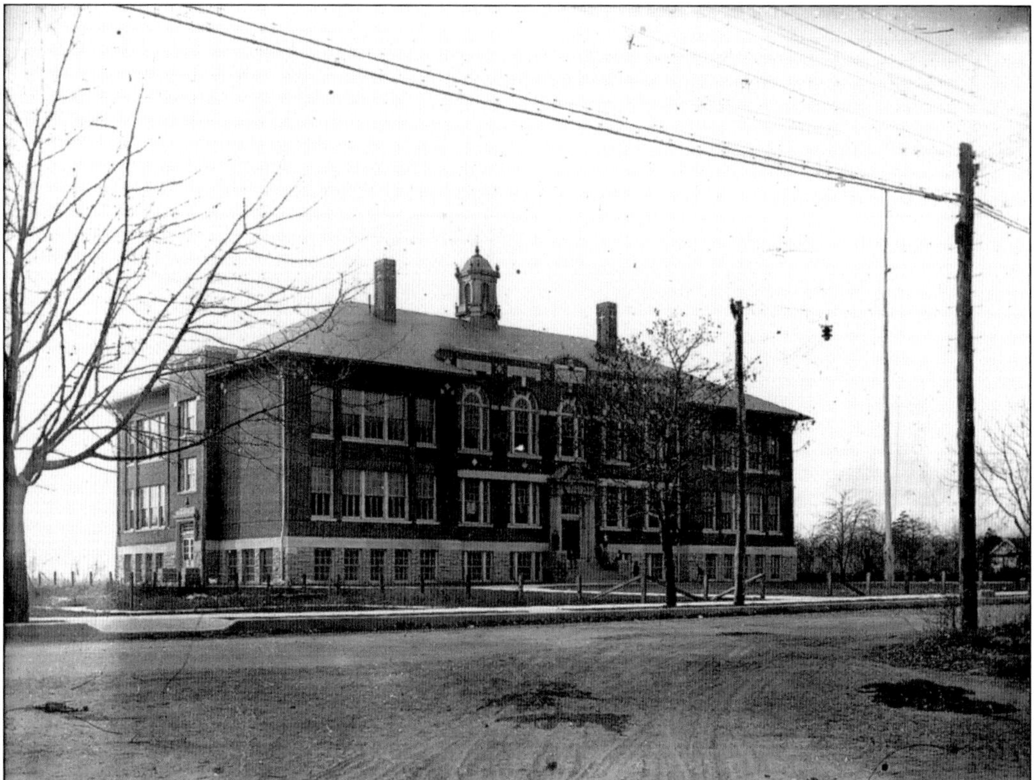

This early view of Paulsboro High School shows the unpaved roadways of the time.

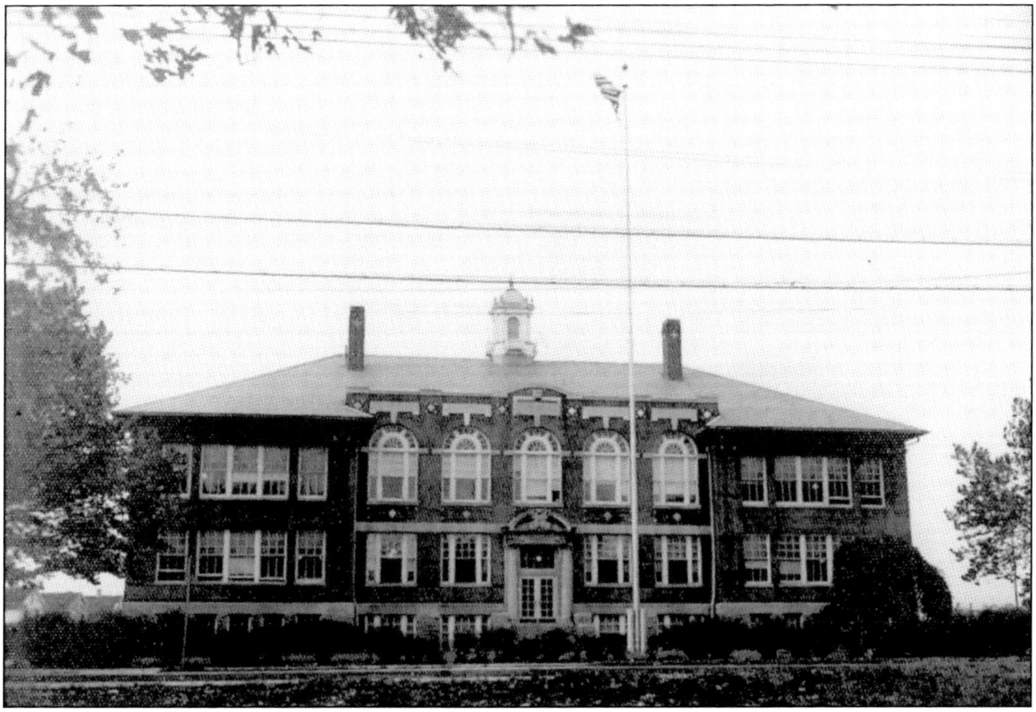

This front view of Paulsboro High School, facing Delaware Street, shows the absence of other structures around the building.

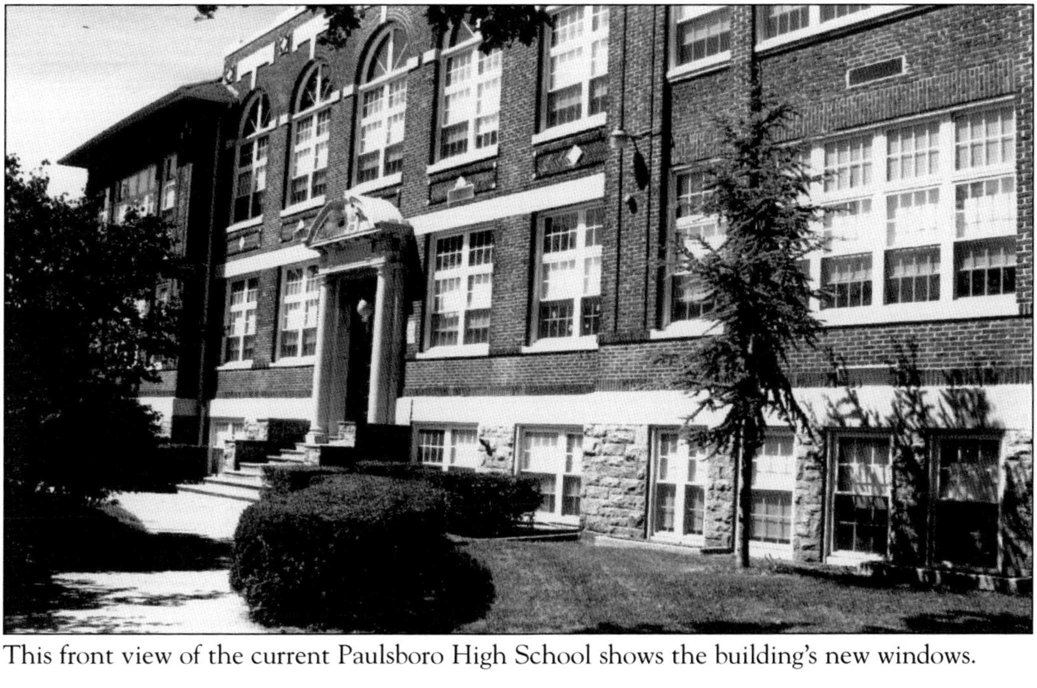

This front view of the current Paulsboro High School shows the building's new windows.

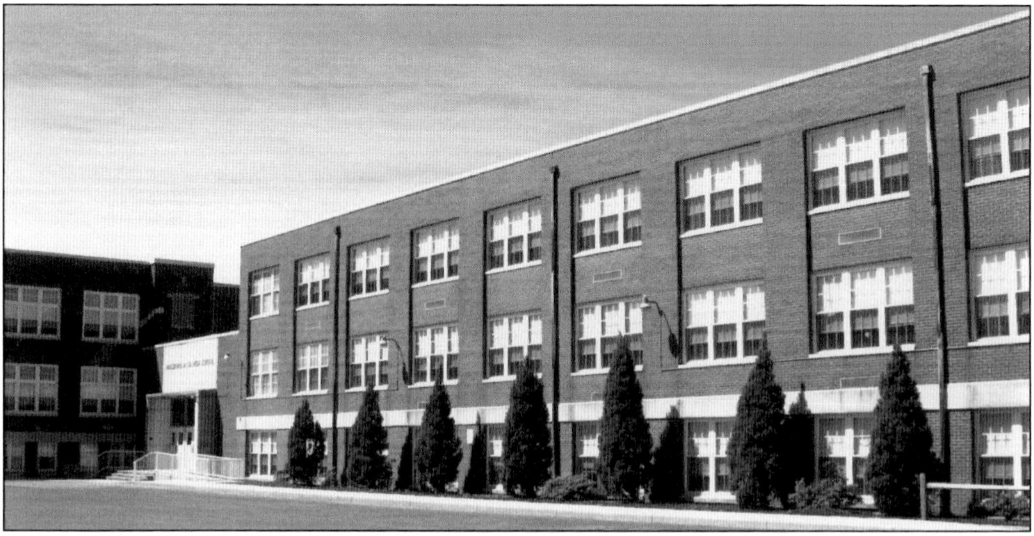

Paulsboro High School has received three additions over the years. This wing was added in 1966.

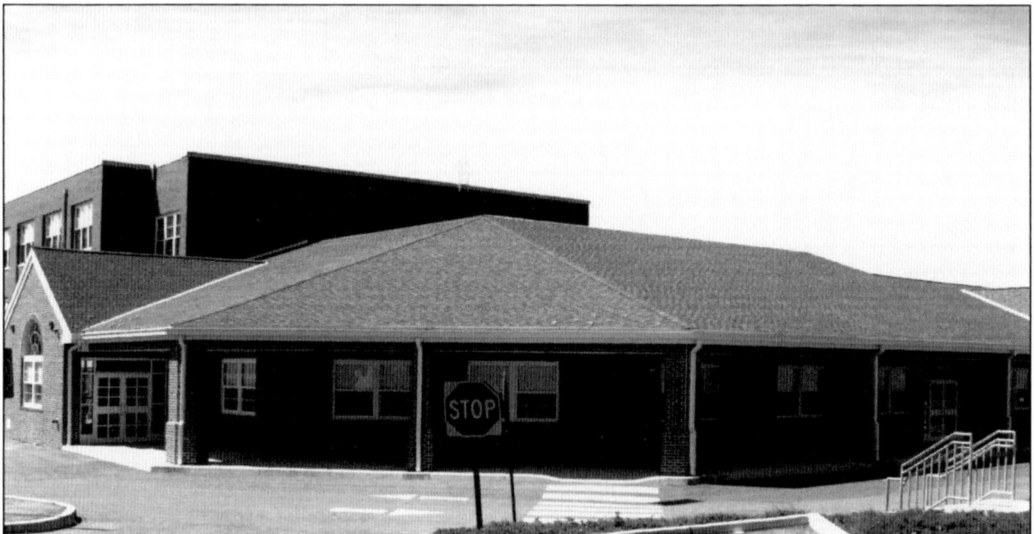

This wide view shows the school's newest addition, which includes the library-media center that was added in 2000.

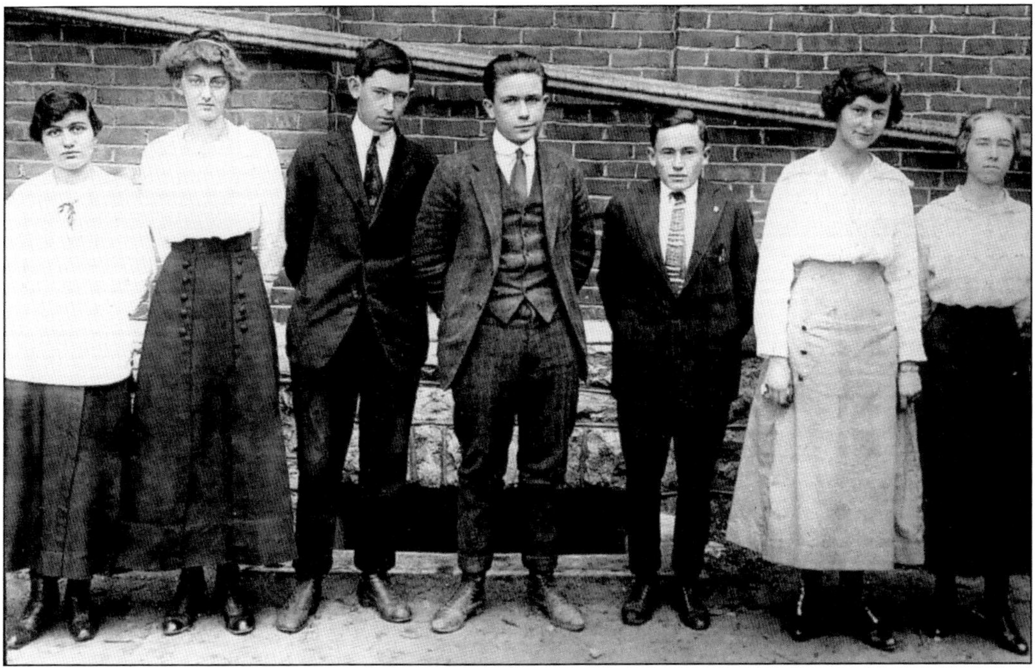

The class of 1917 was the first graduating class of Paulsboro High School's present building. Class members are, from left to right, Millie Reed, Rae Shuster, Edward Bramell, Earle Wonderlich, J. Garnet West, Elsie Risner, and Olive Middleton.

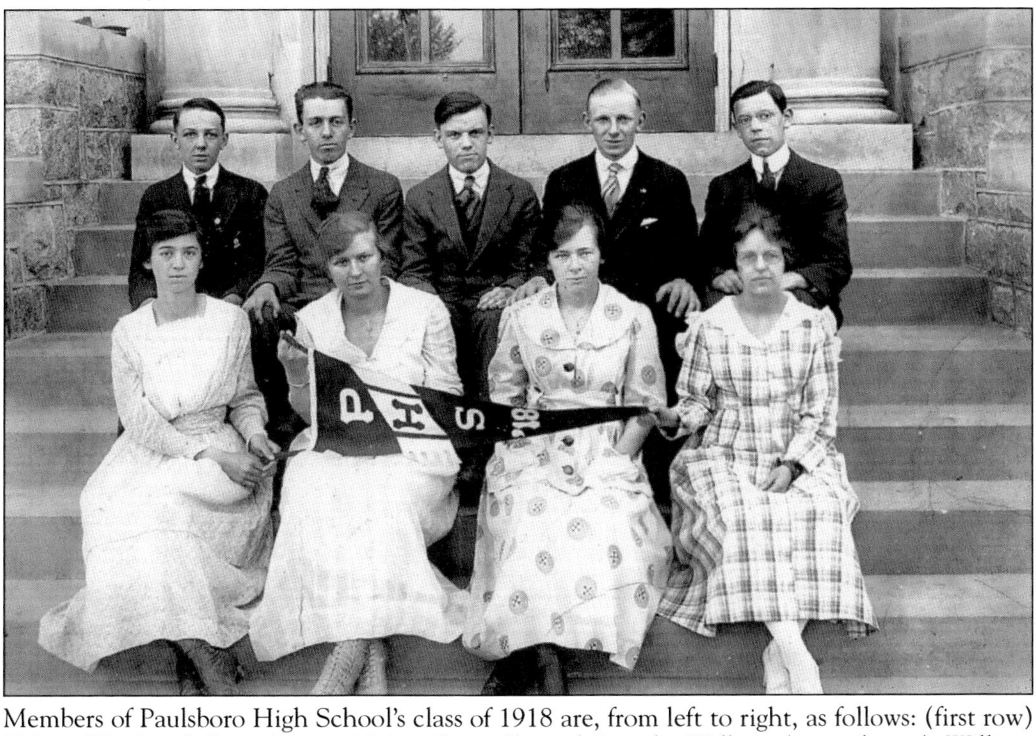

Members of Paulsboro High School's class of 1918 are, from left to right, as follows: (first row) Helen Wright, Lillian Zanes, Helen Bramell, and Lenola Wilkes; (second row) William Lowden, Ralph Adamson, Garland Miller, Clark Gleeson, and Carl Knake.

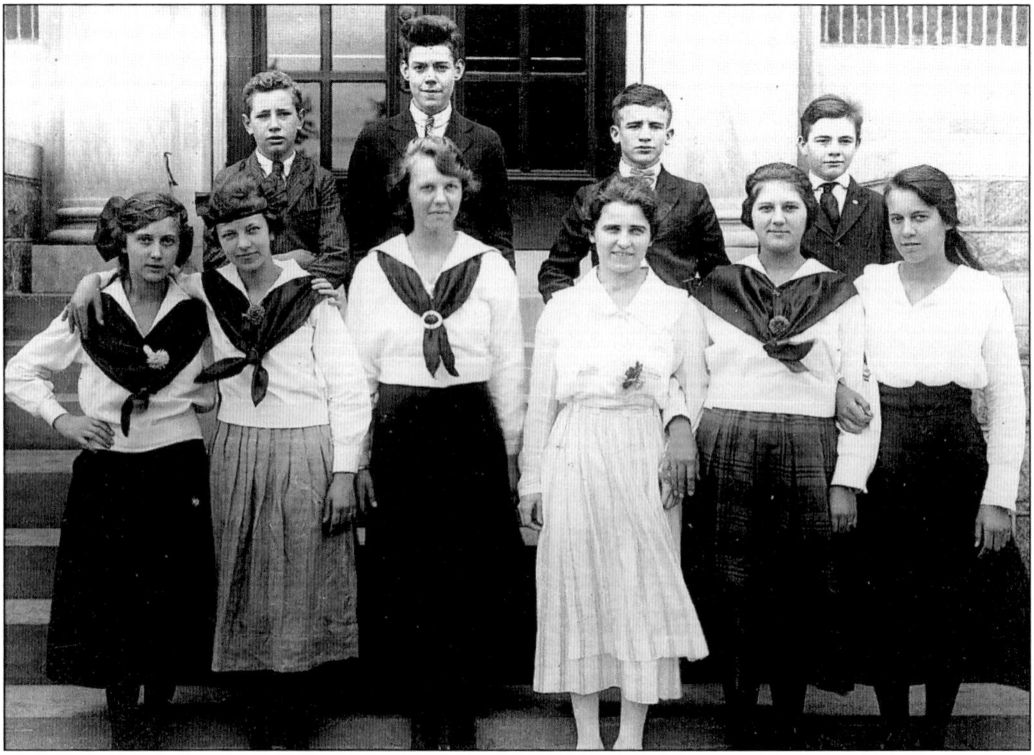

Members of Paulsboro High School's graduating class of 1922 are, from left to right, as follows: (first row) Frances Stanley, Elizabeth Fell, Grace Bell, Grace Burt (teacher), Grace Bundens, and Marian Simmerman; (second row) "Motsy" Plamer, James Bates, Leo Bonner, and Frank Eastlack.

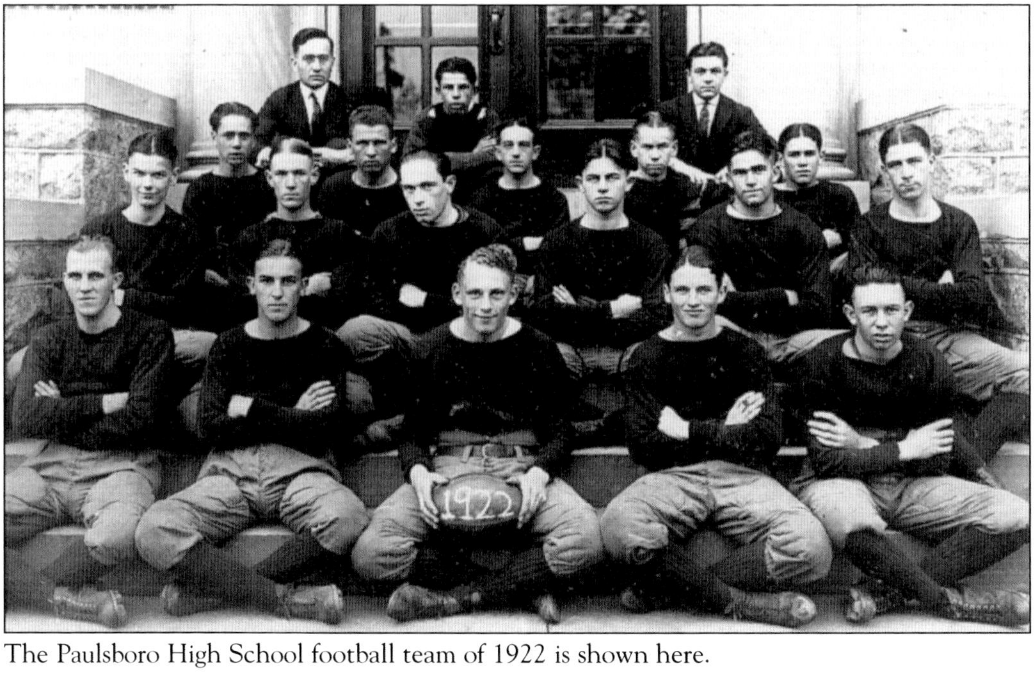

The Paulsboro High School football team of 1922 is shown here.

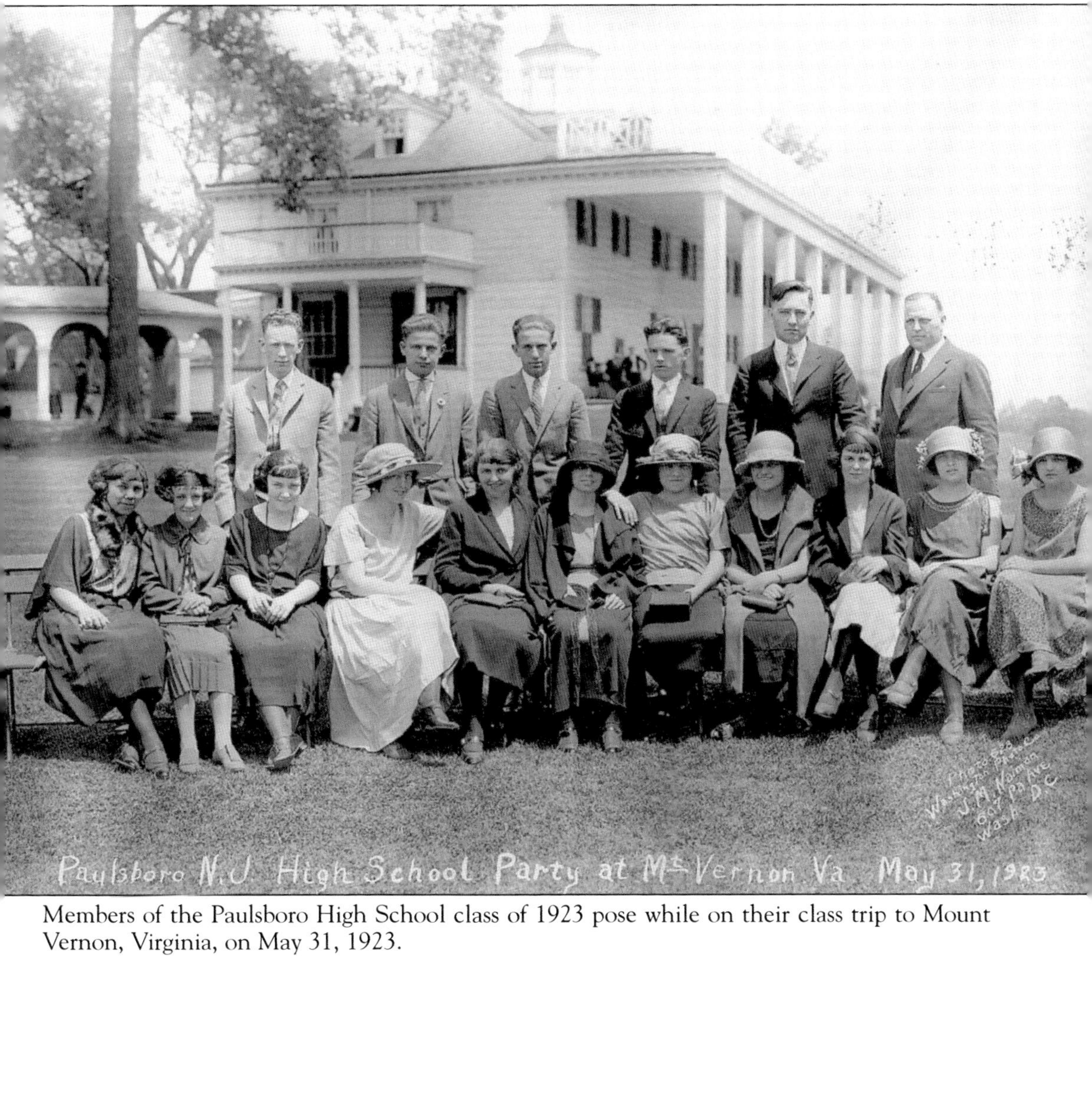

Members of the Paulsboro High School class of 1923 pose while on their class trip to Mount Vernon, Virginia, on May 31, 1923.

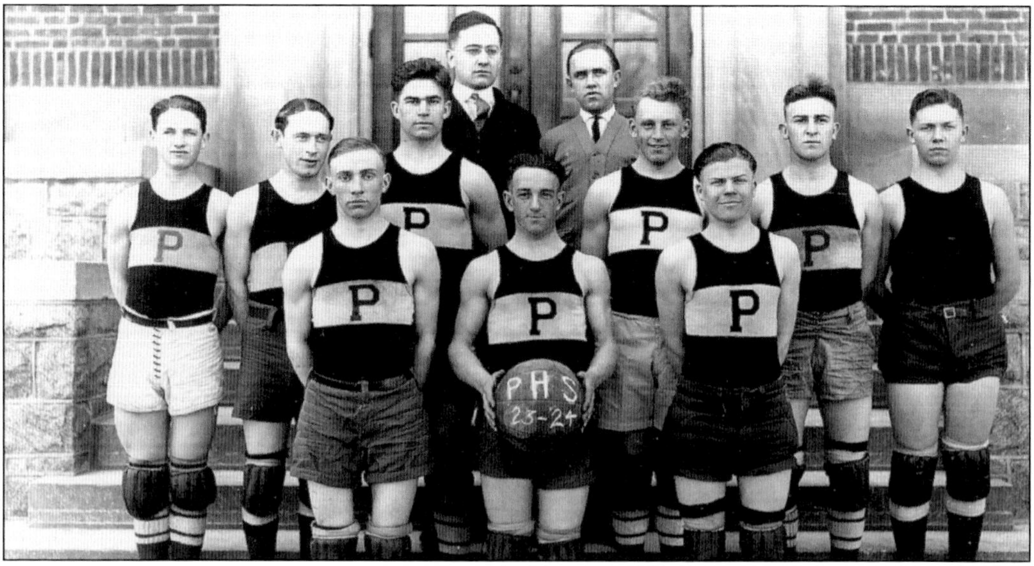

The 1923–1924 Paulsboro High School basketball team is shown here. From left to right are the following: (first row) Mickey Schuman, "Doc" Albert Meyers, and Albert Knestaut; (second row) Pat Roanoe, Bernard Brickman, Casper Hawarth, George Hendrickson, D. West, and Eddie Bunden; (third row) John Shay (coach) and Gerard Stackhouse (manager).

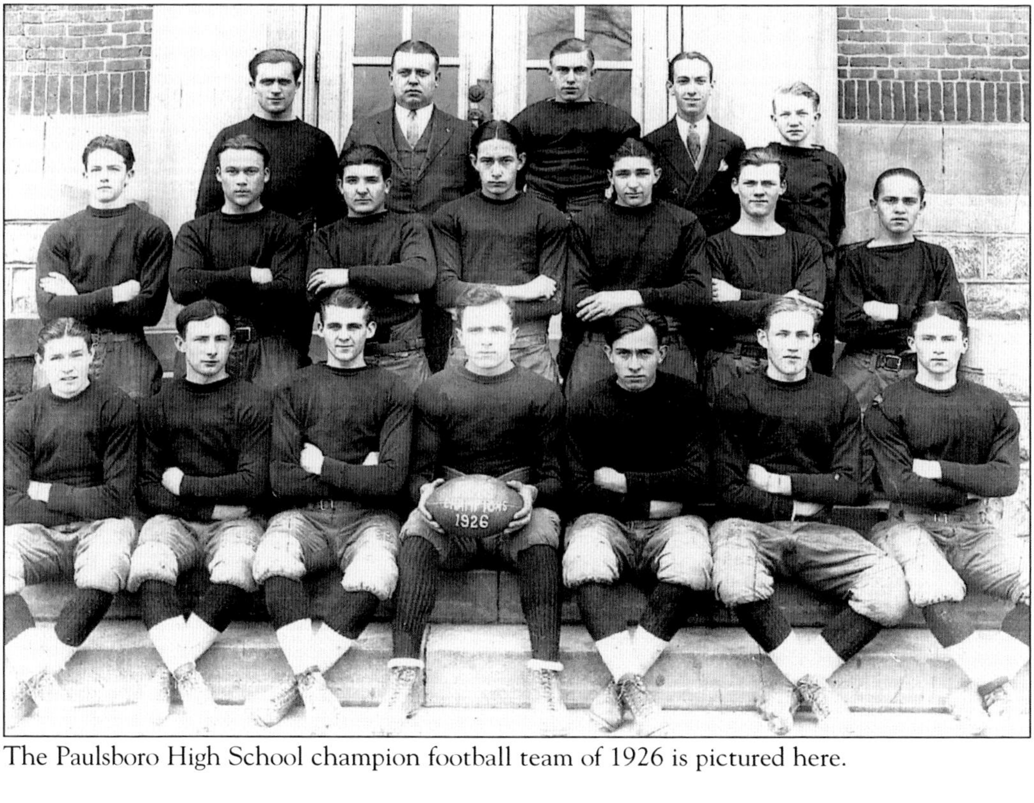

The Paulsboro High School champion football team of 1926 is pictured here.

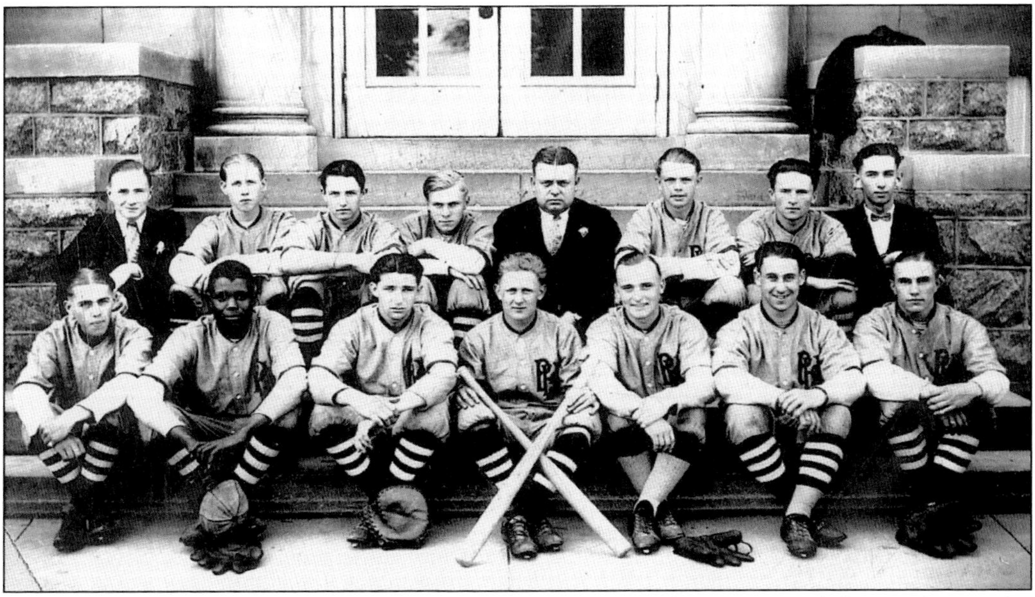

Pictured here is the Paulsboro High School baseball team of 1927. From left to right are the following: (first row) Alvin Folker, James Eli, Willard Hitchner, George Kungler, Joseph Enos, Carl Flack, and Frank Shoeman; (second row) Kenny Adams (manager), Melvin Dubois, Harry Hunter, Harry "Babe" Shoeman, Phil Stump (coach), Newell Langley, Howard Cassidy, and Paul Fink (manager).

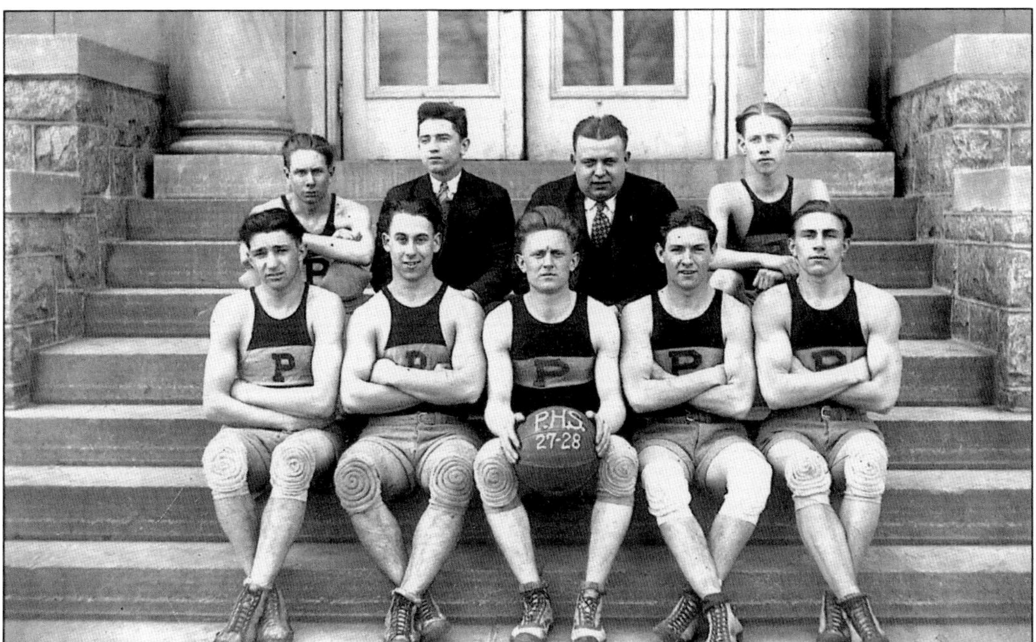

The Paulsboro High School basketball team of 1927–1928 included Willard Hitchner, Carl Flack, George Funzler, John Stuart, Frank Shoeman, ? Washburn, Steve Richards (manager), Phil Stump (coach), and Melvin Dubois.

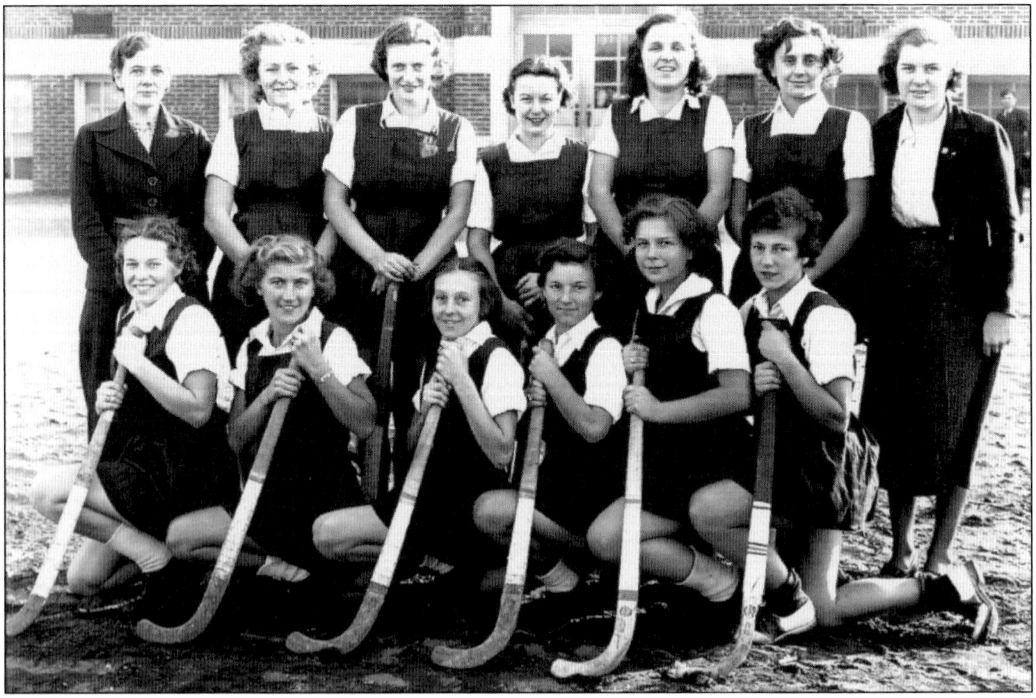

The Paulsboro High School girls' hockey team of 1937 poses here. From left to right are the following: (first row) Betty Turner, Rose Apostoli, Patricia Taylor, Mitzi Gellenthin, Margaret Mogor, and Gert McCarson; (second row) Dot Roper (coach), Dot Moran, Grace Bibihaus, Josephine Kayser, Mary Kelly, Florence Schuler, and Irma Kamman. (Donated by Margaret Mogor Owen.)

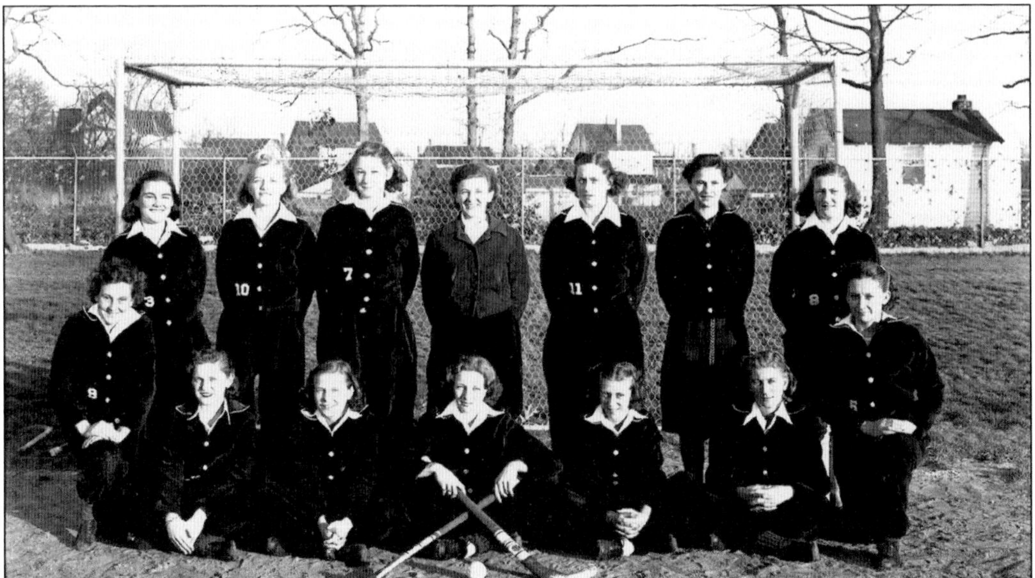

The Paulsboro High School girls' hockey team of 1938 included Pat Taylor, Martha Wolfrom, Margaret Mogor, Gladys Thompson, Gert McCarson, Rose Apostoli, and Everlyn Driscoll. (Donated by Margaret Mogor Owen.)

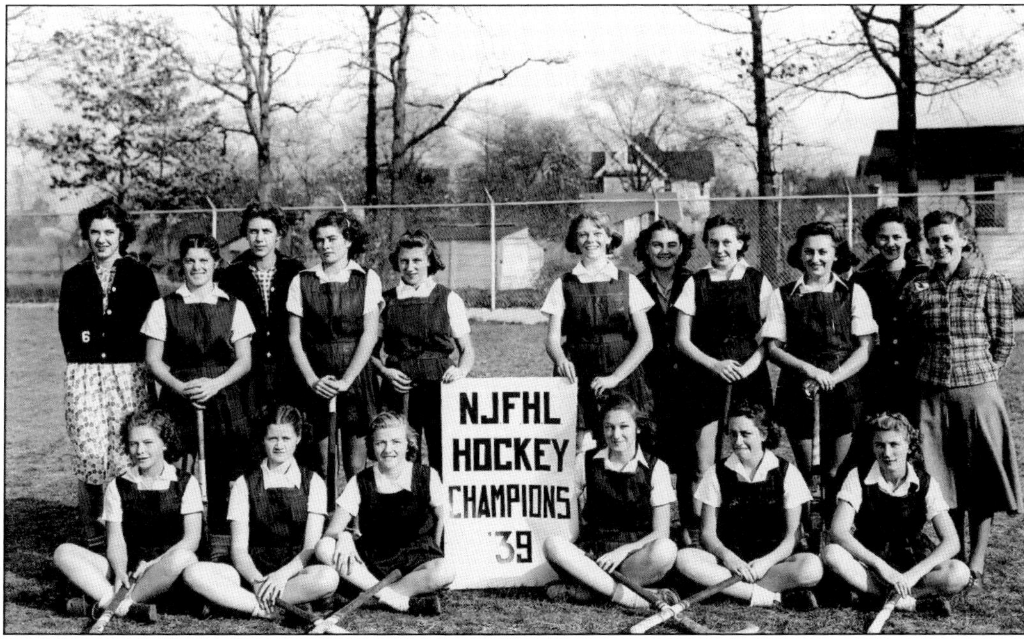

The members of the Paulsboro High School girls' champion hockey team of 1939 are, from left to right, as follows: (first row) Margaret Mogor, Elaine Heritage, Mary Gesty, Carolyn Carl, Anna Miller, and Rose Apostoli; (second row) Jean Adan, Theresa Croce, Elizabeth Wingate, Rose Wilson, Gert McCarson, Isabel Marple, Mary DiNardo, Pat Taylor, Evelyn Driscoll, Betty Owen, and Dot Roper (coach). (Donated by Margaret Mogor Owen.)

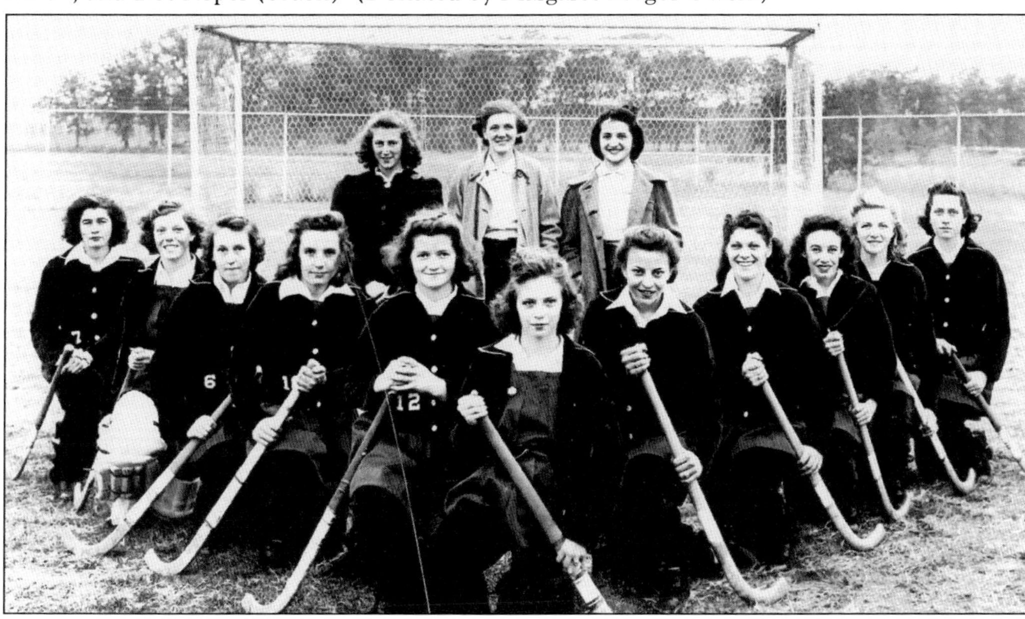

Members of the Paulsboro High School girls' hockey team of 1940 are, from left to right, as follows: (first row) Rose Wilson, Isabel Marple, Pat Taylor, Helen Raively, Sally Hertiage, Mickey Reynolds, Anna Sindoni, Theresa Croce, Grace Miller, Mary Gesty, and Anna Miller; (second row) Gert McCarson, Dot Roper (coach), and Jean Gezzi. (Donated by Margaret Mogor Owen.)

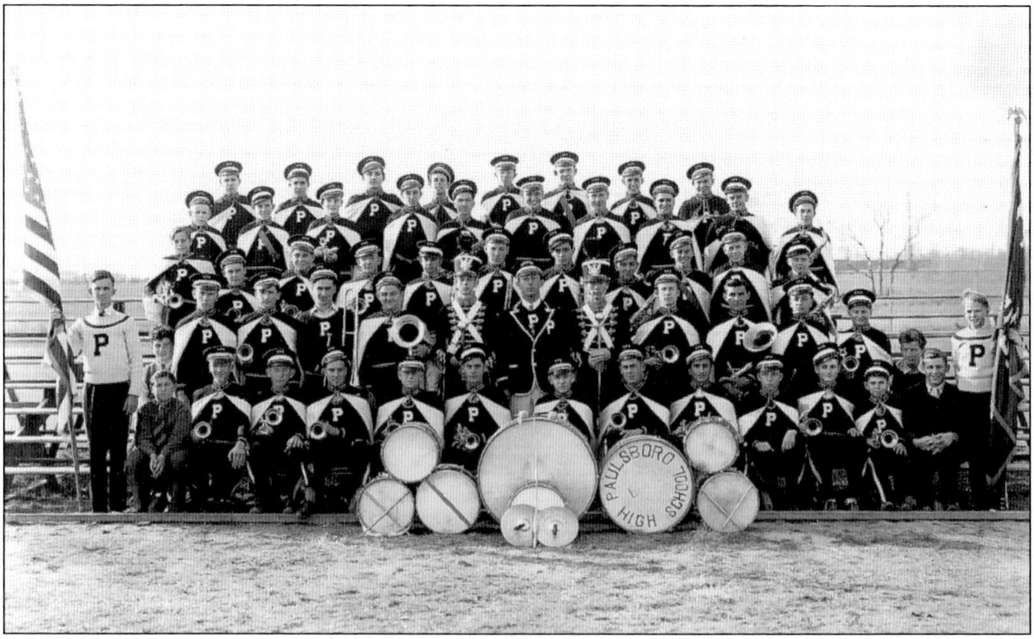

The members of the 1940 high school band pose for a photograph. (Donated by Naomi and Harry Snyder.)

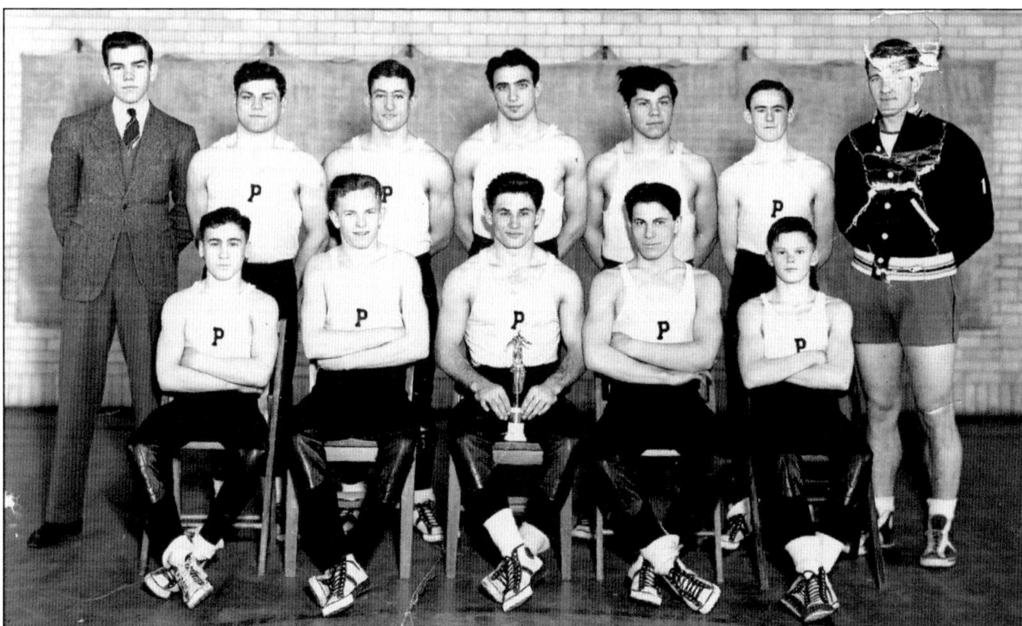

The Paulsboro High School wrestling team of 1941 includes, from left to right, the following: (first row) Frank Gattuso, Wilburn Webber, Anthony Gattuso, Michael Croce, and Peter Munyan; (second row) Jack Rule, Peter Limanni, John Gattuso, Anthony Carbone, John Limanni, Jack Haughey, and Norman Hangen (coach). (Photograph courtesy of Paul Morina.)

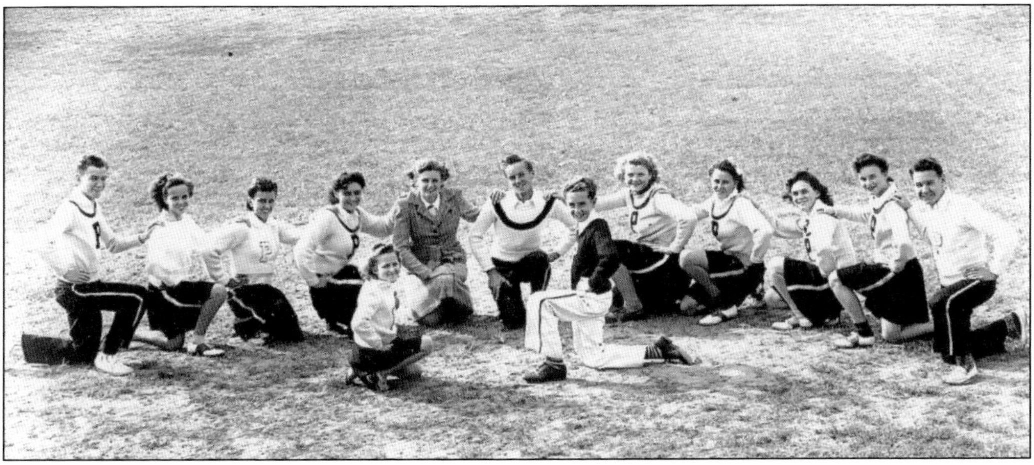

Members of the Paulsboro High School cheerleading squad of 1943 are, from left to right, as follows: (first row) Florance Malin and Howard Lipsett; (second row) Rudy Hagenbarth, Ruth Reeves, Kathryn Vilykis, Ruth Manchester, J. Marie Anderwald (coach), Jimmy Bernard, Sara Llyod, Lucinda Hinman, Naomi Fogg, Janet Ailes, and Howard Cox. (Donated by Naomi and Harry Snyder.)

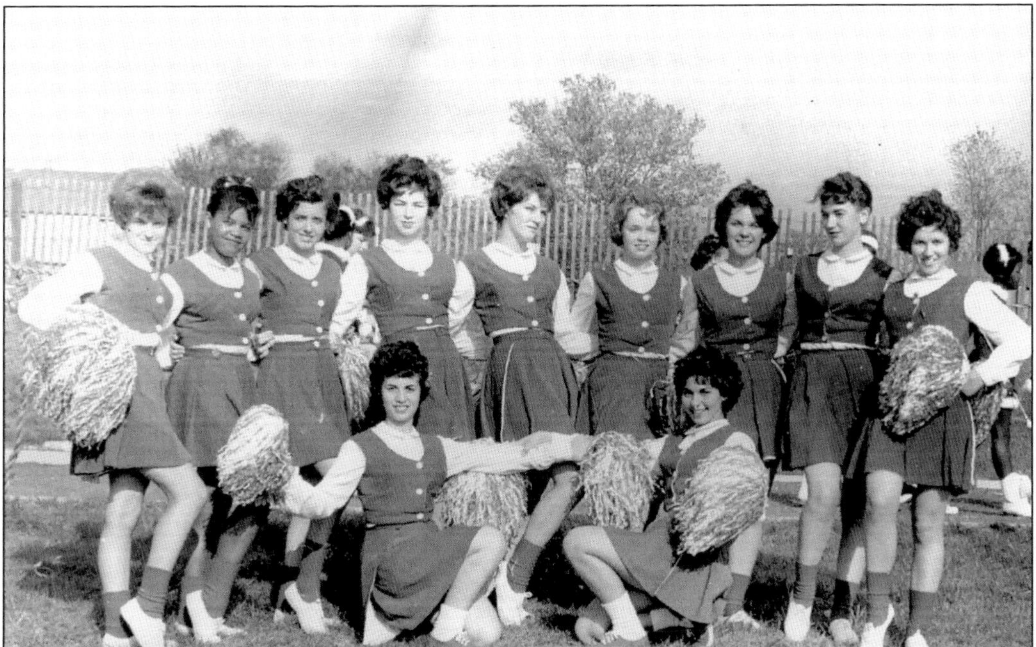

The members of the 1962 Paulsboro High School cheerleading squad are, from left to right, as follows: (first row) Joann Mercantino and Jane Dellaratta (cocaptains); (second row) Carol Piel, Hazel Roots, Beverly Duffy, Karen Drummond, Sheila Brayton, Vicki Weller, Carol Langen, Ann DeHart, and Donna Brown. (Donated by Vicki Weller Kumpel.)

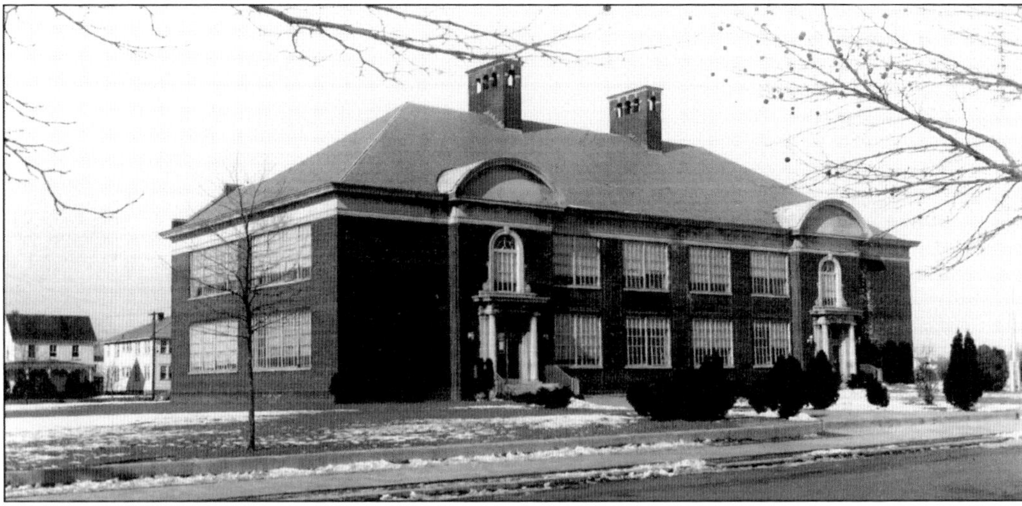

This July 3, 1950, photograph shows the front of Billingsport School facing Greenwich Avenue. When the school's doors opened for students on September 10, 1924, the boys had to use one entrance of the building while the girls used the other.

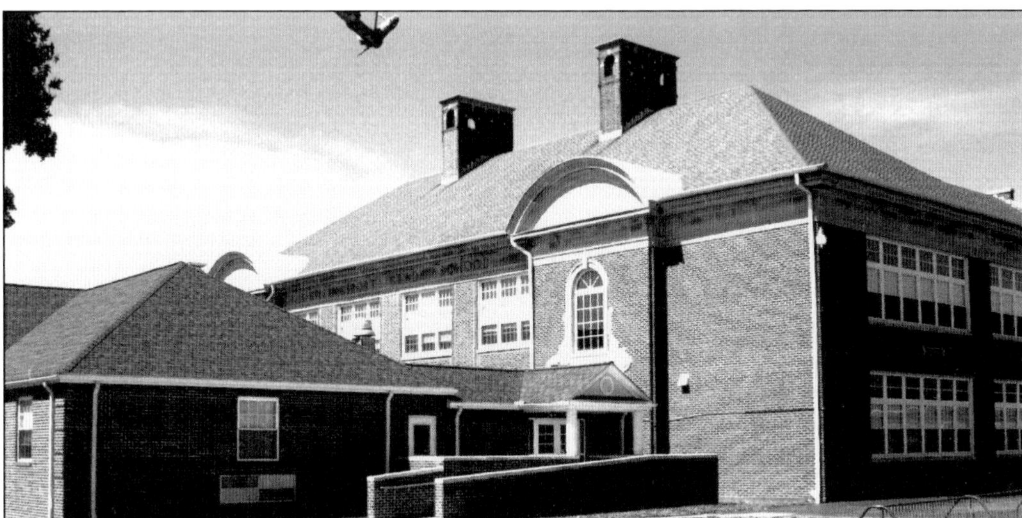

A different angle of Billingsport School shows the 1999 addition of the library-media center. The addition forced the main entrance of the building to be moved from Greenwich Avenue to Nassau Avenue.

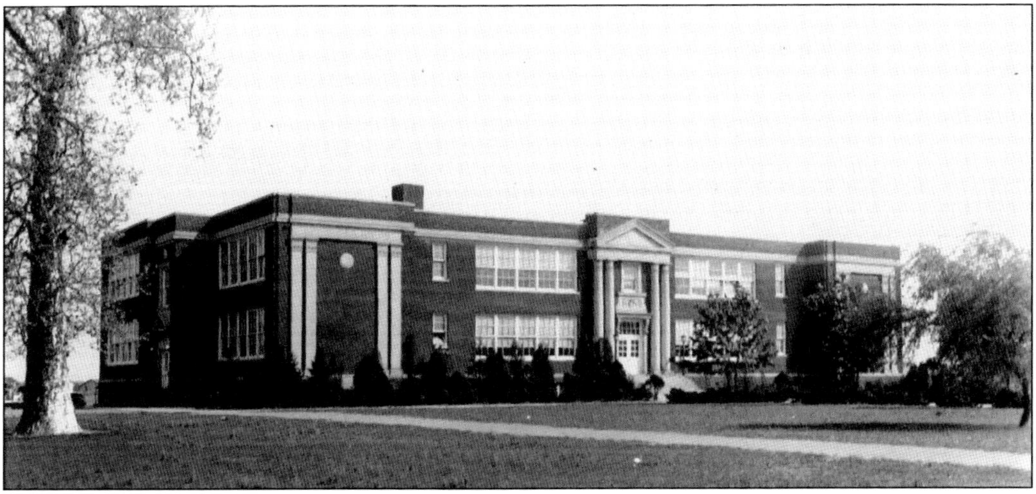

This *c*. 1940 photograph shows the Loudenslager School facing Swedesboro Avenue.

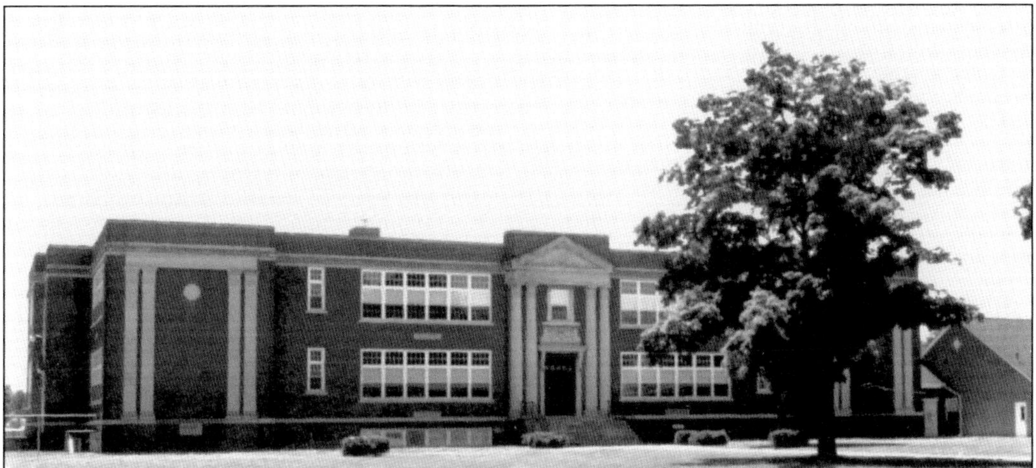

This photograph of Loudenslager School shows the 1999 addition of library-media center.

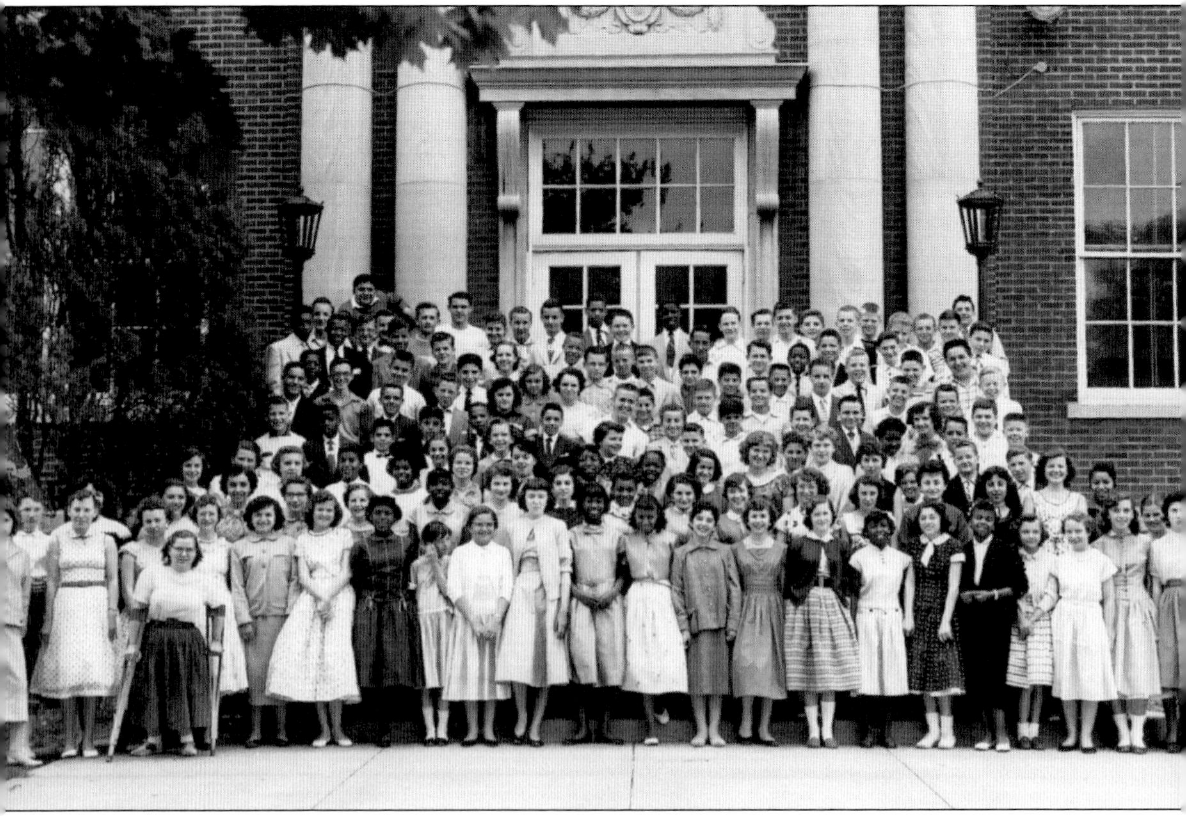

Students pose in front of Loudenslager School c. 1955.

Five

BUSINESSES

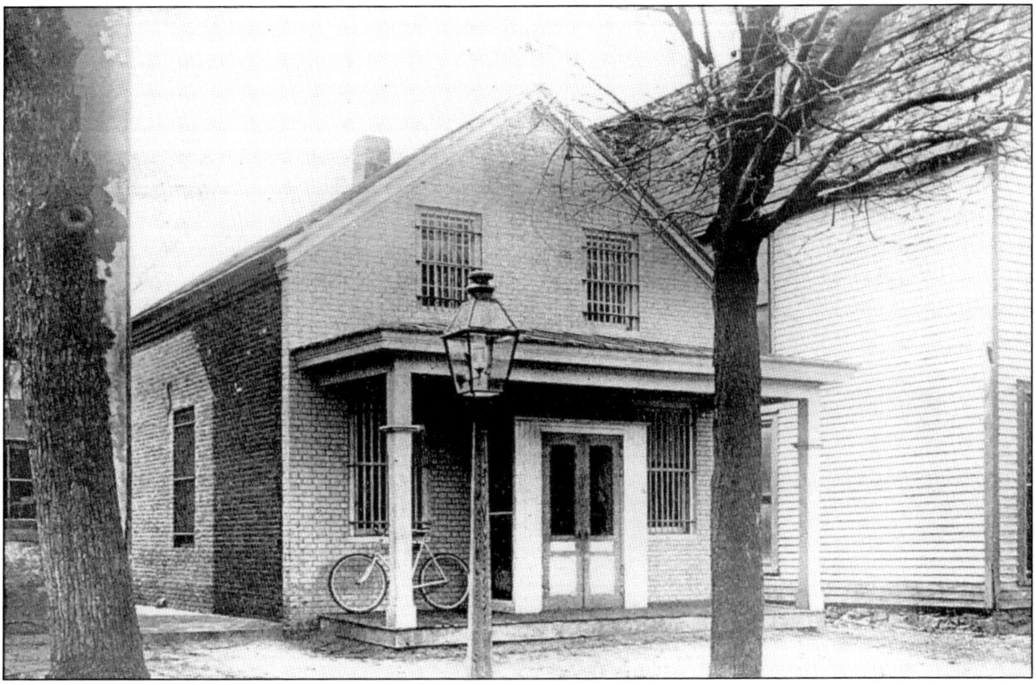

The original building of the First National Bank in Paulsboro is featured here. The bicycle in the front is said to have belonged to Judge Reed *c.* 1906.

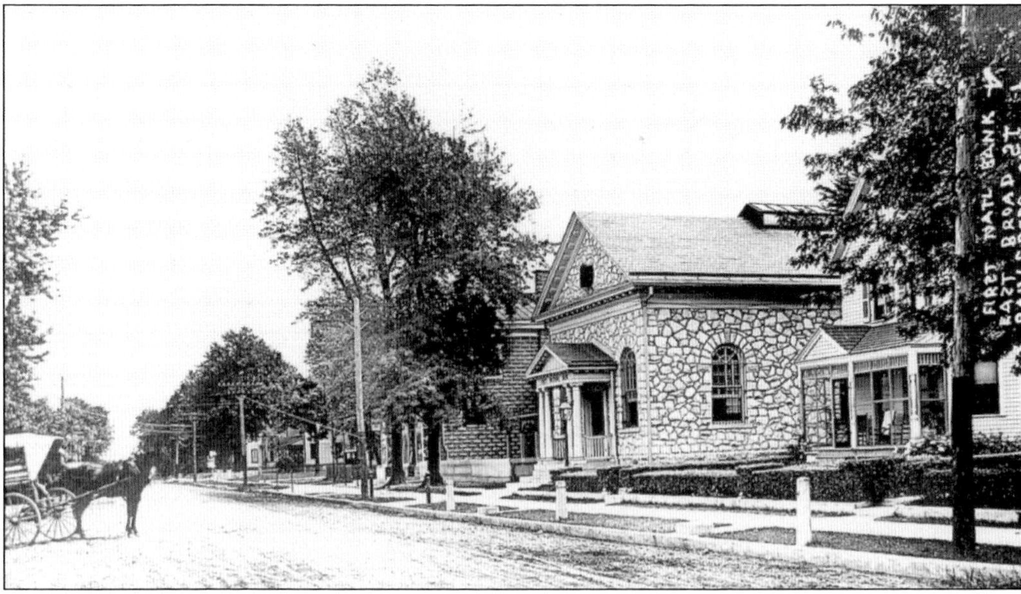

The second building of the First National Bank is shown in this *c.* 1910 photograph. Notice the horse and buggy traveling along the dirt road.

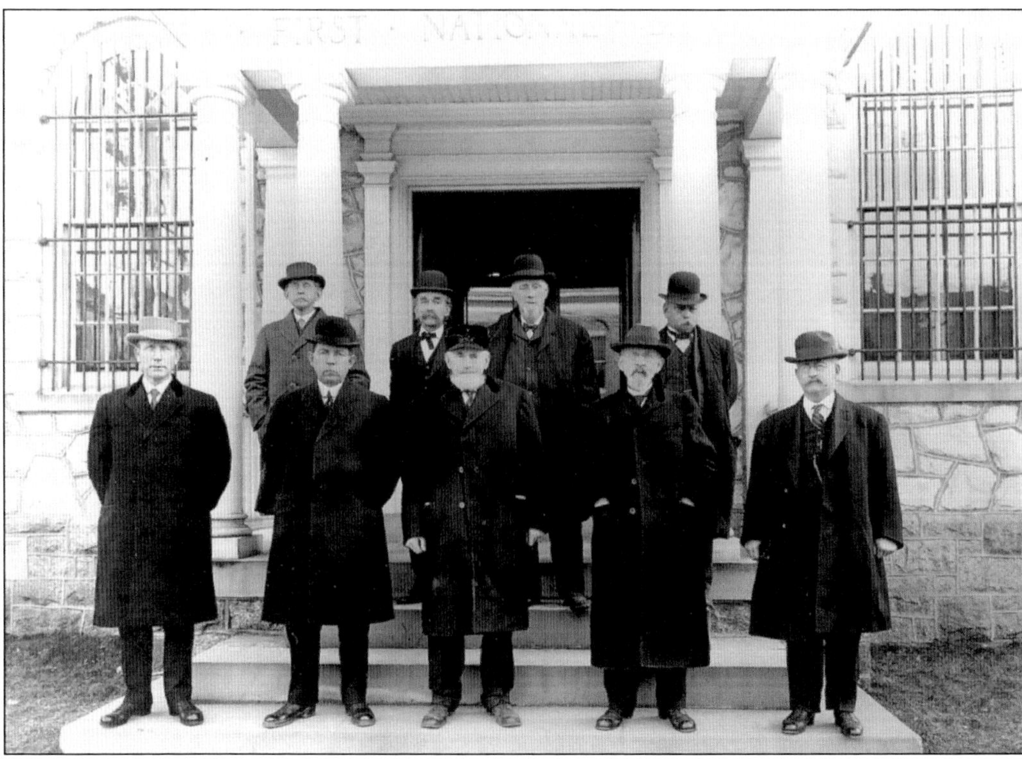

Members of the first board of directors of the First National Bank are, from left to right, as follows: (first row) B. G. Paul (president), Richard Richards (vice president), Christian Wolferth, Isaac Haines, and Edward P. Henry; (second row) William Helmes, James Cox, James DeVault, and Bowman S. Cox.

The old Paulsboro Borough Hall, seen here decorated with flags, was formerly the second home of the First National Bank, until bank built a new building in 1929. This building is now the Paulsboro Senior Citizen Center.

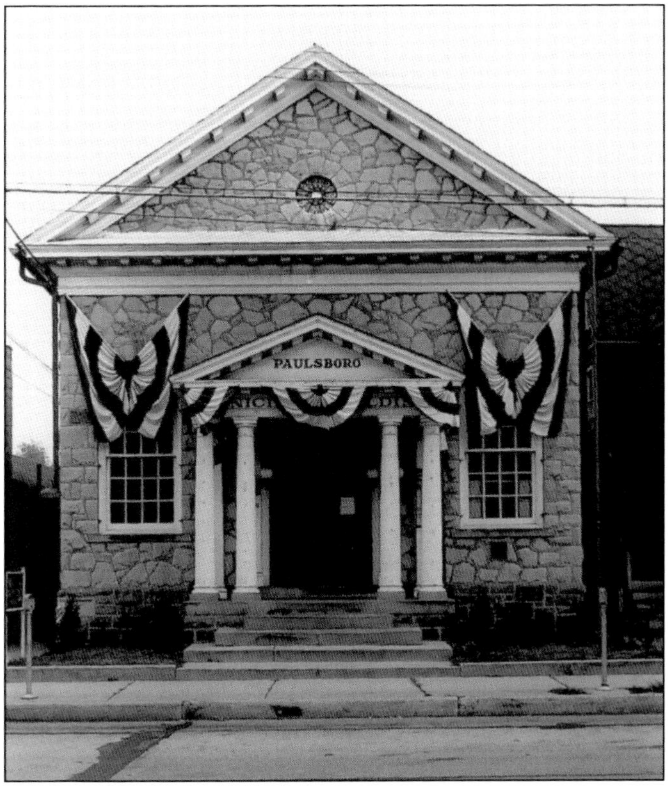

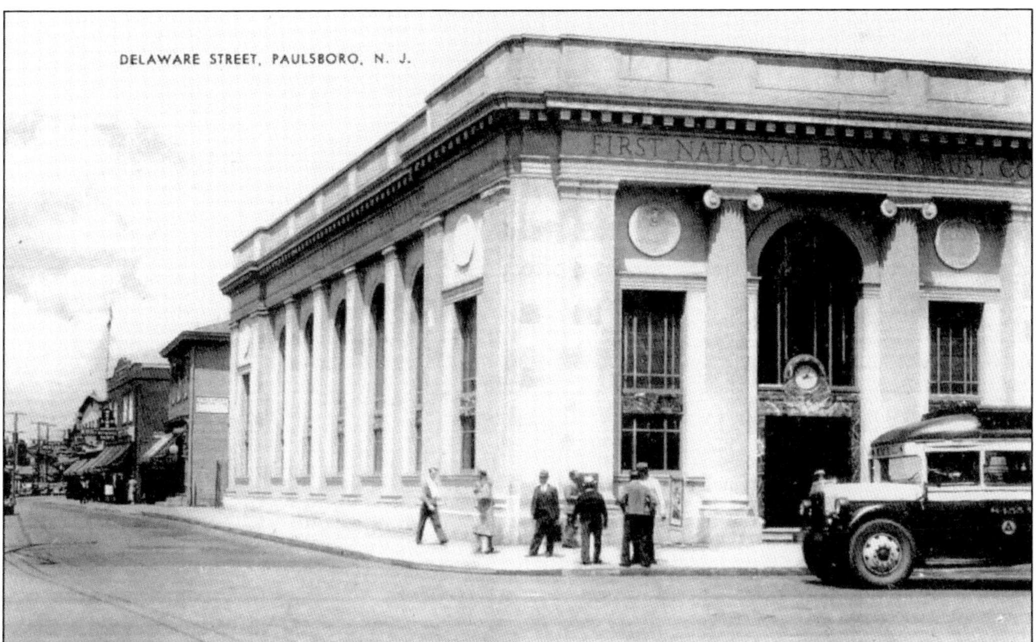

The third structure built by the First National Bank was this building, which was built in 1929 on the corner of Broad and Delaware Streets.

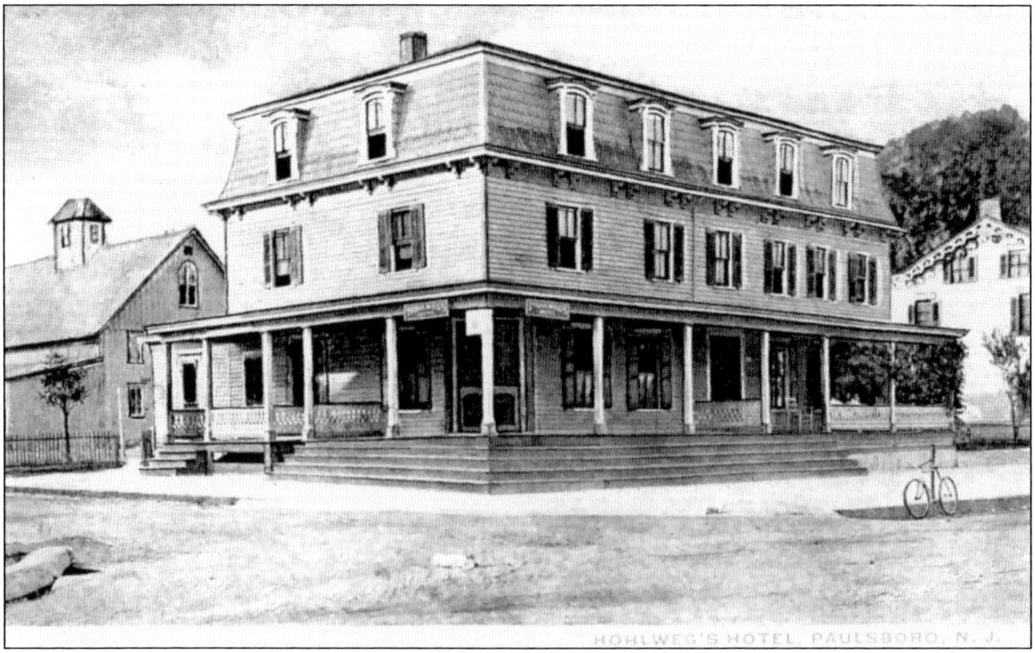

Hohlweg's Hotel, located on Broad Street, later became the Paulsboro Hotel and was eventually torn down. (Postcard by W. J. Moore.)

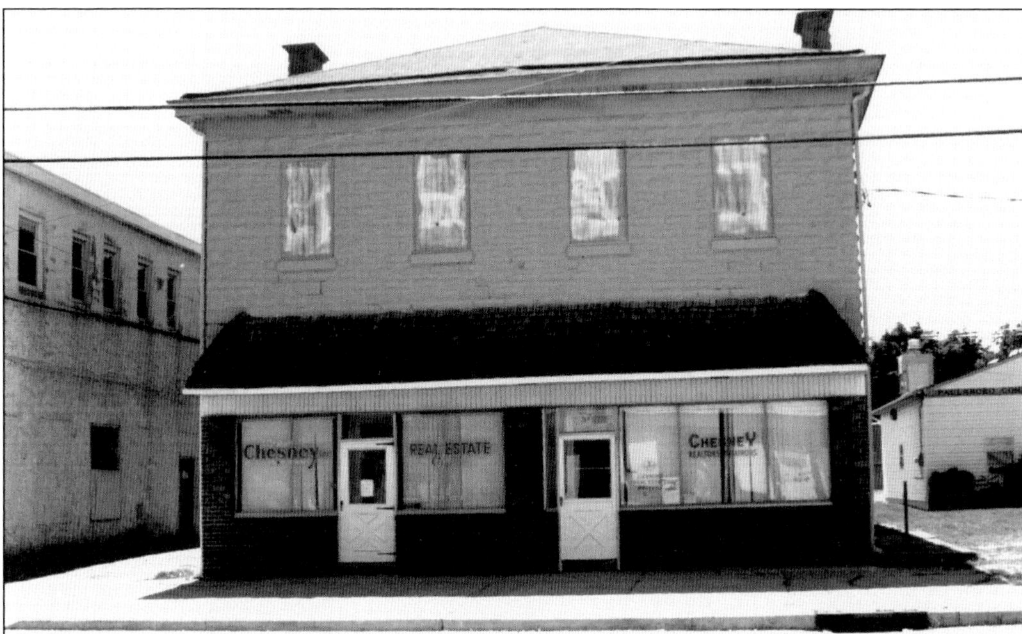

Chesney and Flowers Real Estate & Insurance was located on Broad Street. Now known as Chesney Real Estate & Insurance, the business is still operating at the same location today.

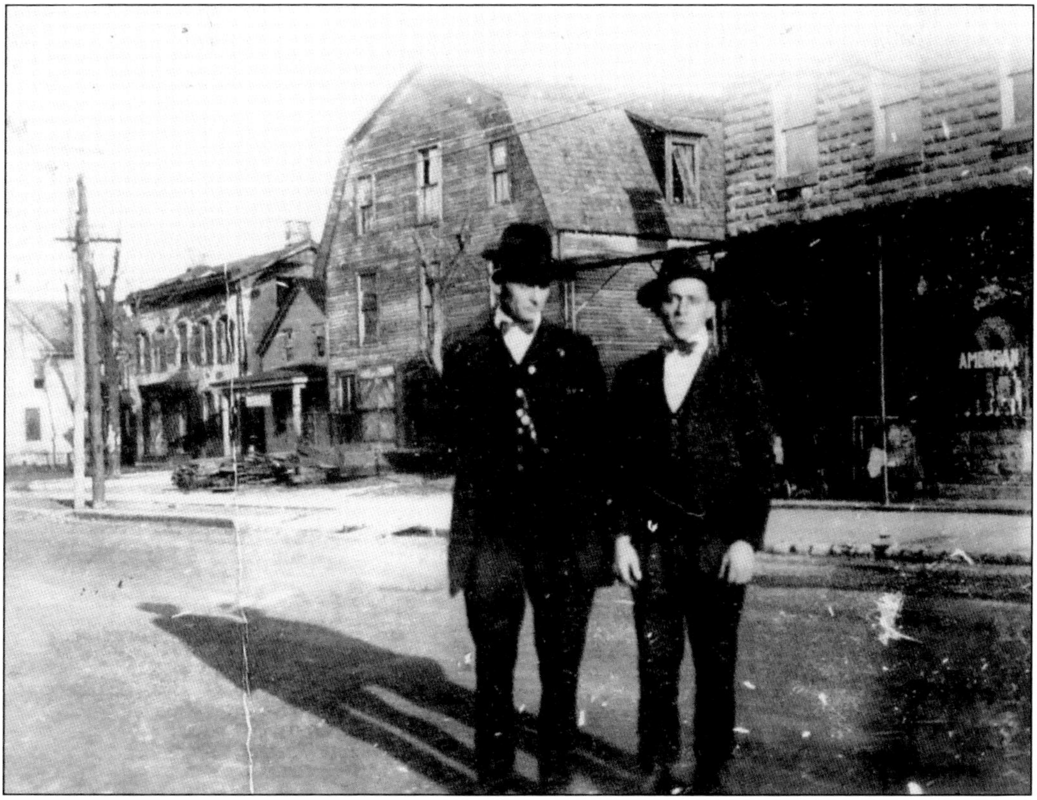

The Cox Brothers wagon works occupied the large structure seen in the background of this photograph taken in the summer of 1919. The men in the photograph are Charles Burroughs and Joe Mitgerald, ironworkers at Vacuum Oil.

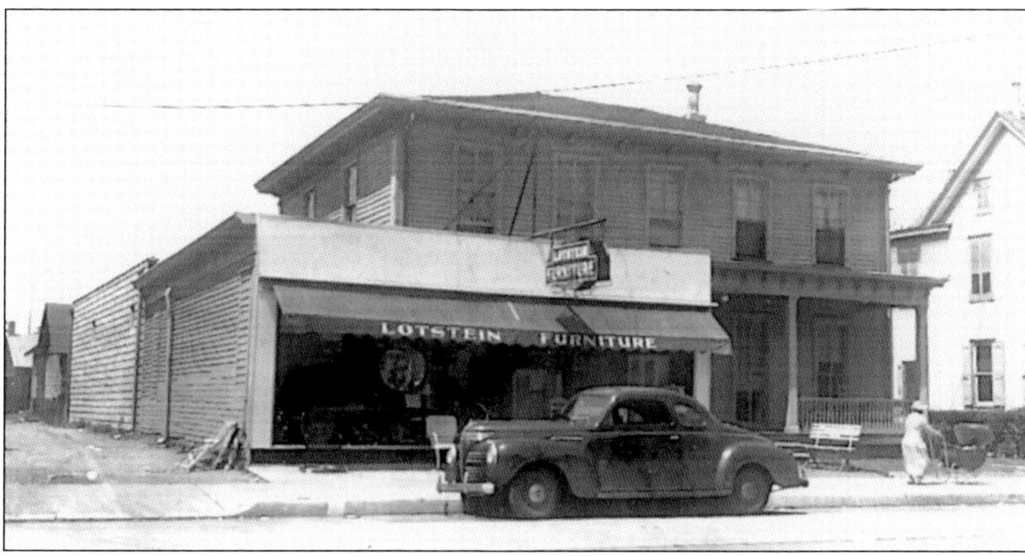

Lotstien Furniture was located at 17 West Broad Street. To the right is a woman strolling with a baby carriage.

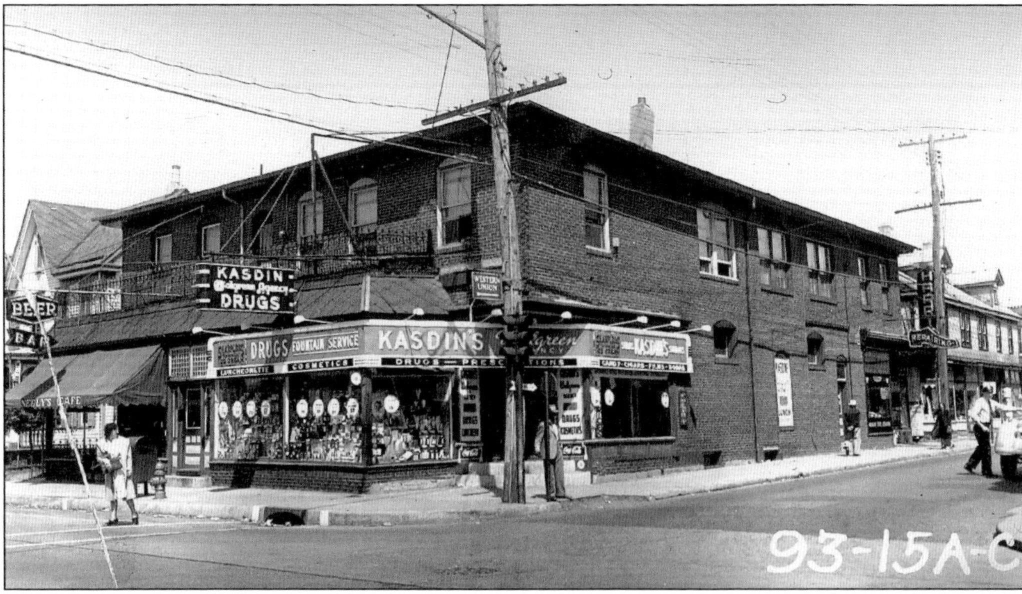

Kasdin's, a drugstore on the corner of Broad and Delaware Streets, is now the Underwood Medical Clinic.

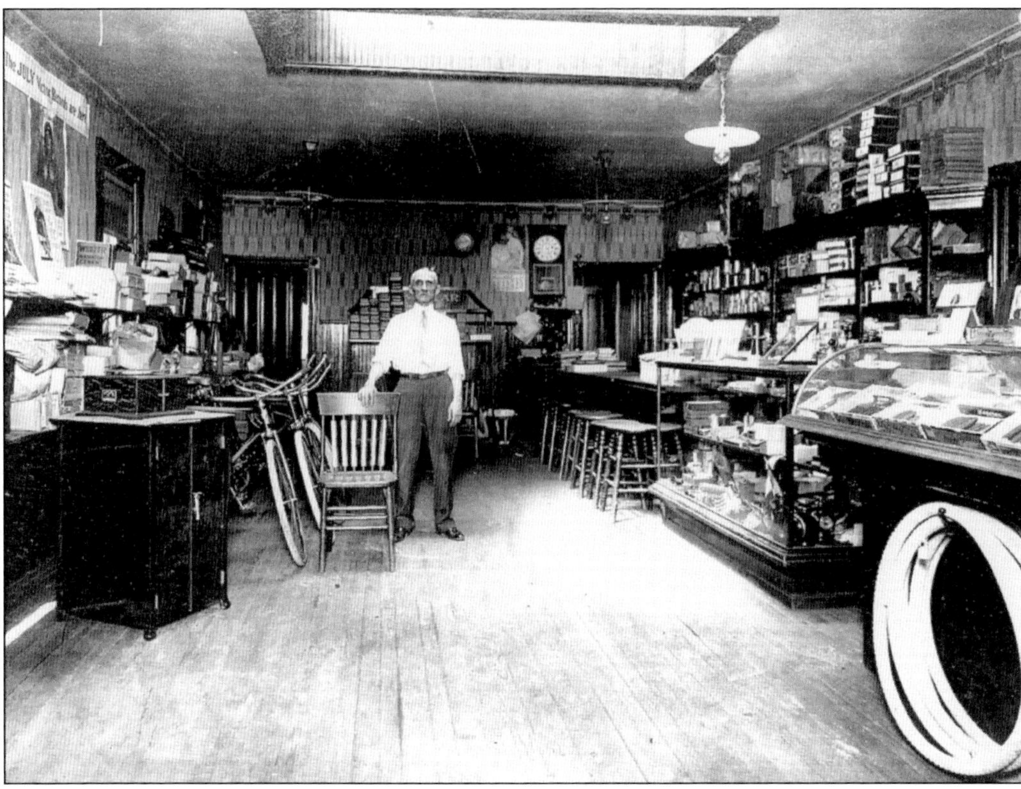

Ambler "Gampy" Stetser is seen in this *c.* 1905 photograph in his establishment where he sold and repaired bicycles.

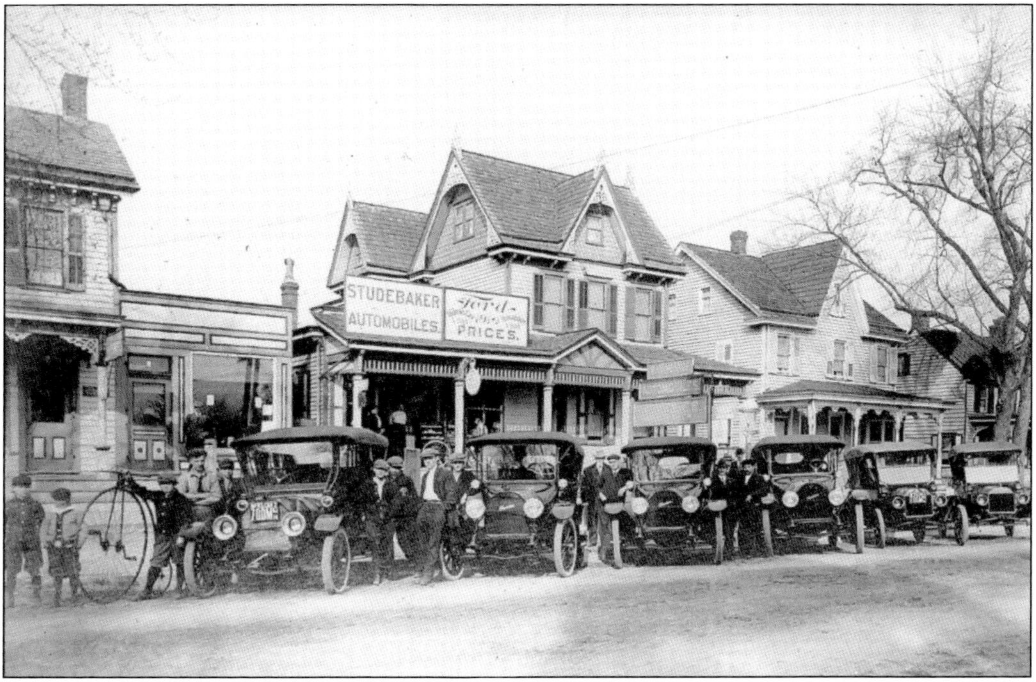

Stetser is seen in 1914 selling Fords and Studebakers in his establishment on Broad Street.

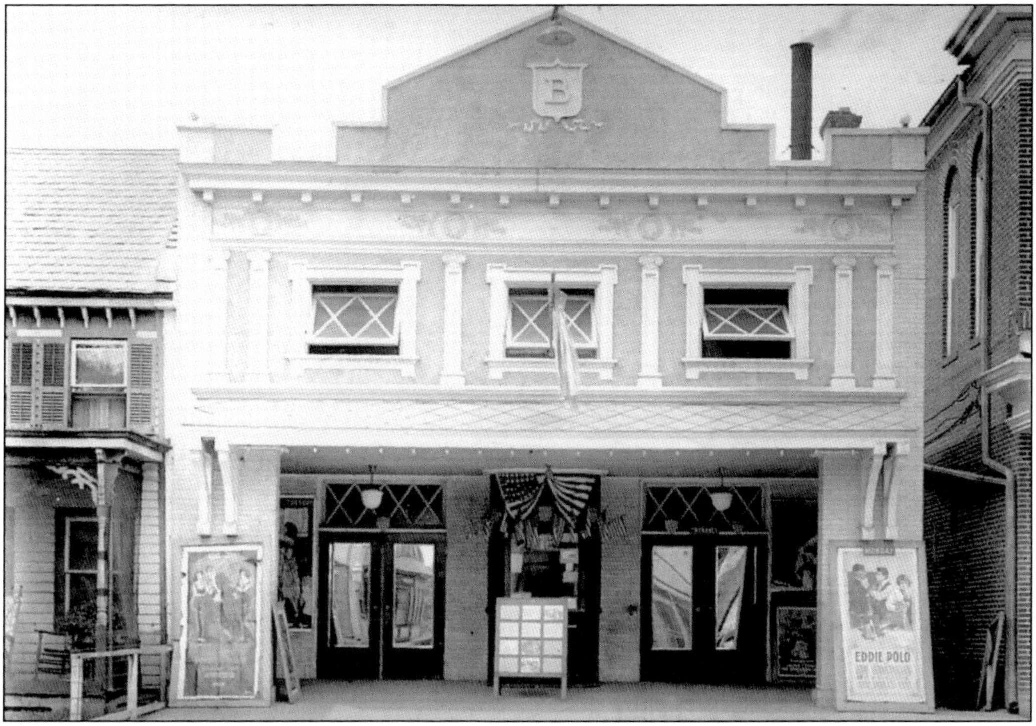

The Bailey theater was built after 1916. In the good old days, the cost of a Saturday matinee and a bag of peanuts was 5¢ each.

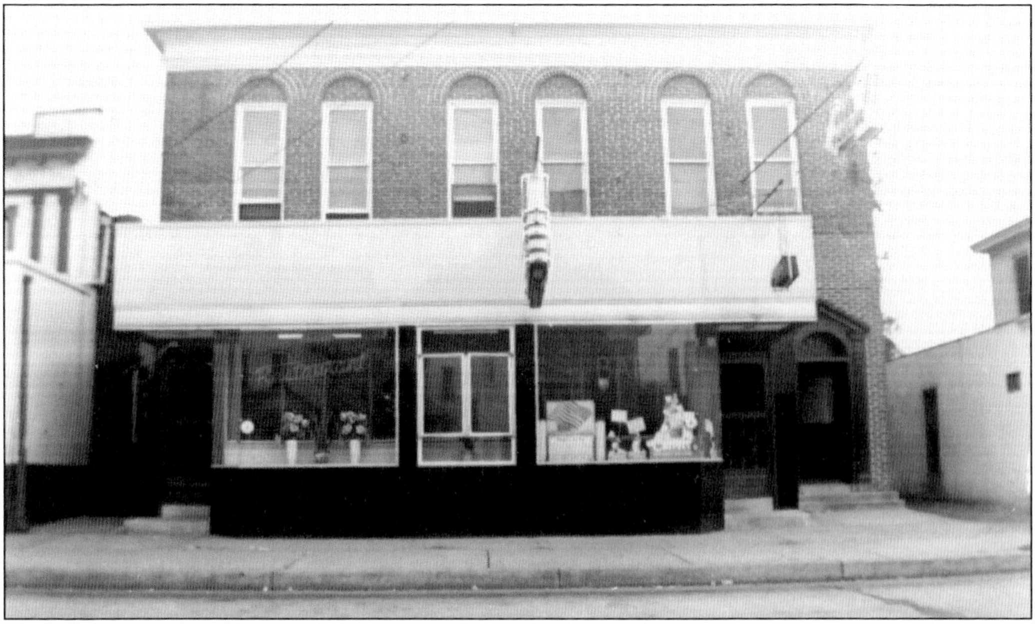

This is a front view of Fitzgerald's Bar, located in the Bailey Building, on Broad Street. Visible on the left is a small part of the Bailey theater. (Photograph courtesy of Lorraine Jones.)

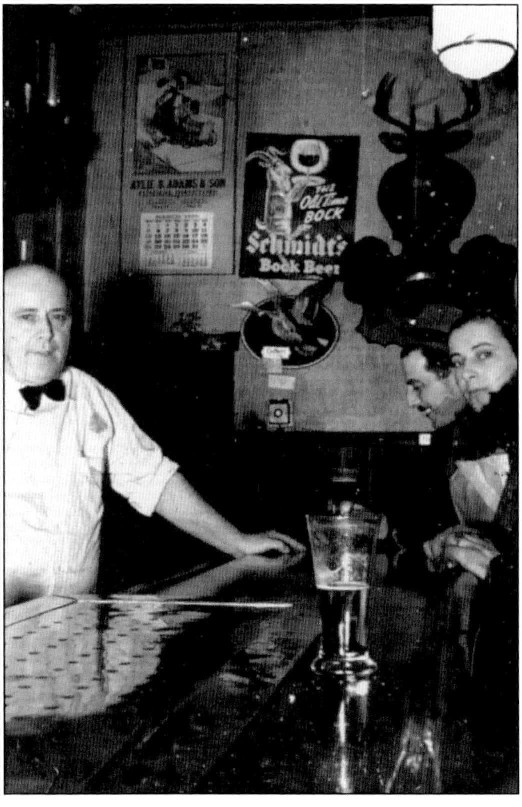

John Fitzgerald is on the left in this photograph of Fitzgerald's Bar, located on Broad Street. The other individuals in the photograph are unidentified. (Photograph courtesy of Lorraine Jones.)

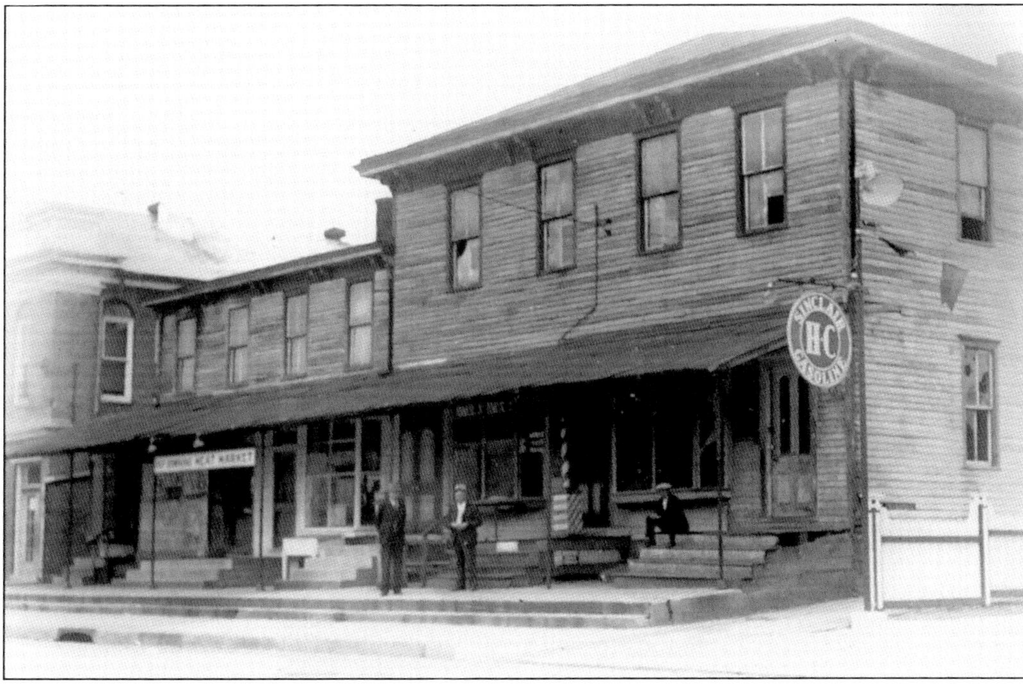

The Law's building, located on the corner of East Broad and Chestnut Streets, is seen here. A corner of the Bailey Building is visible on the left side of photograph.

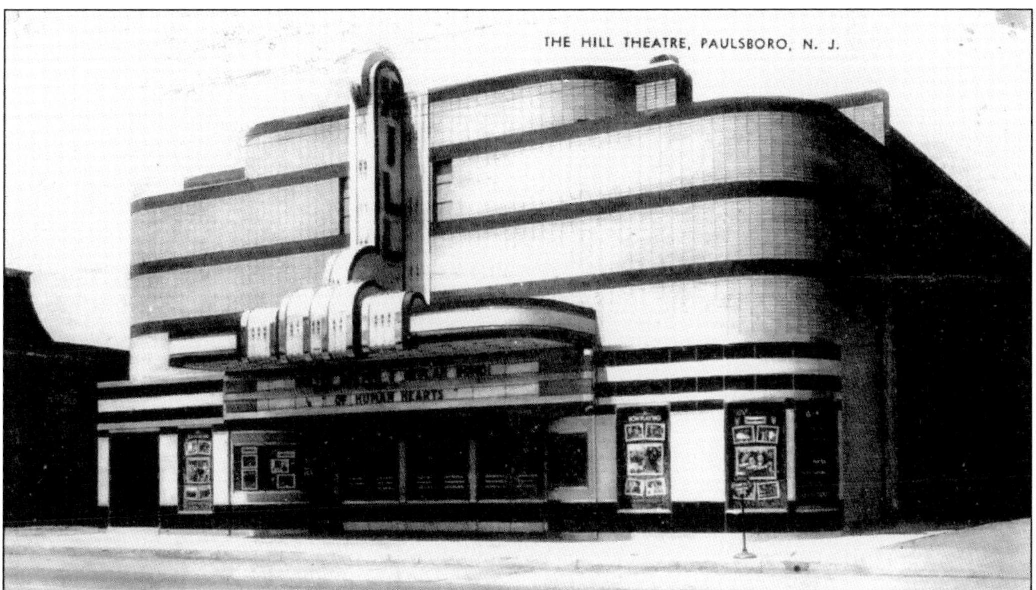

The Hill Theatre, located at 37 West Broad Street, displayed posters of upcoming movies. Today this theater is a busy studio used for commercials and other filming productions.

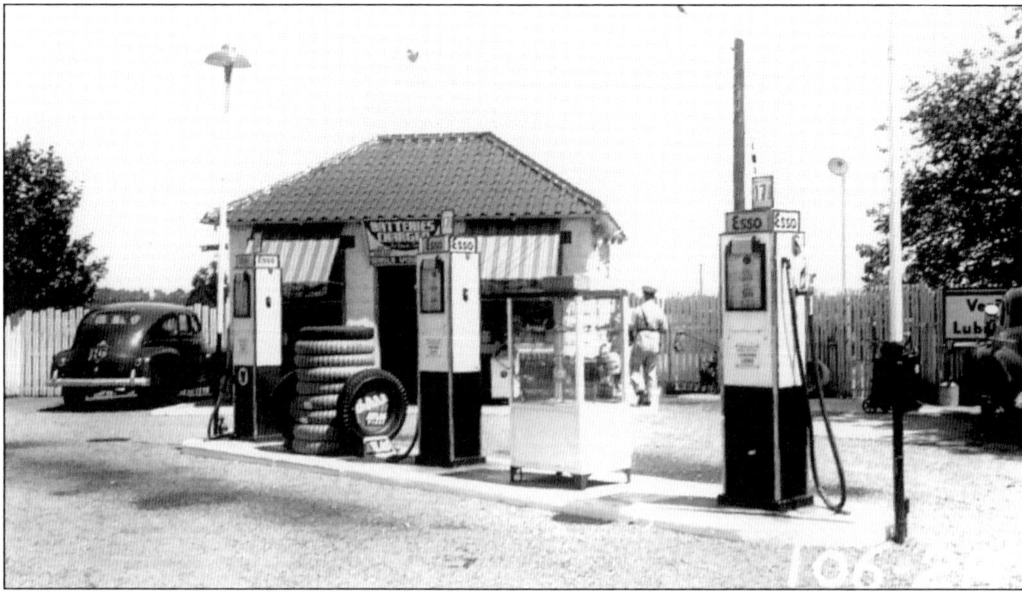

Gas could be purchased for 17¢ a gallon at the Esso gas station located on Broad Street.

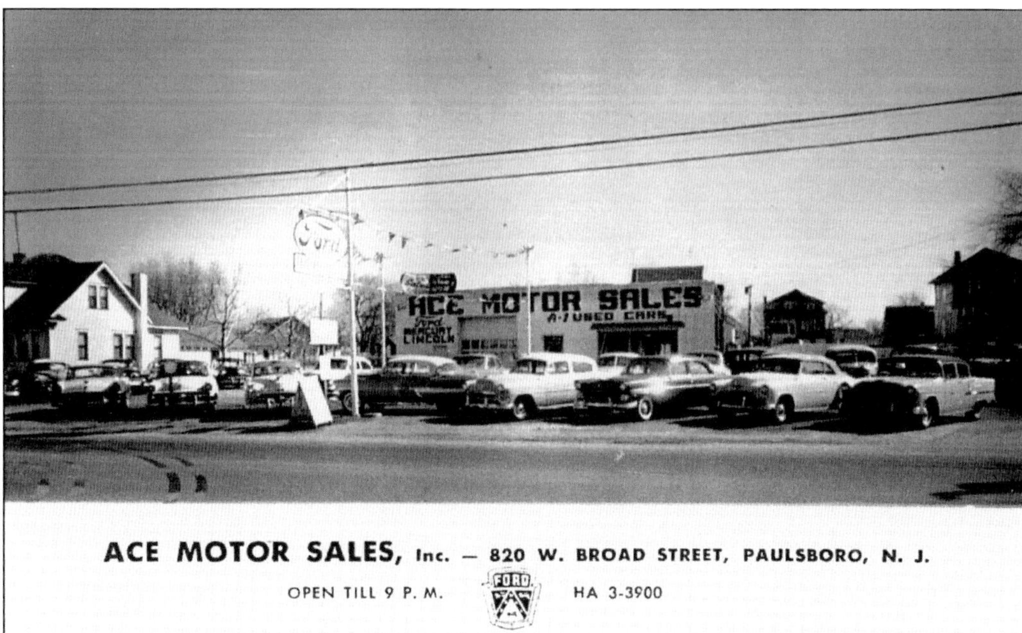

Ace Motor Sales is shown here at its 820 West Broad Street location in Paulsboro. The business also had a location in Woodbury.

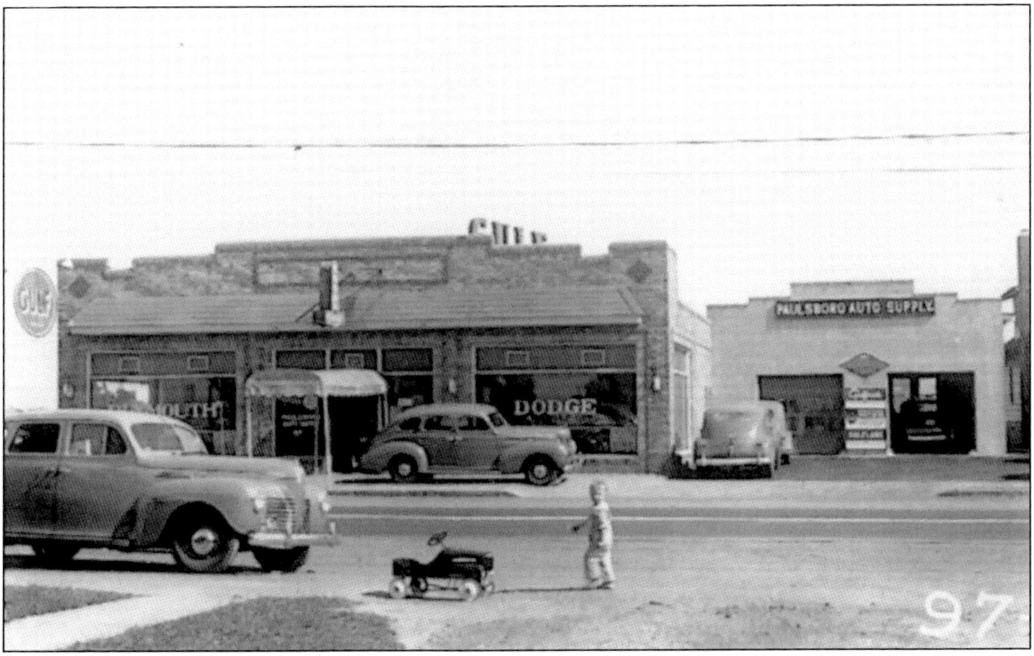

The Plymouth Dodge building, at 416 West Broad Street, is now the South Jersey Antique Fire Battalion. Notice the little boy with his own toy car.

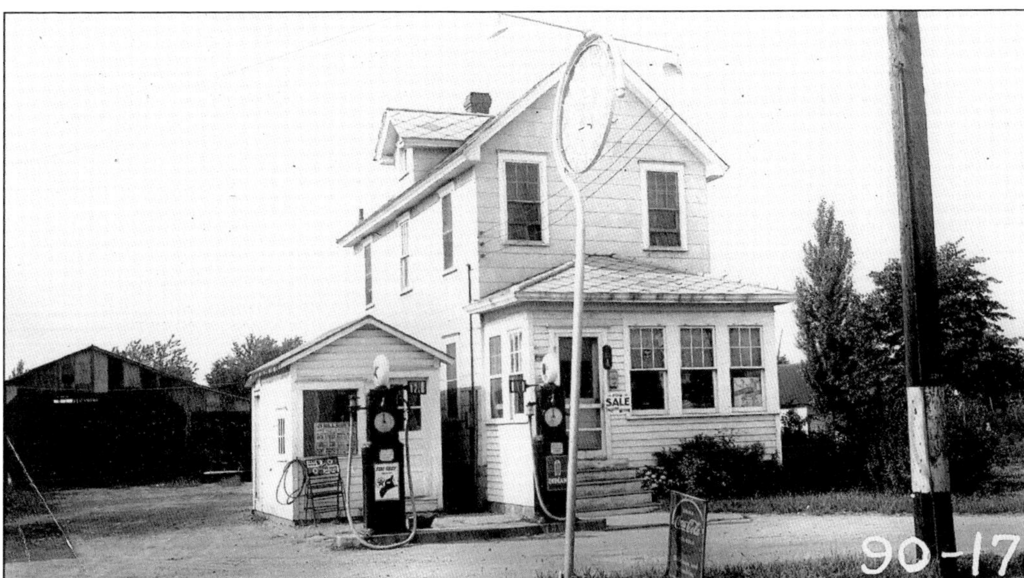

Gas was also 17¢ a gallon at the Texaco station at 421 West Broad Street.

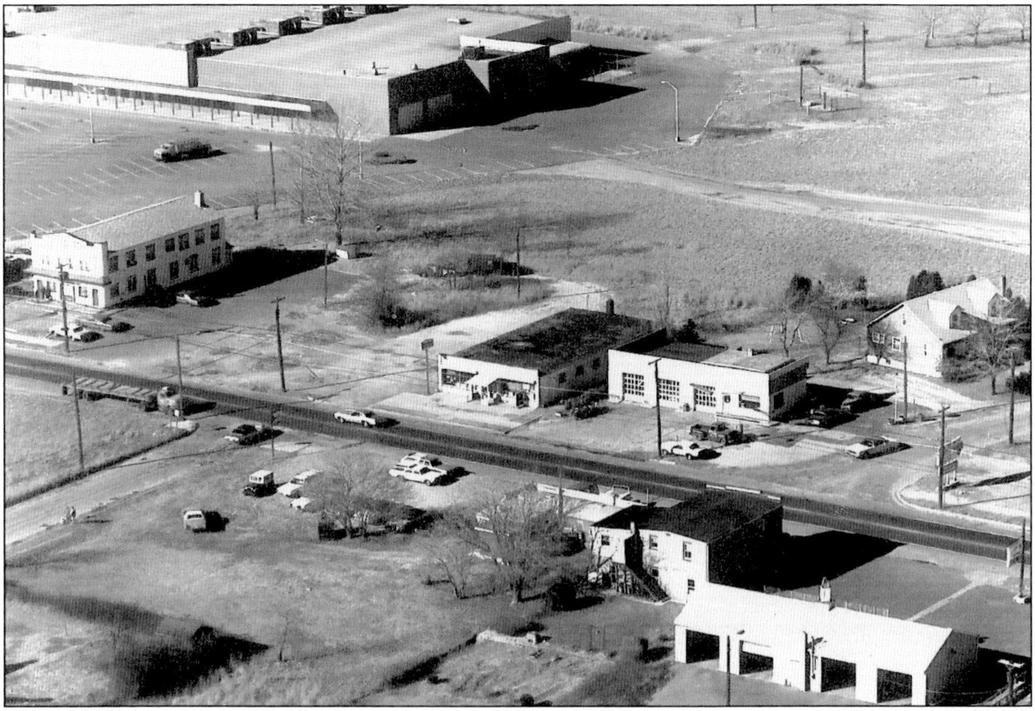

This photograph shows Conte's Bakery before the Burger King was built across the street. The Burger King is now Pat's Pizza. Paulsboro Plaza can be seen at the top left, and farther down is the Star Dust, which is now the Sons of Italy. Conte's Bakery is in the middle. Carol's Diner is behind a tree in the center, and the car wash is in the bottom right corner. (Photograph courtesy of Anthony Conte.)

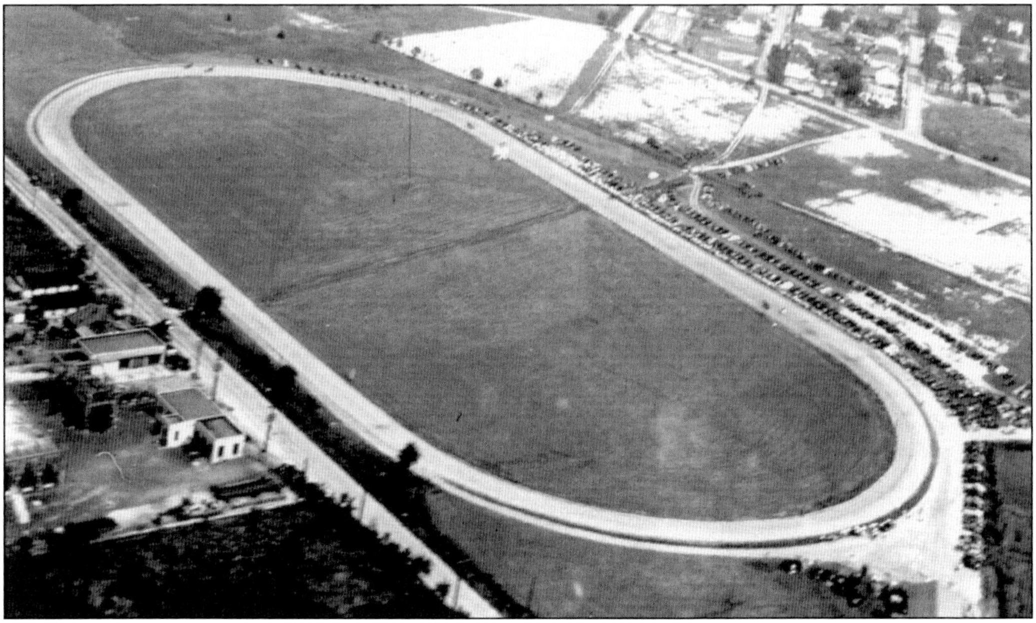

The area where the Paulsboro Horse Race Track was located, shown in this aerial view, is now the home of the Paulsboro Plaza.

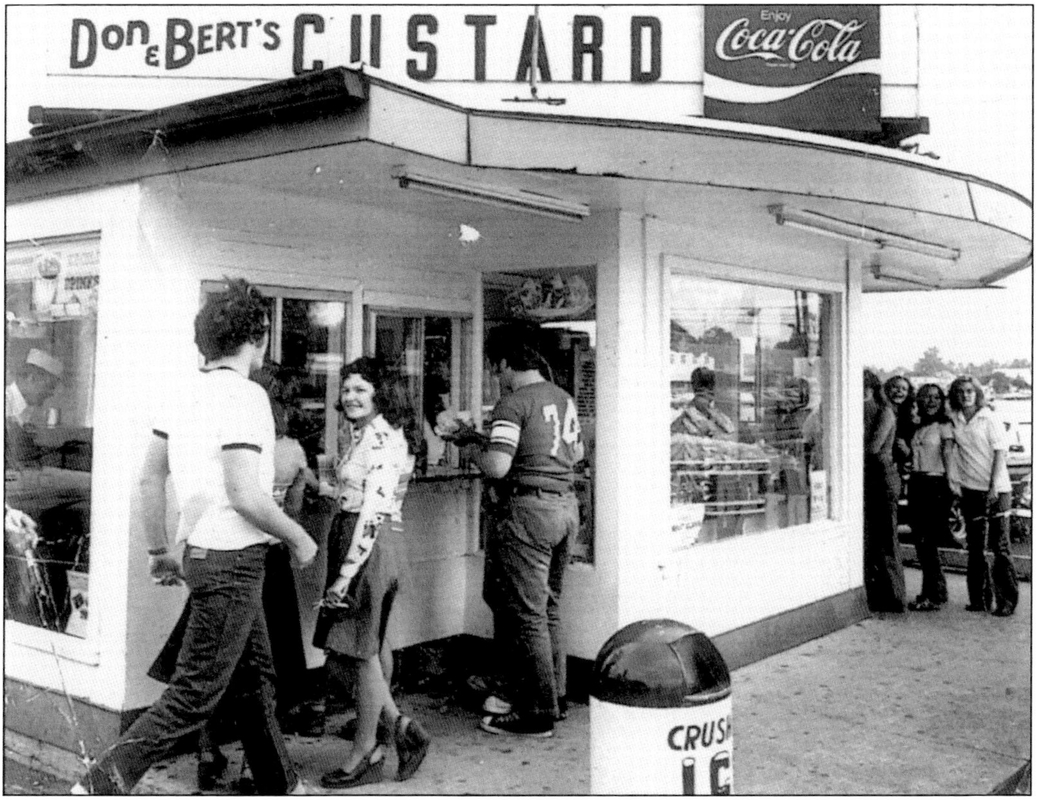

Don & Bert's Custard, located on West Broad Street, was built in 1953. In 1968, a new building was built at the same location and the old structure was moved to another site. This photograph, taken in the 1970s, shows the old building. (Photograph courtesy of Don Reed.)

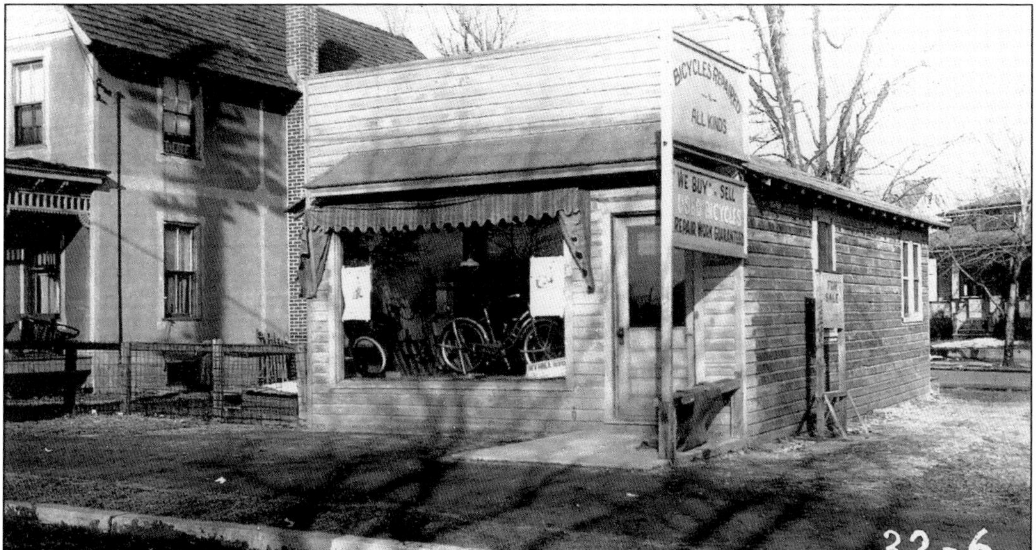

This *c.* 1930s photograph shows an old bicycle shop located at 521 North Delaware Street.

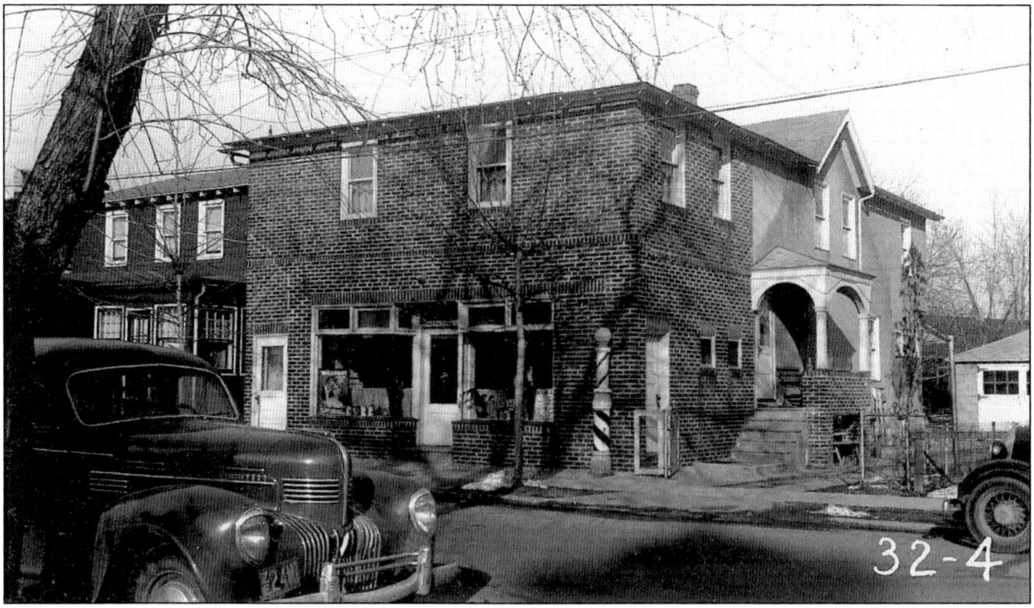

This barbershop, located at 649 North Delaware Street, is captured in a *c.* 1930s view.

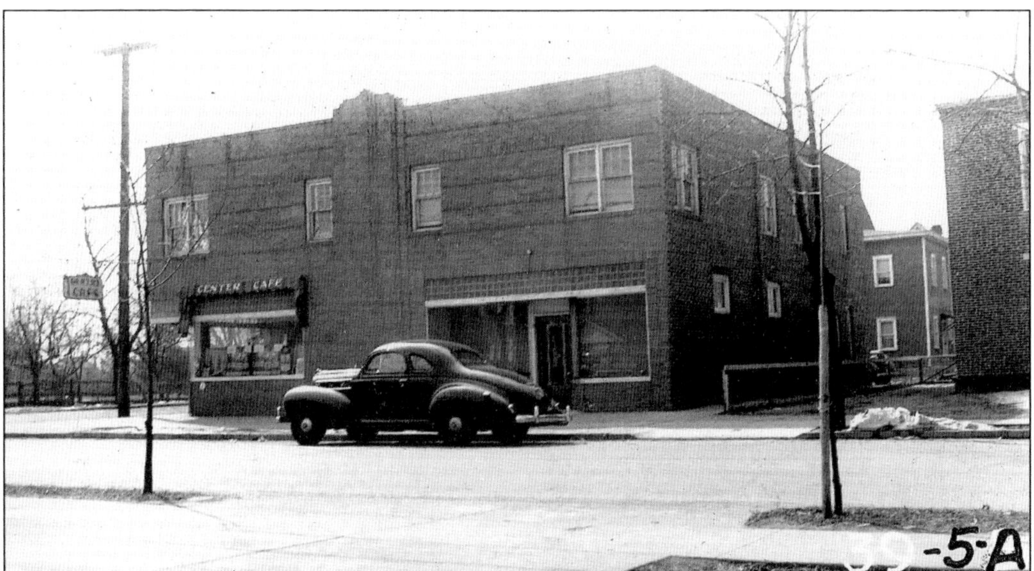

The Center Café, seen in this *c.* 1930s photograph, was located at 718 North Delaware Street.

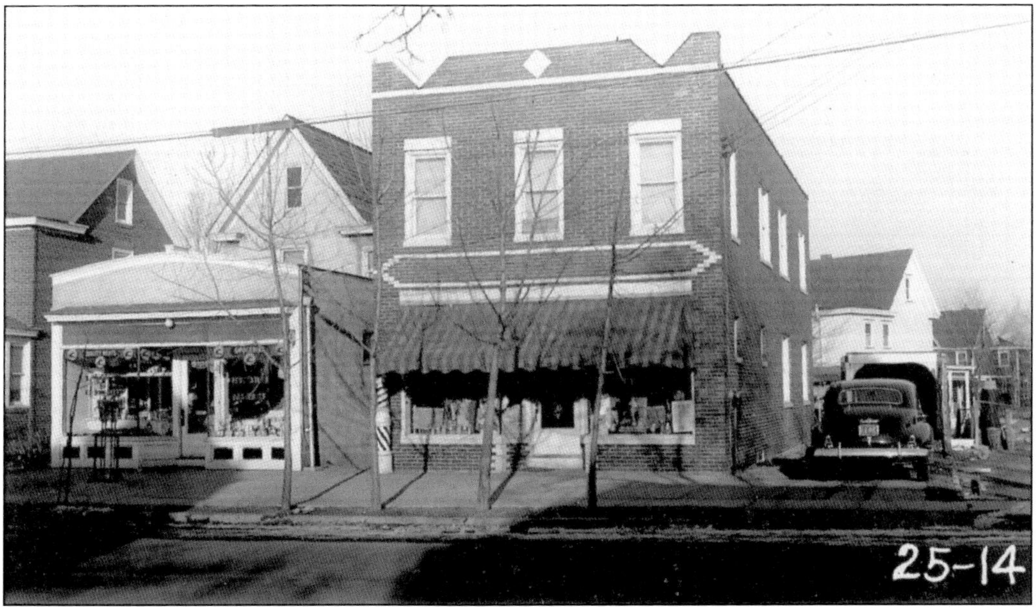

This *c.* 1930s photograph shows another barbershop in Paulsboro. The shop was located at 719 North Delaware Street.

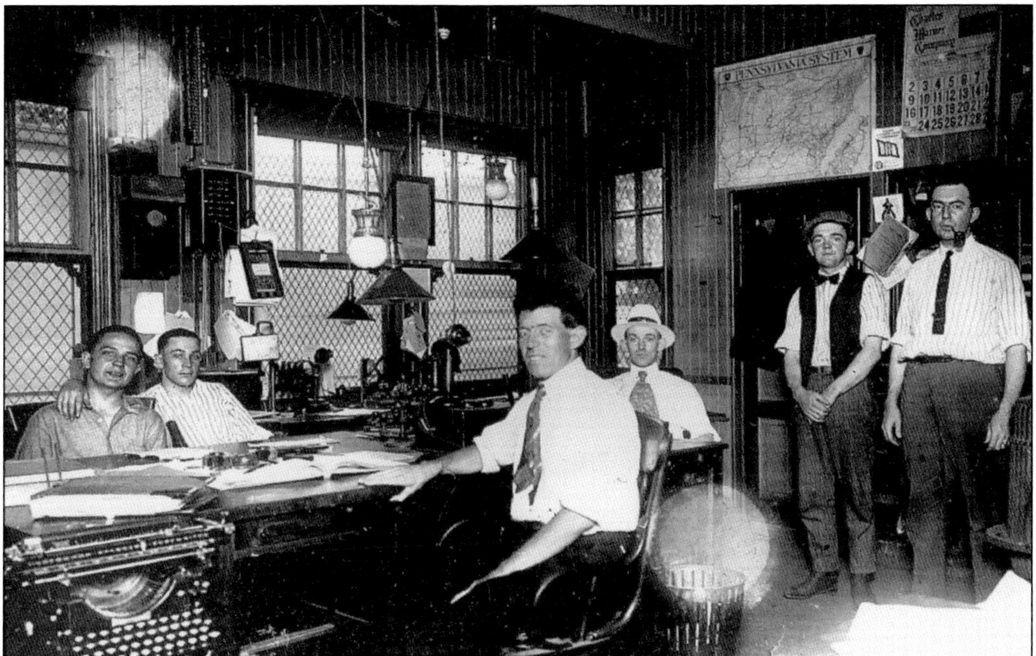

Workers pose inside the freight office at the railroad station in Paulsboro.

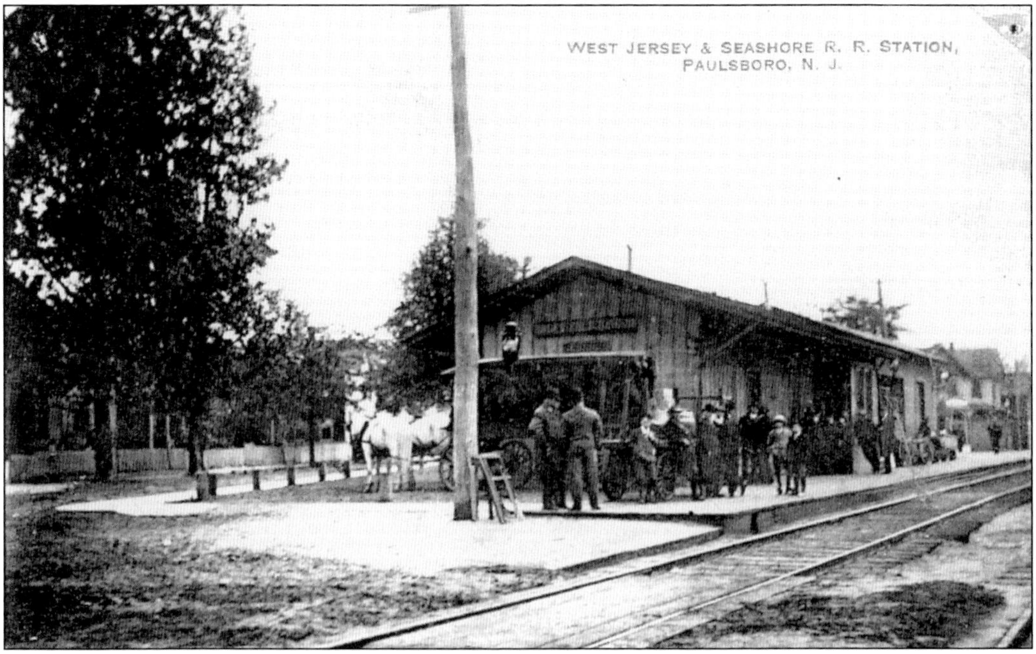

Passengers and workers gather outside of the West Jersey & Seashore station in Paulsboro. (Postcard by W. J. Moore.)

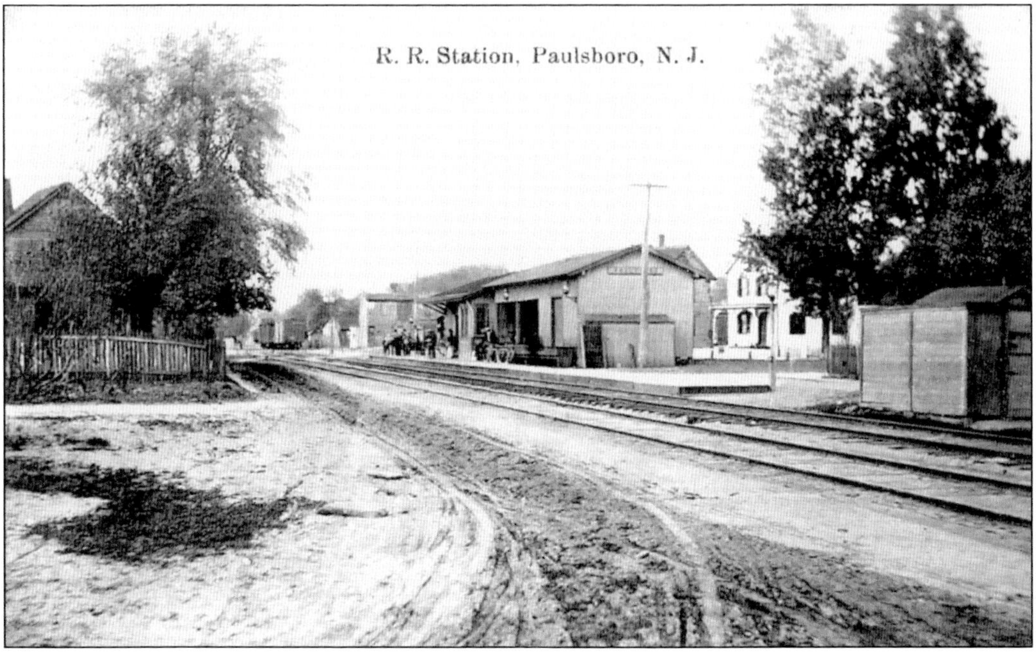

This wider view of the railroad station shows the houses in the area. (Postcard by B. F. Furry.)

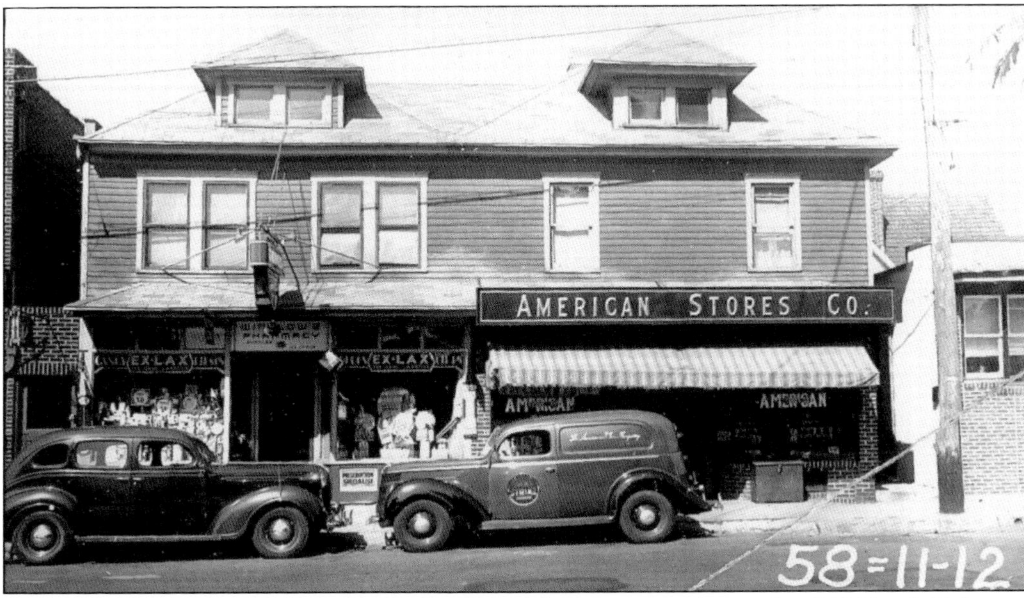

The American Stores Company and Windlow's Pharmacy were located at 760 North Delaware Street. This site later became the location of Nastase's, a drugstore.

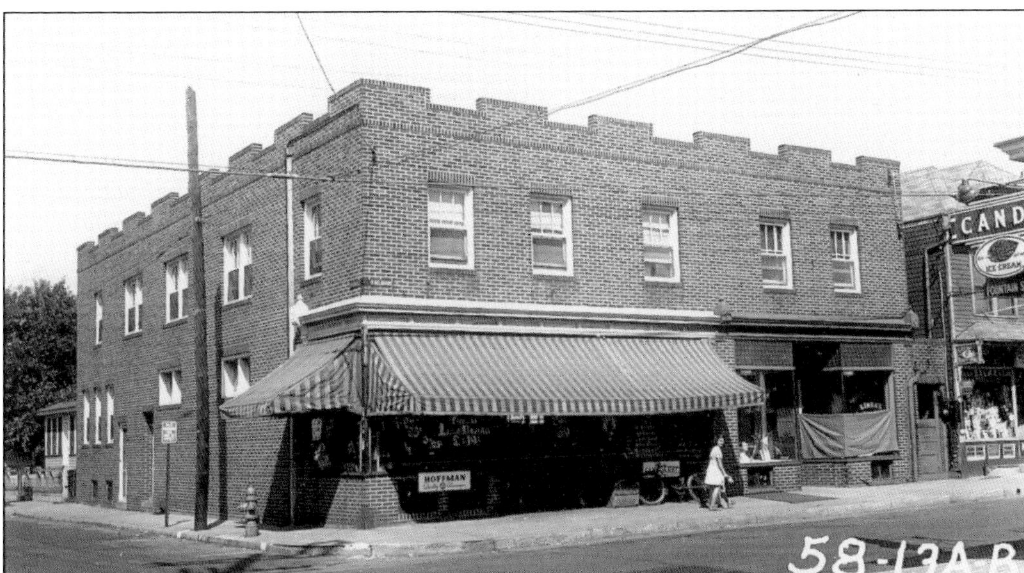

A girl poses for this *c.* 1930s photograph in front of store located at 766 North Delaware Street.

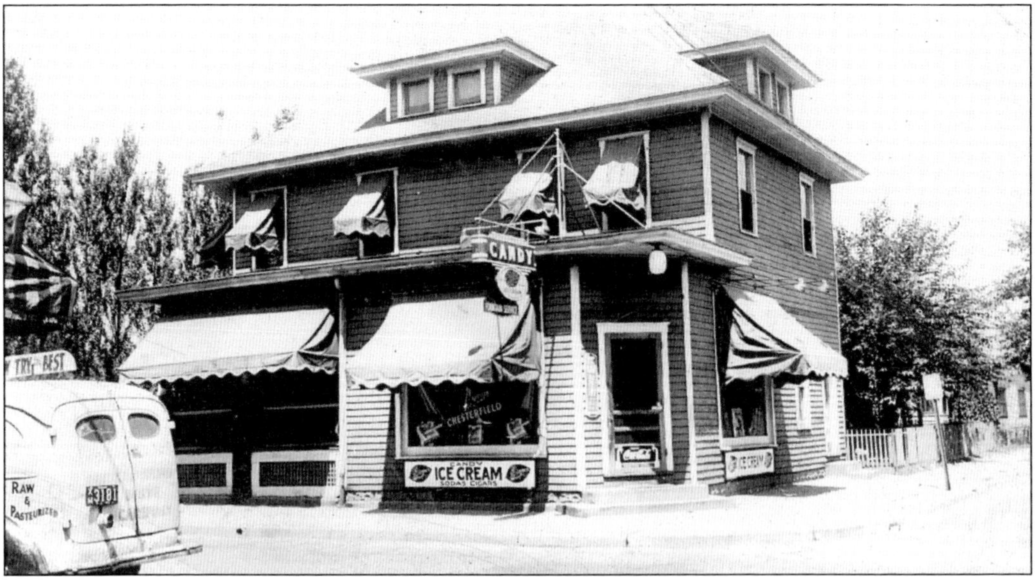

This candy store was located at 771 North Delaware Street. Note the milk delivery truck with the slogan "You've had the rest, now try the best."

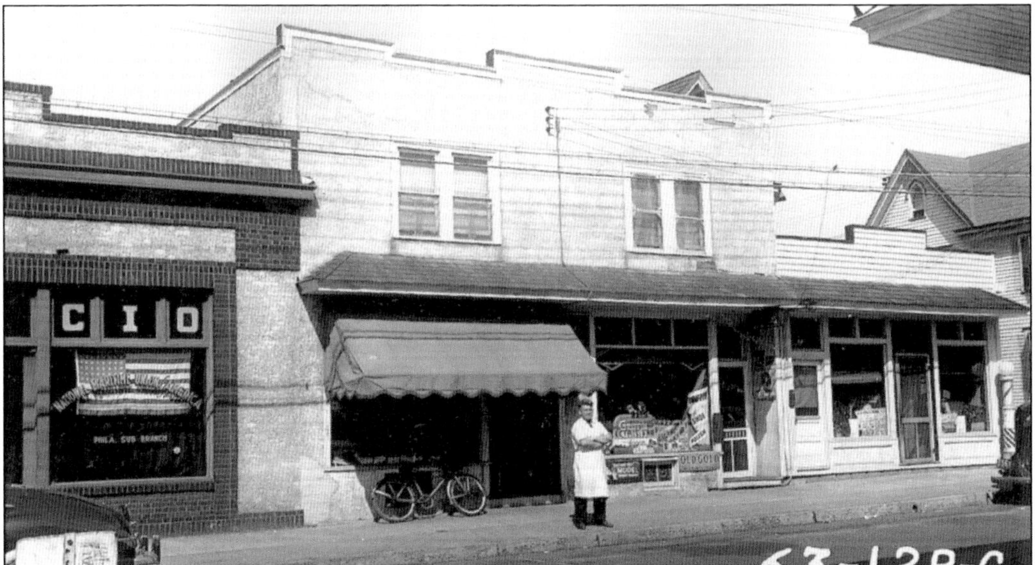

An unidentified man is seen in front of store located at 808 North Delaware Street.

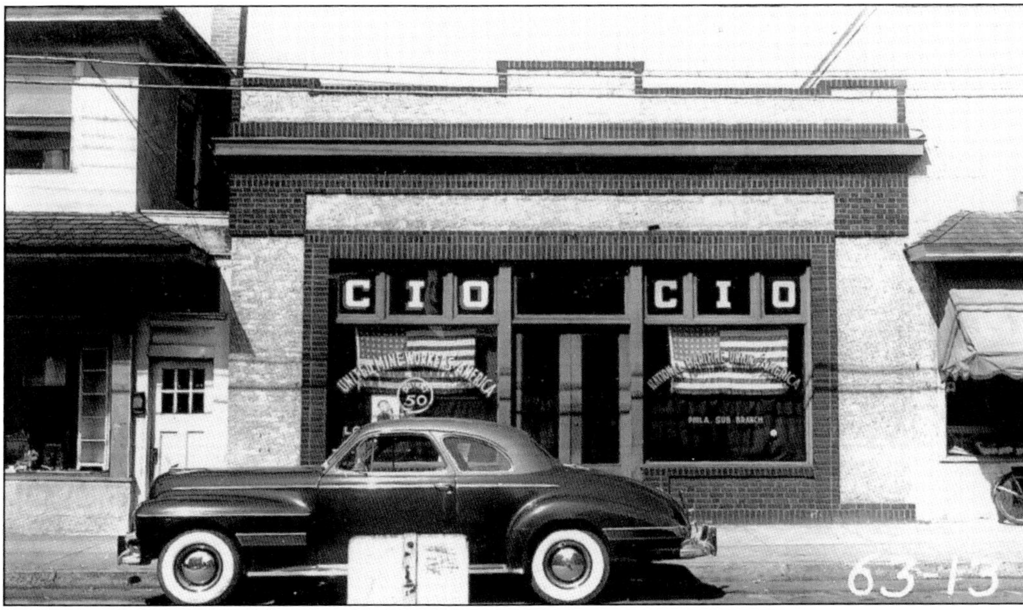

The former CIO union headquarters was located at 812 North Delaware Street.

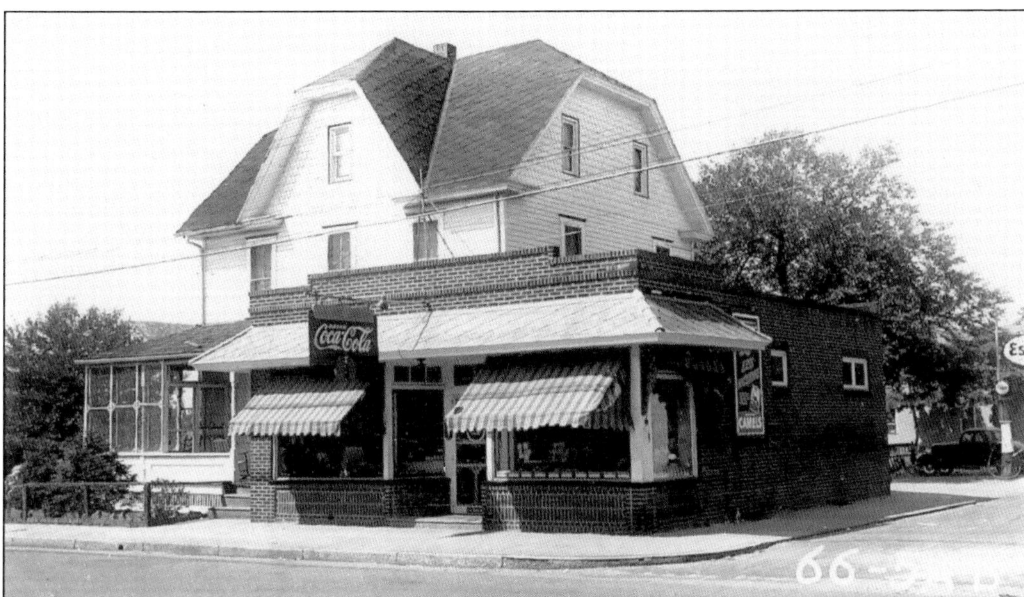

This photograph of a storefront, located in the 900 block of North Delaware Street, shows the Esso gas pump behind the store.

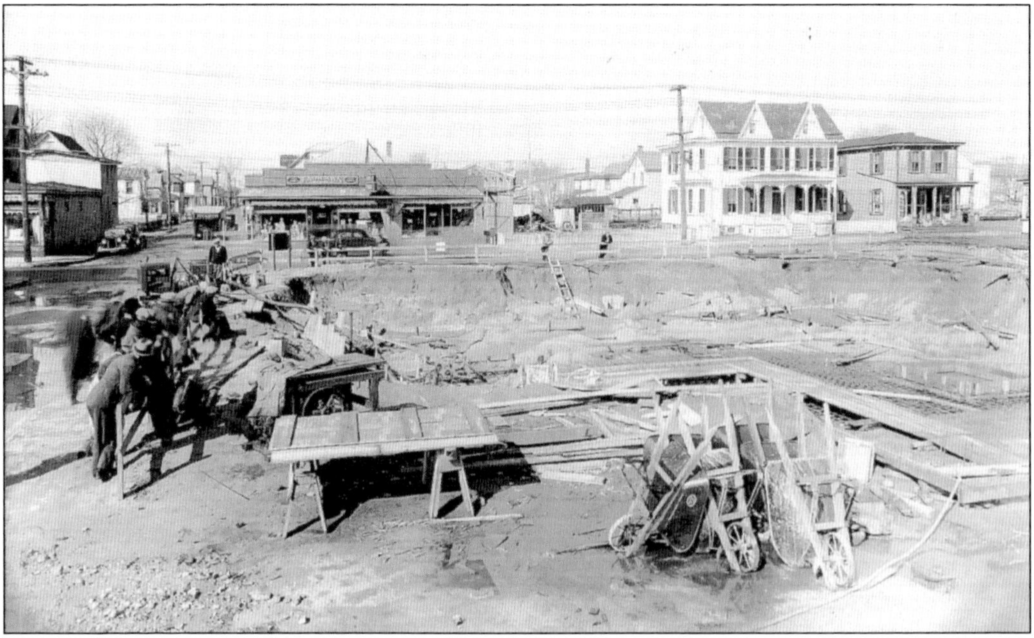

Construction of the Paulsboro post office began on March 28, 1939. The federal government appropriated $72,000 for the purchase of the site and construction of the new building. Mutual Construction Company was awarded the contract to build the new post office.

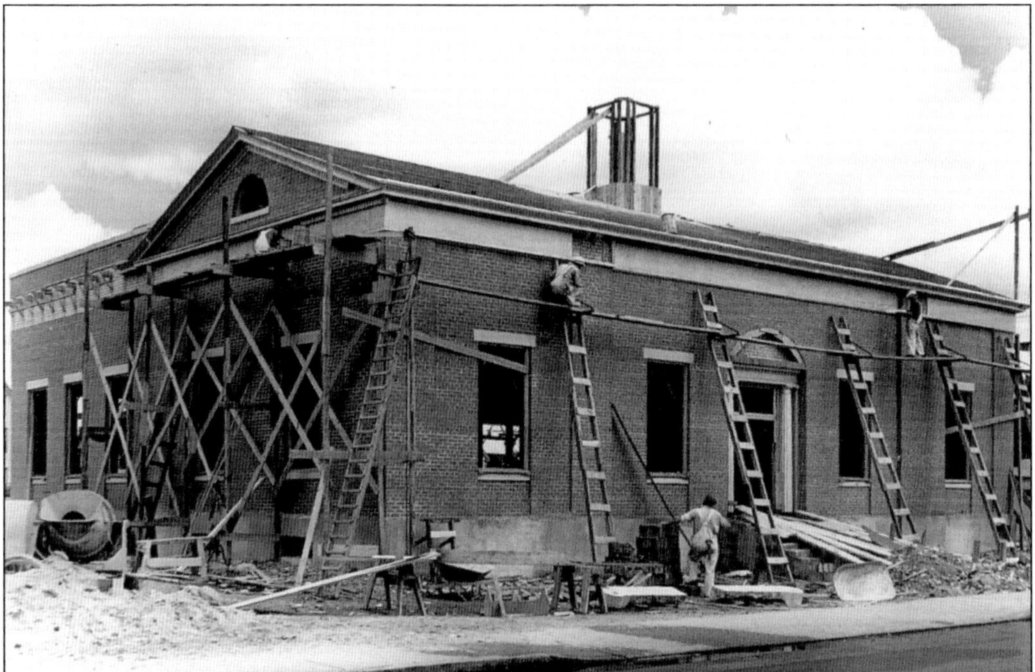

This photograph dated July 31, 1939, shows the building progress of the brickwork on the new Paulsboro post office.

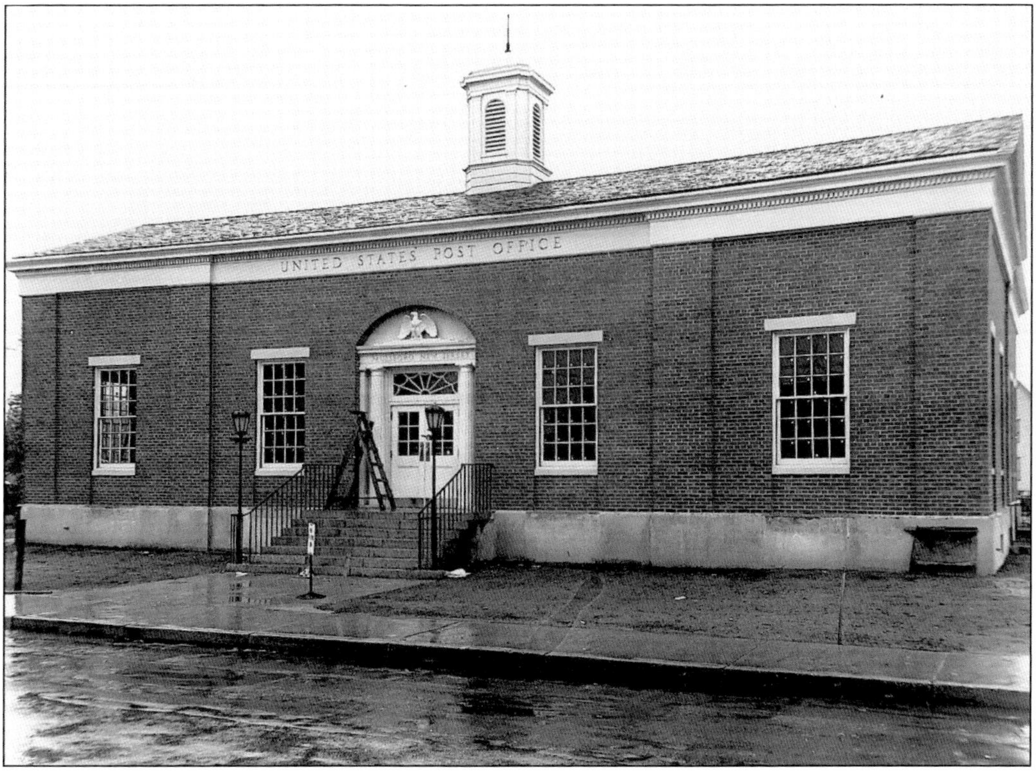

At the time of this November 5, 1939, photograph, construction on the new post office was nearing completion.

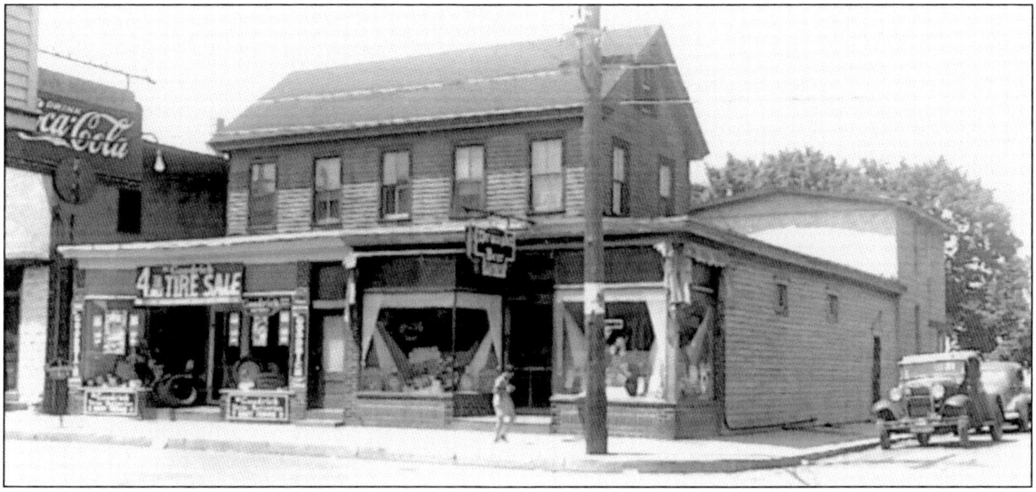

An unidentified person poses outside an auto store, located at 1100 North Delaware Street. Note the old car parked on the side street.

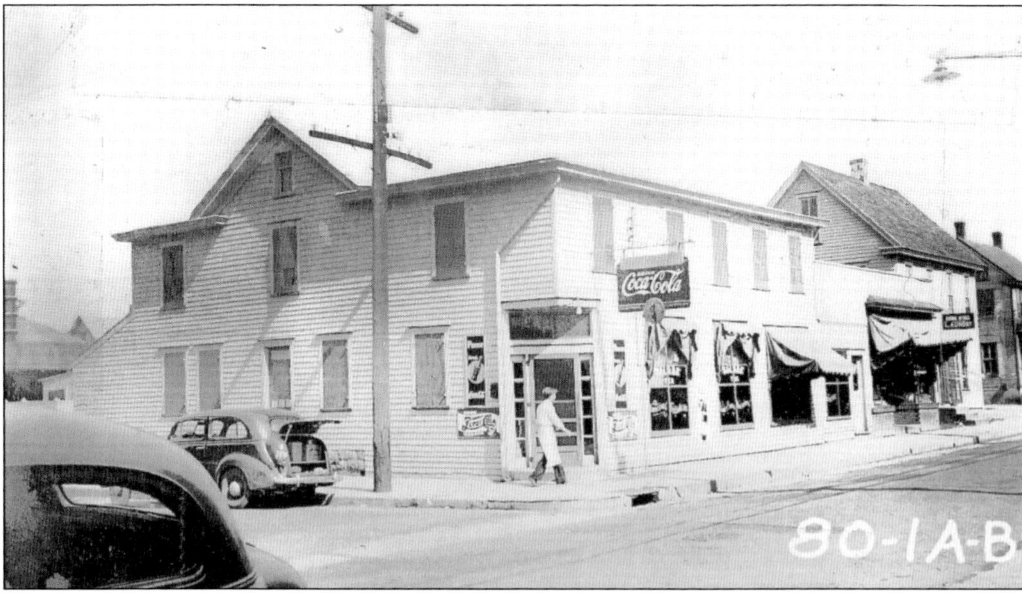

A delivery is being made to this store, located on corner of 1101 North Delaware and Adams Streets.

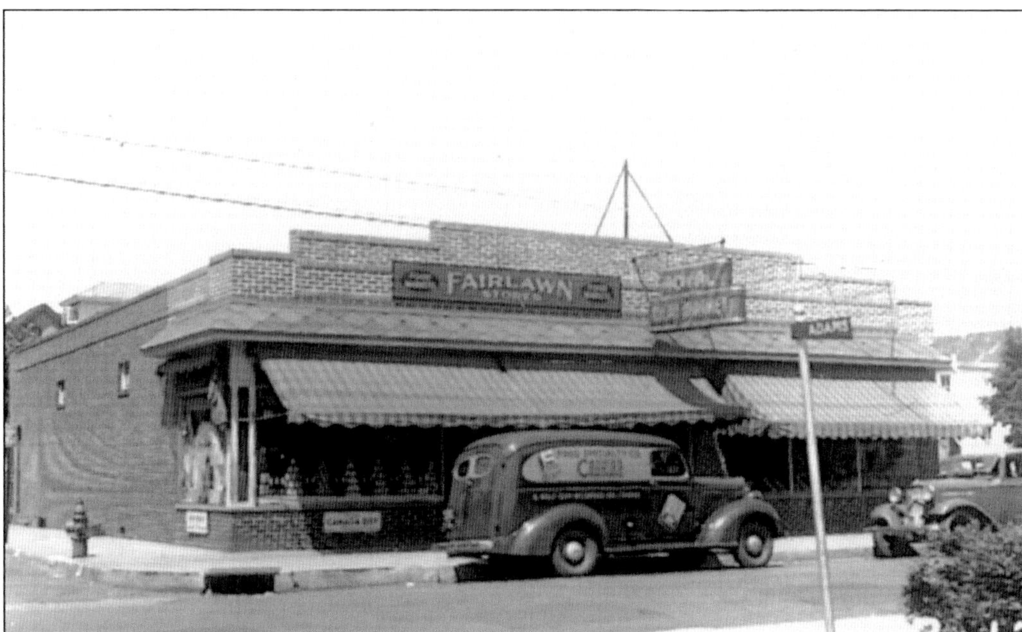

Royal Meat Market, located at 1014 North Delaware Street, was established in 1925. Shown is the second building, which was built across the street from the original structure.

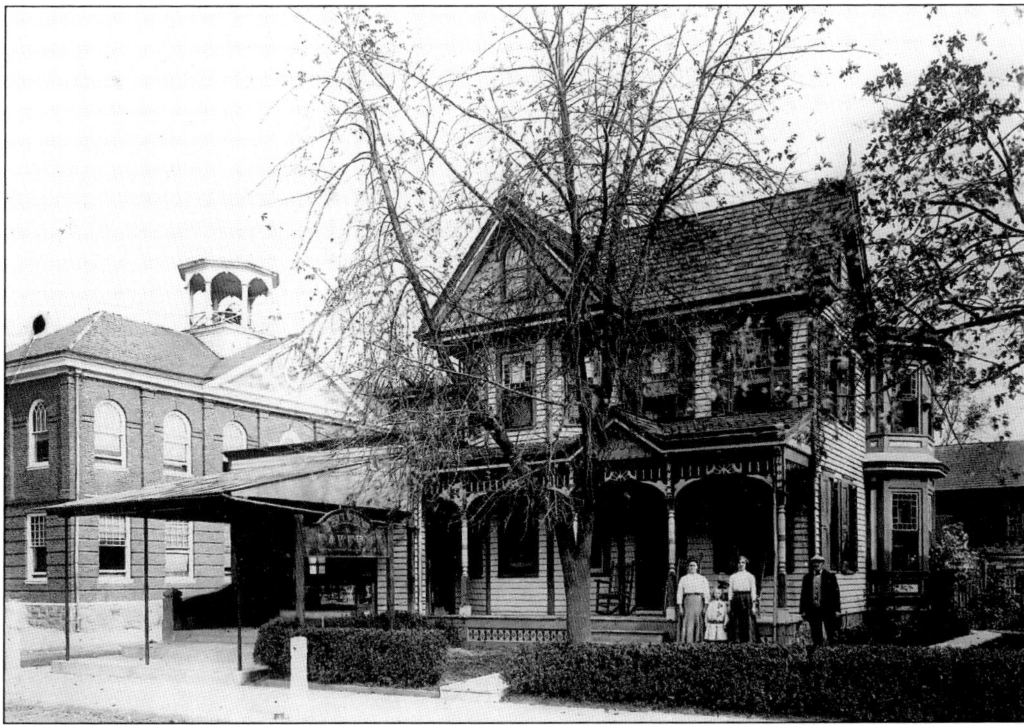

This photograph of the Edward Feiler Bakery and MacMullin Funeral Parlor was taken sometime after 1905. The old Buck Street School can be seen in the background.

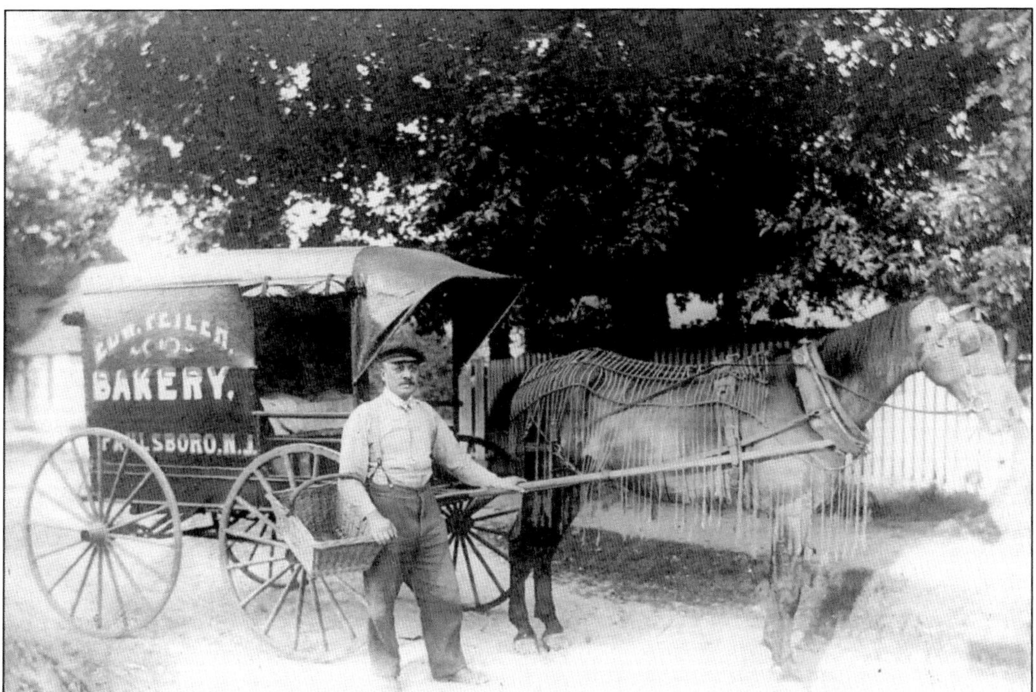

Edward Feiler makes deliveries with his bakery wagon in 1906.

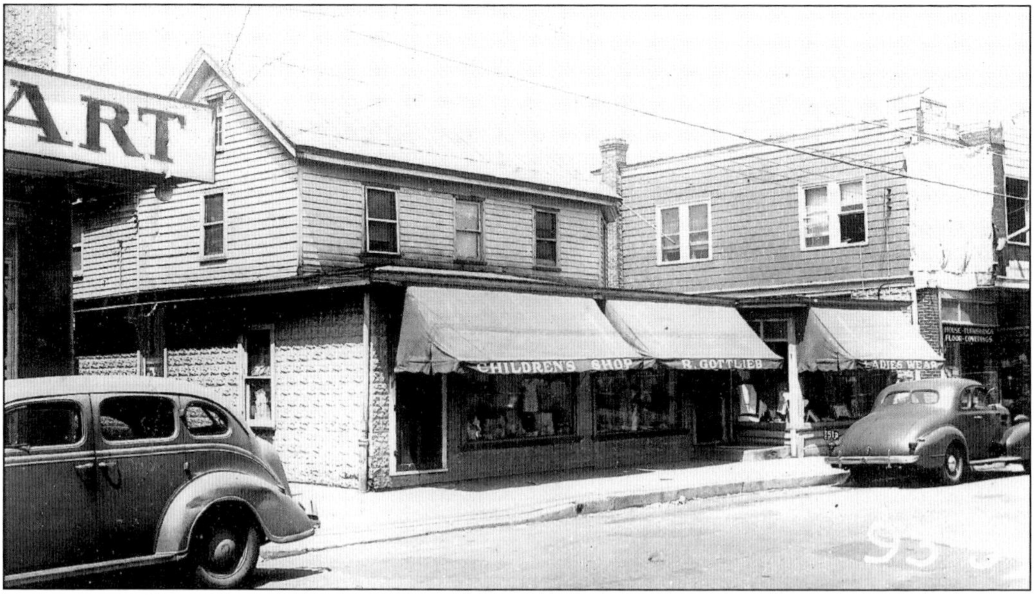

Connie's Ladies & Children's Shop, located at 1306 North Delaware Street, is still in business today.

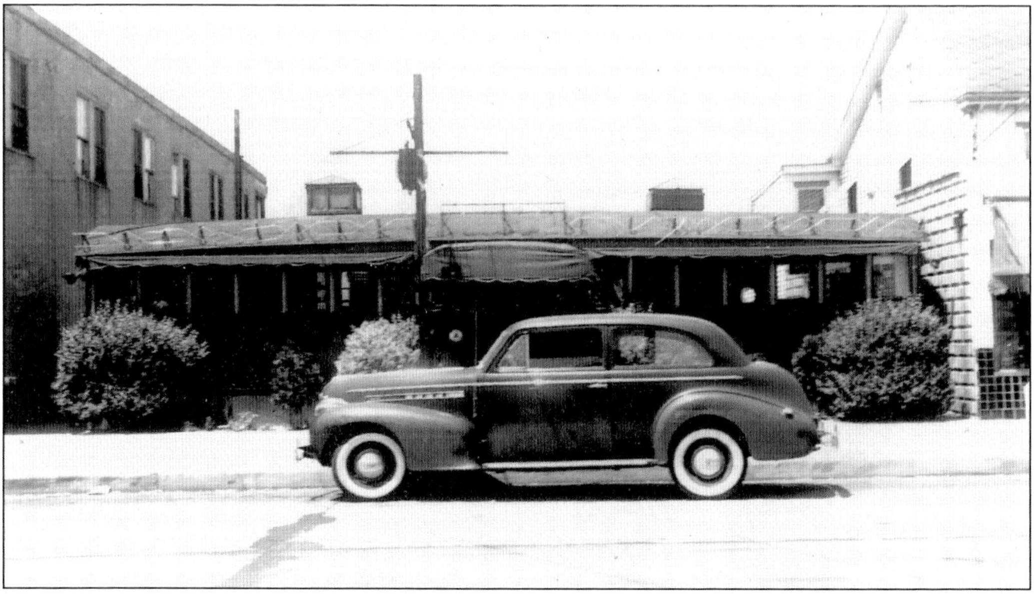

This small diner was located on North Delaware Street.

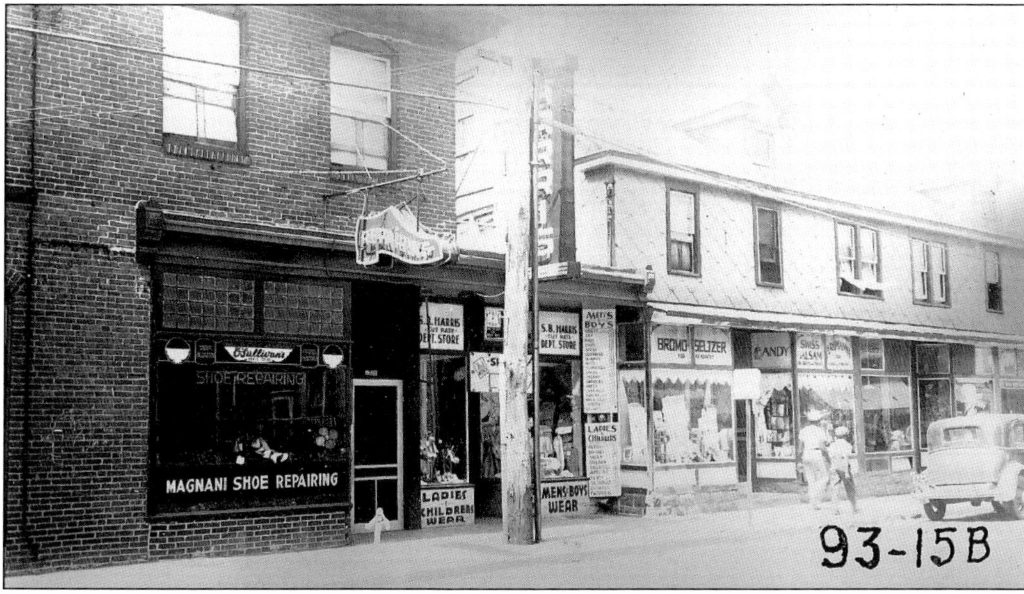

Magnani Shoe Repair, the Harris department store, and other stores located on North Delaware Street are seen in this photograph.

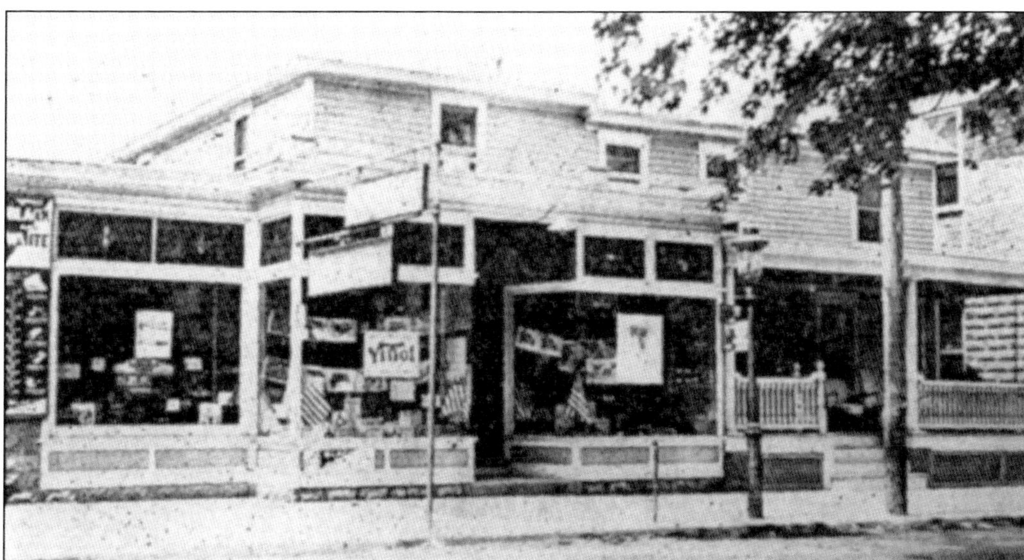

The W. J. Moore drugstore was located on North Delaware Street.

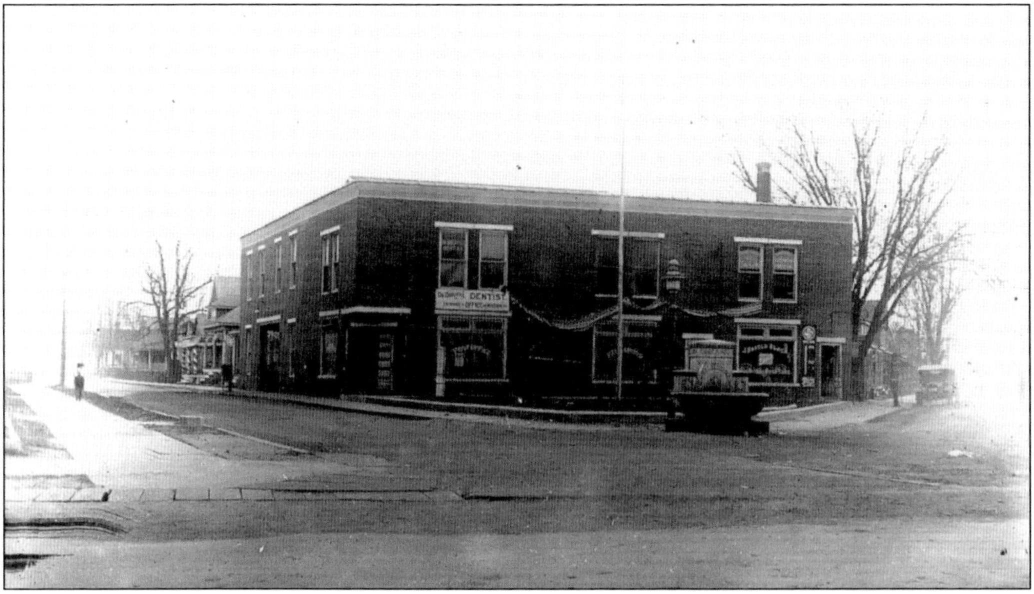

The post office is shown when it was at its original location, on the corner of South Delaware and Swedesboro Avenues. The photograph was made from a glass-plate negative.

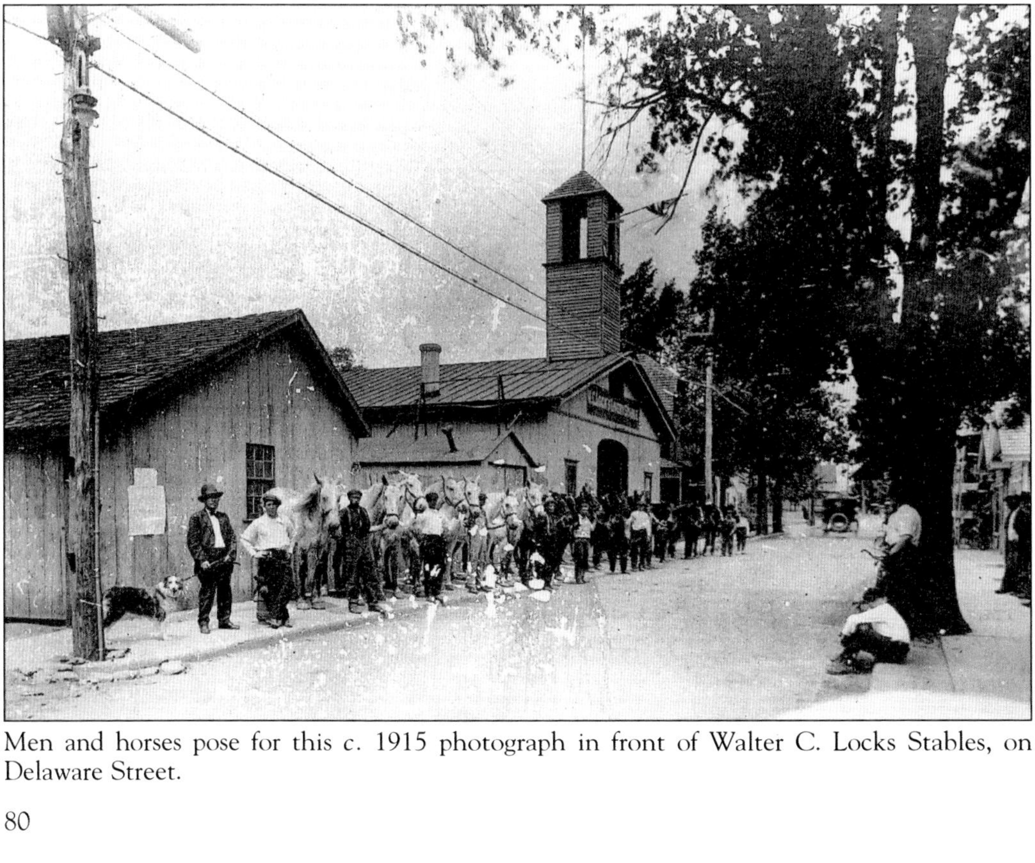

Men and horses pose for this c. 1915 photograph in front of Walter C. Locks Stables, on Delaware Street.

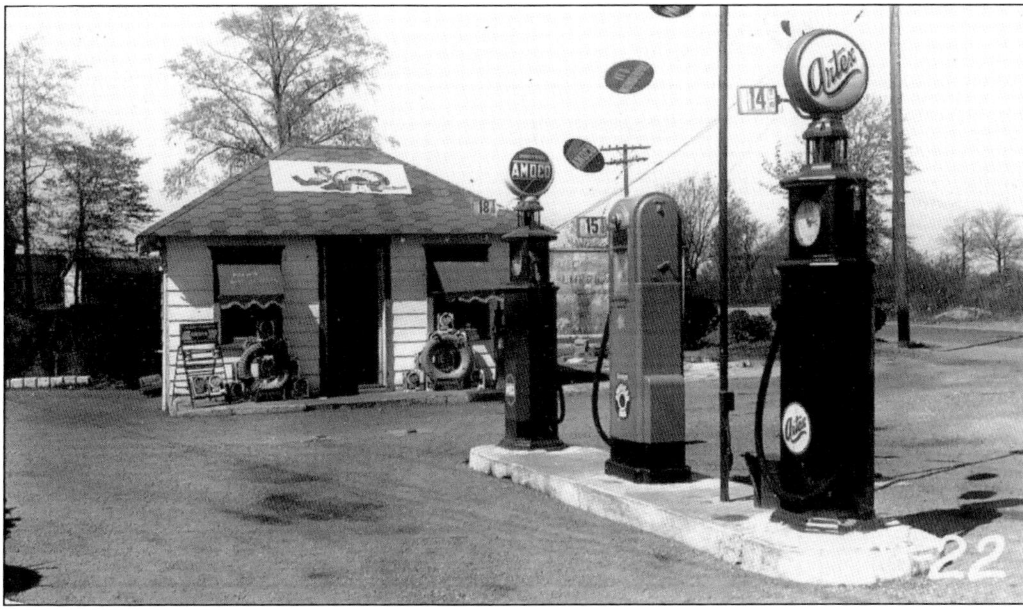

These old gas pumps in front of the Amoco station were located on South Delaware Street. Gas is advertised for as low as 14¢ a gallon.

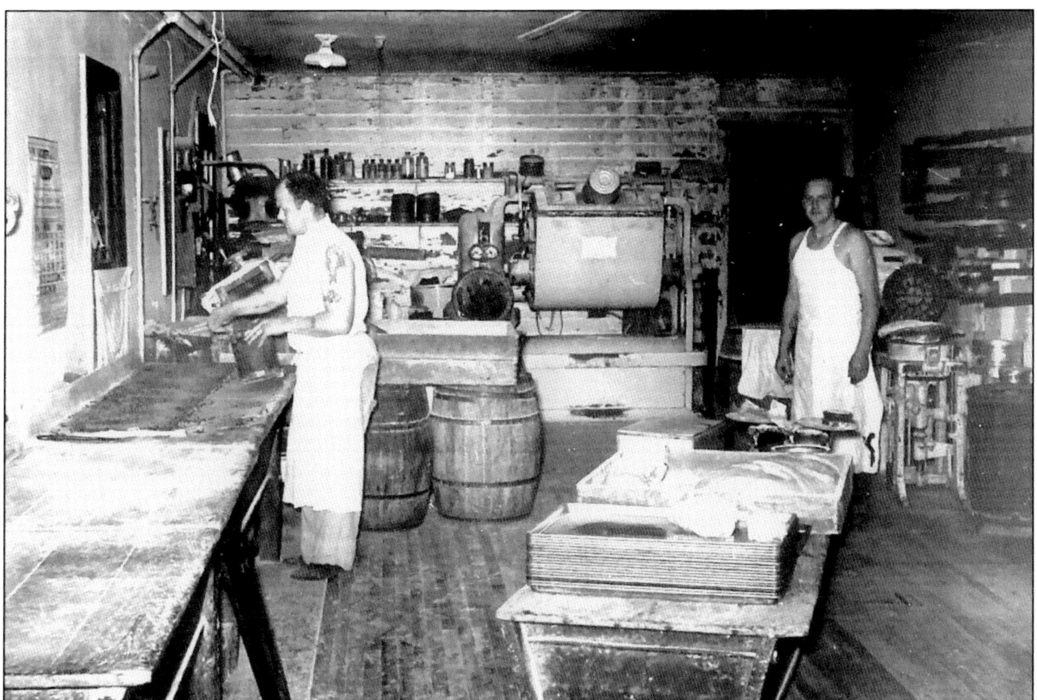
Nick Blum, on the left, and Adam Blum are seen working inside Blum's Bakery, located at 446 Billingsport Road.

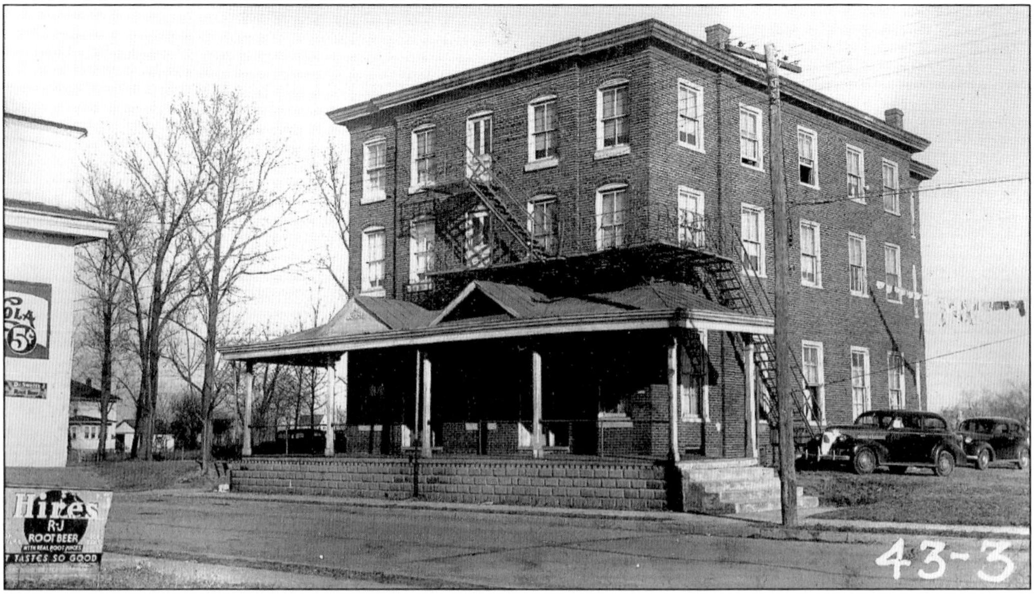

This photograph shows the Brick Hotel, located on Billingsport Road. The hotel became apartments and was later torn down.

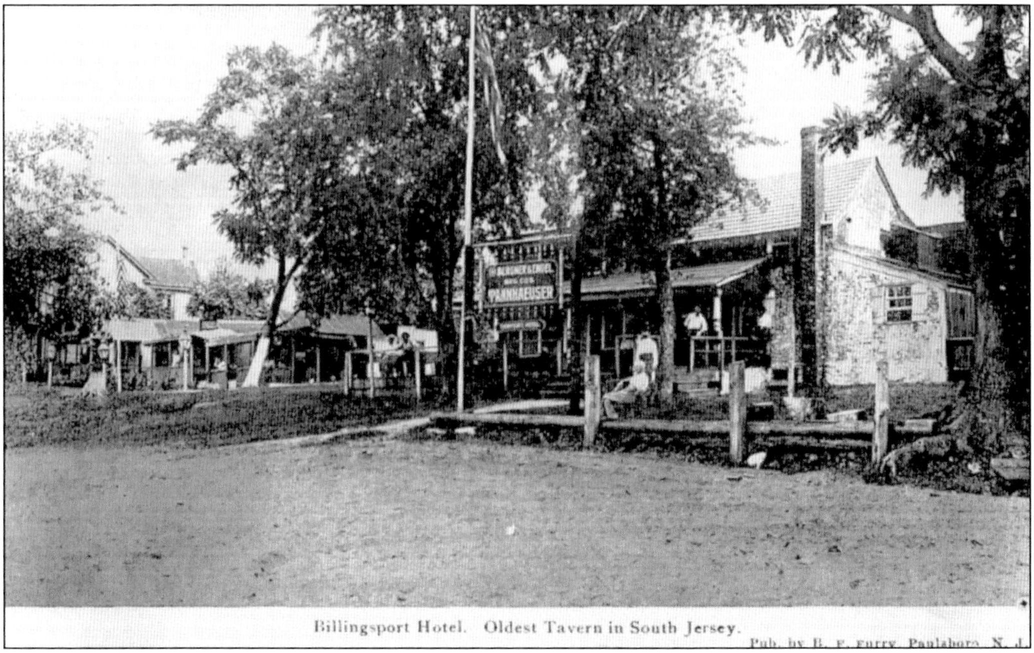

At one time, the Billingsport Hotel was the oldest tavern in South Jersey. (Postcard by B. F. Furry.)

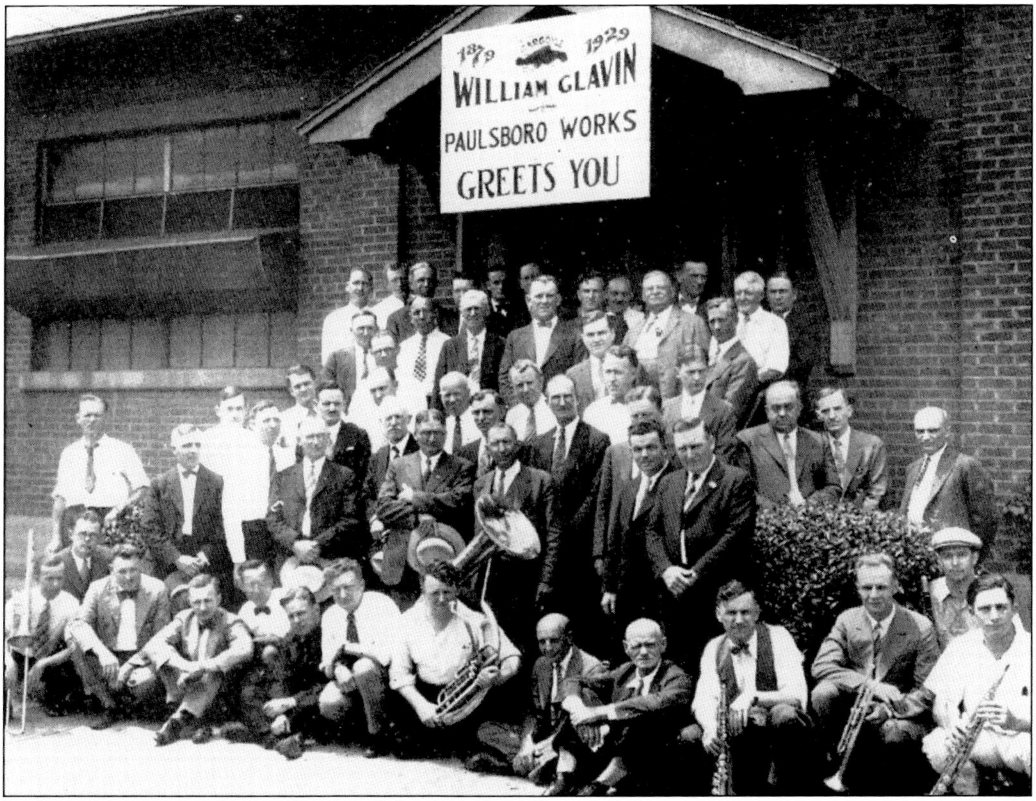

This celebration at the Vacuum Oil works is in honor of William Glavin, who put in 50 years of service, from 1879 to 1929. Glavin is shown with department heads, foremen, and members of the company orchestra.

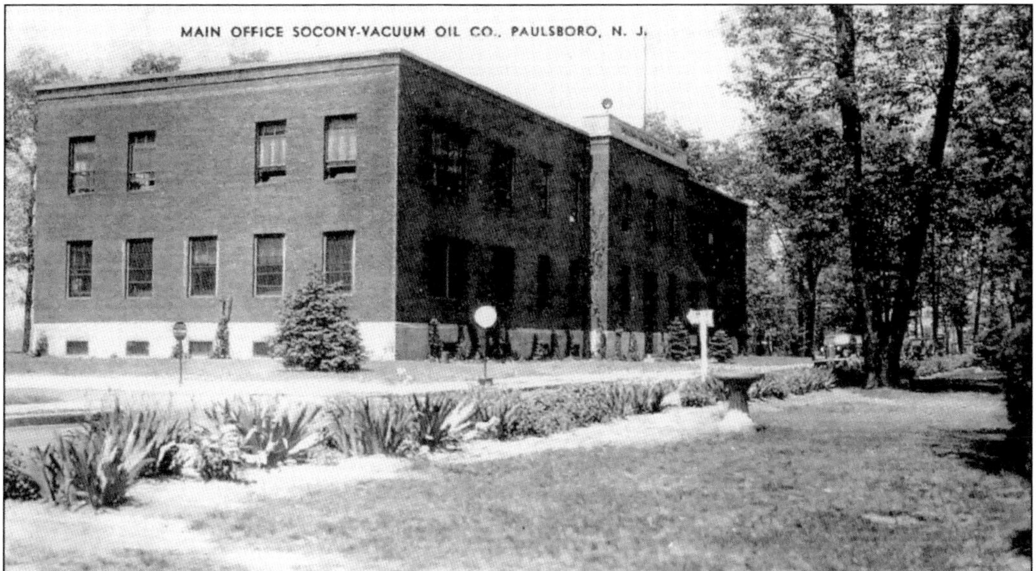

The main office of the Socony-Vacuum Oil Company is shown in this photograph.

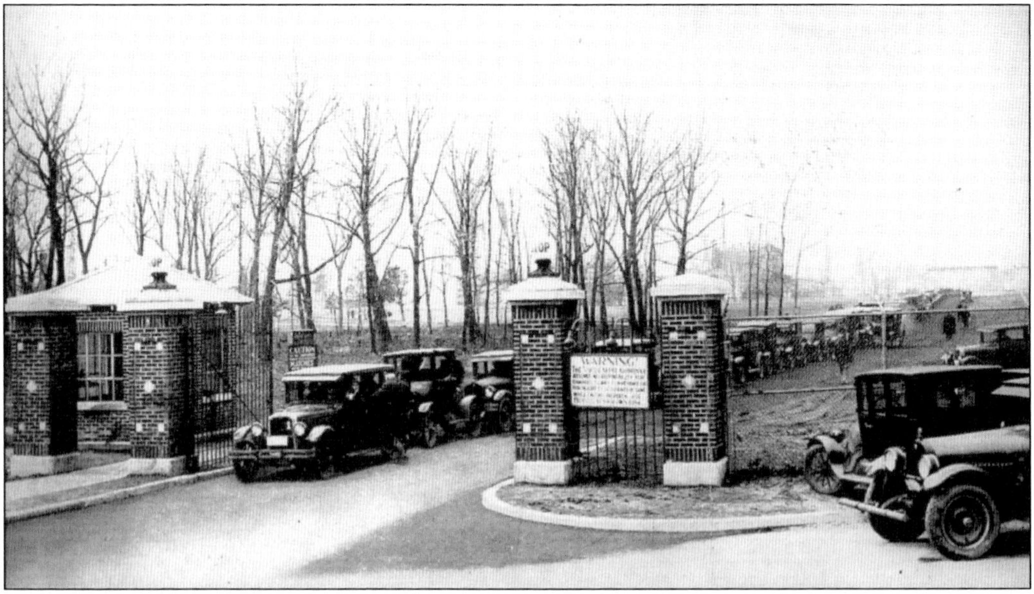

This *c*. 1928 photograph shows how busy the main gate at Socony-Vacuum Oil became during shift changes.

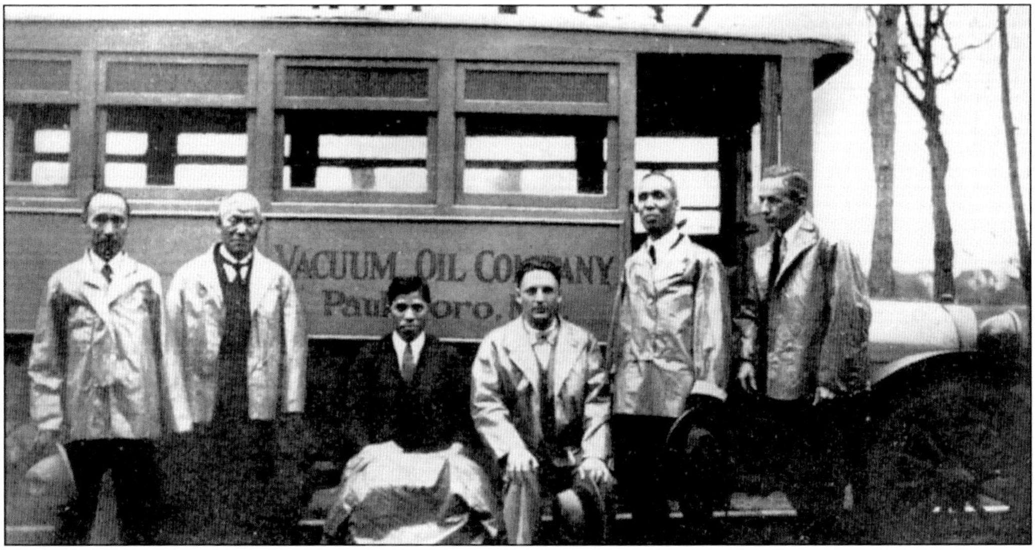

Several officials of the Fujikura Electric Cable Work of Tokyo visit Vacuum Oil in Paulsboro in 1929 to get ideas as to the methods used in other countries in the manufacturing of high-tension cables.

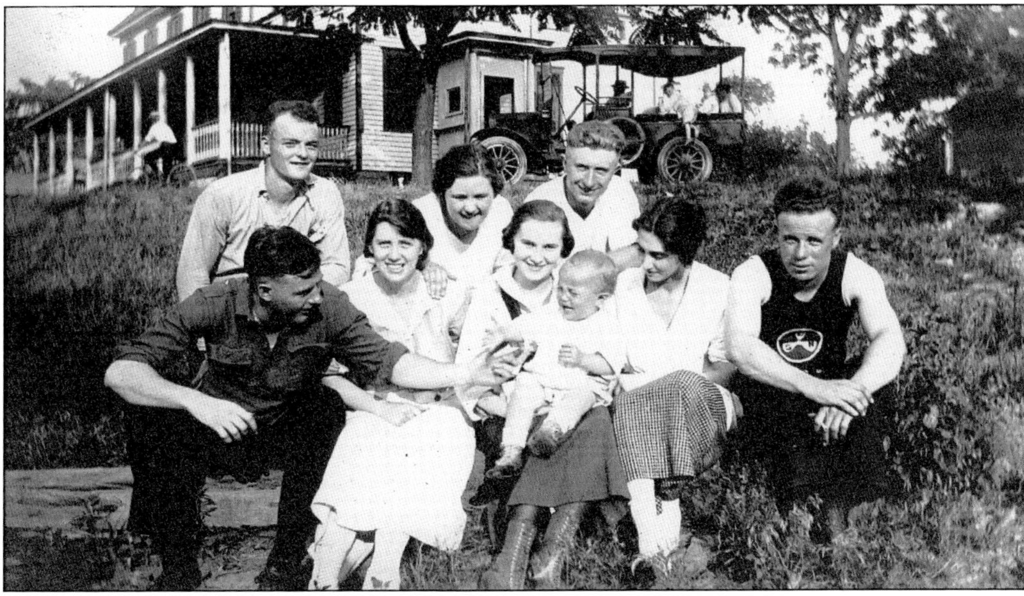

The old Thompson Hotel can be seen in the background of this family photograph.

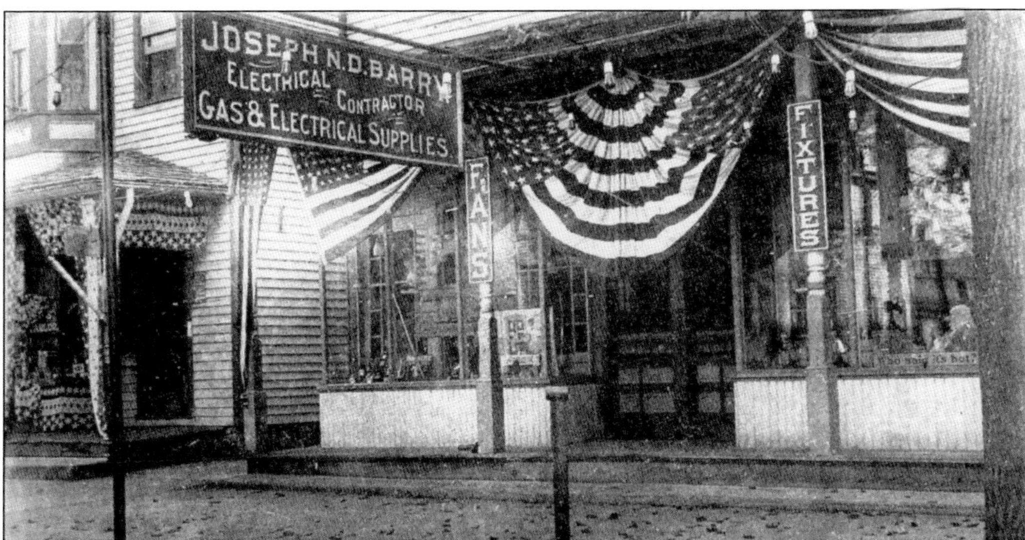

This photograph shows the Joseph N. D. Barry gas and electrical supplies store decorated for the Fourth of July.

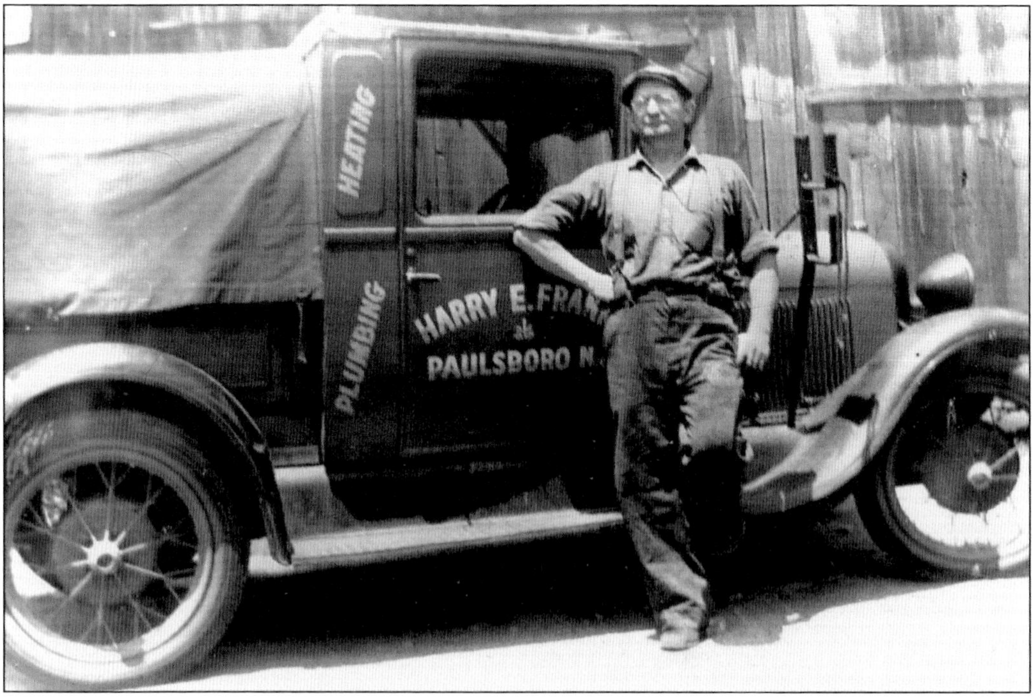

Harry E. Frank poses with his truck, which advertises his plumbing and heating business.

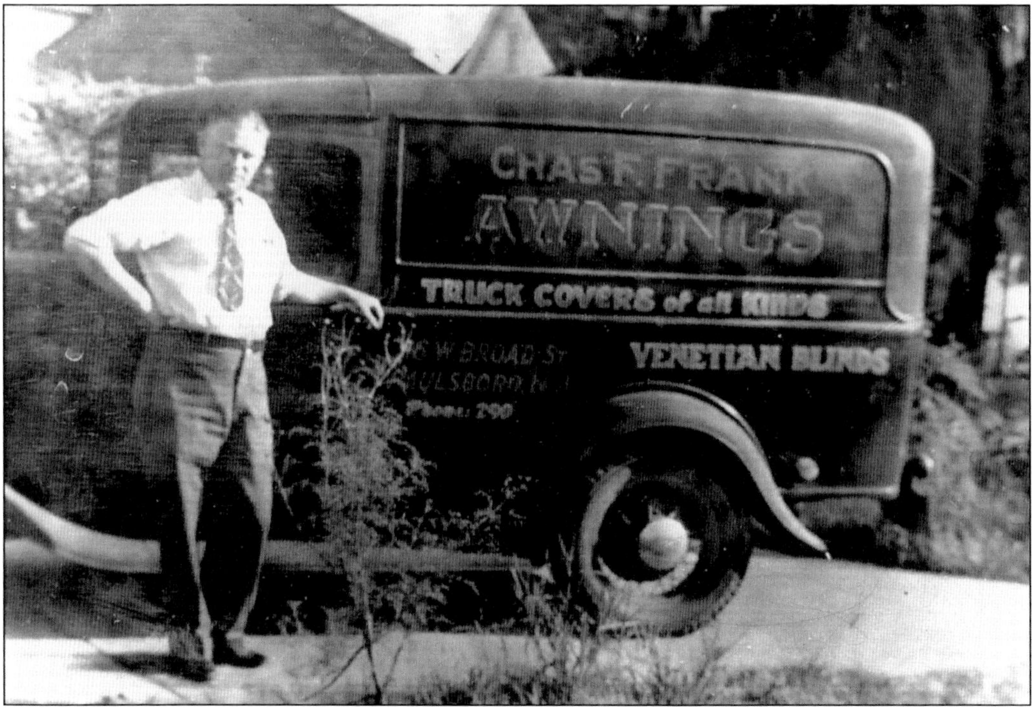

Charles F. Frank poses with his van, which shows advertisements for his business of awnings, truck covers, and venetian blinds.

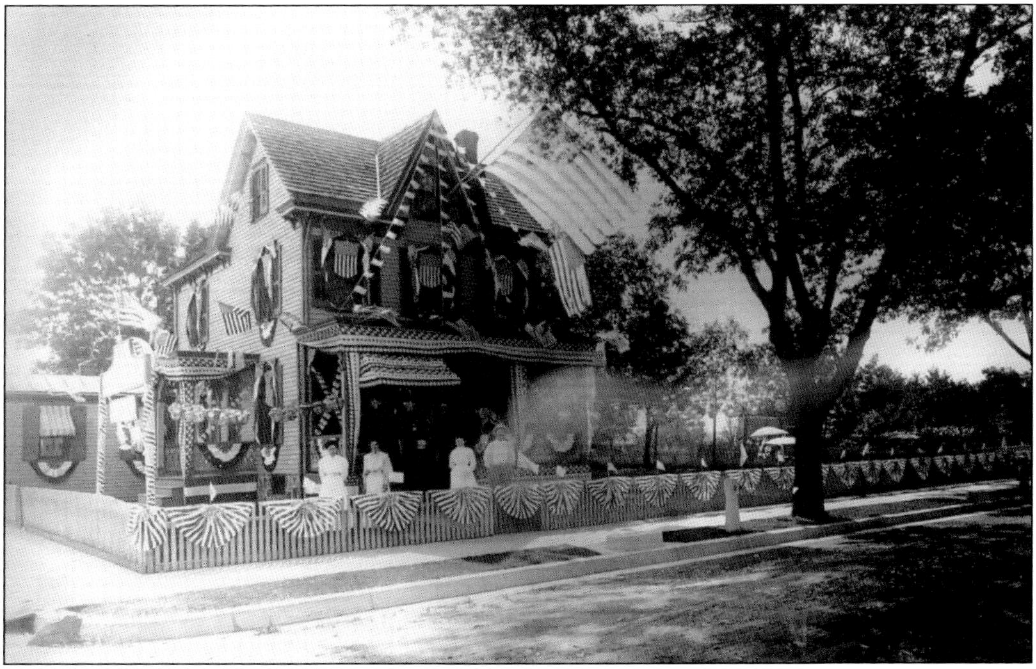

The Hannold house is all decorated for the Fourth of July parade in this c. 1870 photograph.

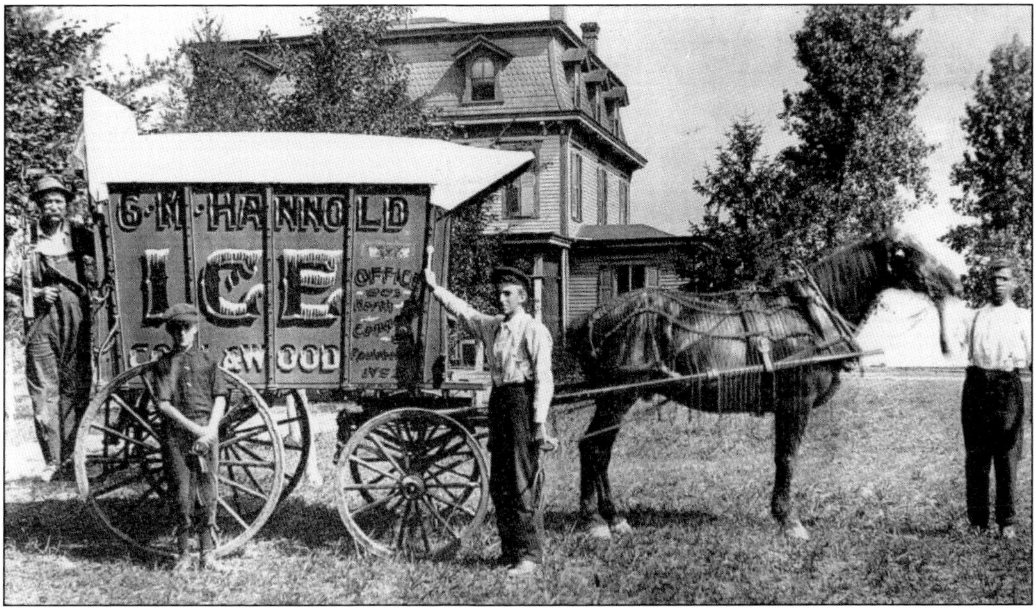

This c. 1912 photograph shows the G. M. Hannold Coal, Wood, and Ice Company with a horse-drawn wagon in front of the Duffy house. William Tredway is on the left, and Ike Vannaman can be seen at the far right. The two people in the center are unidentified.

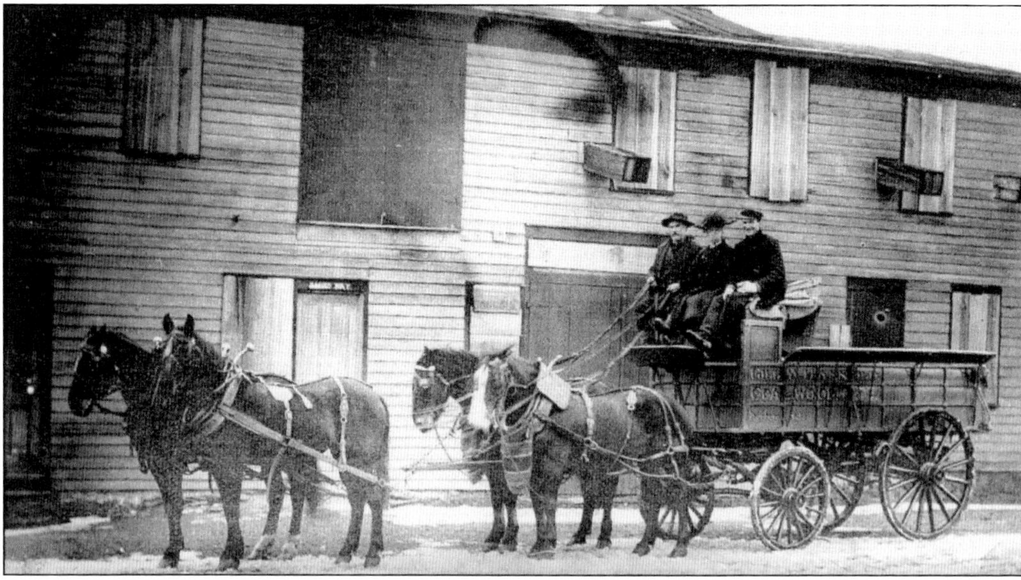

Pictured here is one of G. M. Hannold's rigs at Chestnut and Monroe Streets with a basket factory seen in the background. Samuel Garwood is sitting in the wagon to the left, and Burt Hepperd sits to the right. The man in the middle is unidentified.

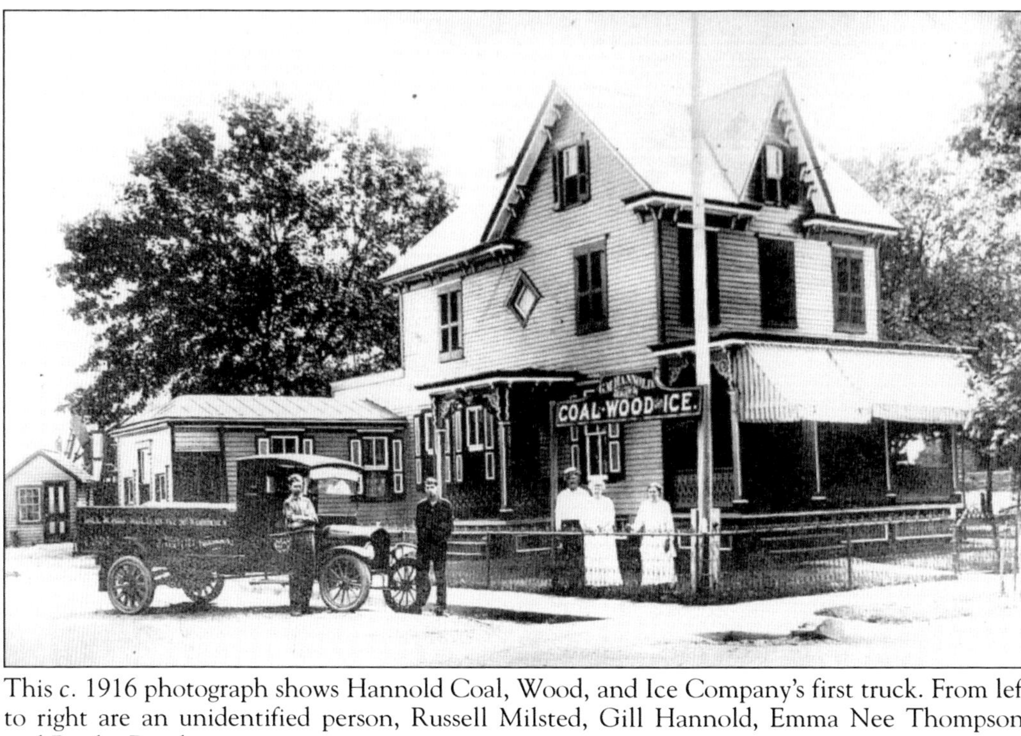

This c. 1916 photograph shows Hannold Coal, Wood, and Ice Company's first truck. From left to right are an unidentified person, Russell Milsted, Gill Hannold, Emma Nee Thompson, and Bertha Rambo.

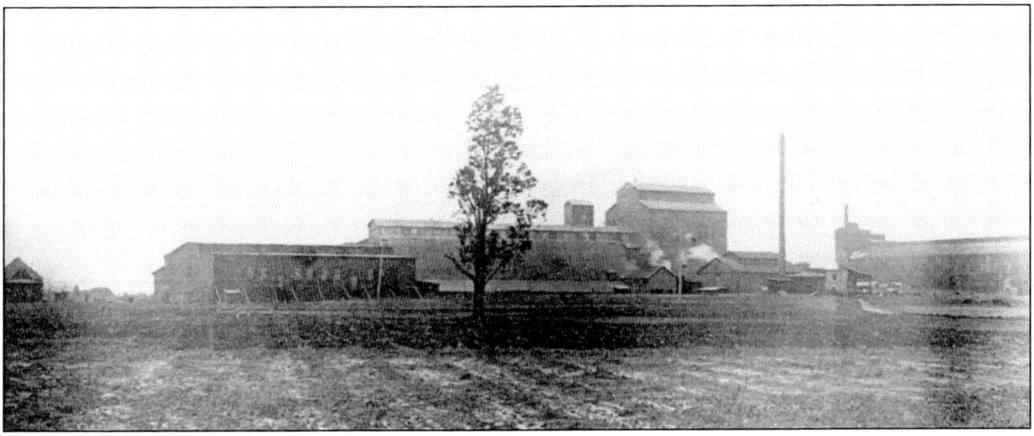

This c. 1912 photograph shows the I. P. Thomas & Company Works, which first located here in 1880. This tract of land originally belonged to the Paul family when they first settled in Paulsboro. The Paul burial ground was located here and was later moved to St. Paul's Methodist Church Cemetery.

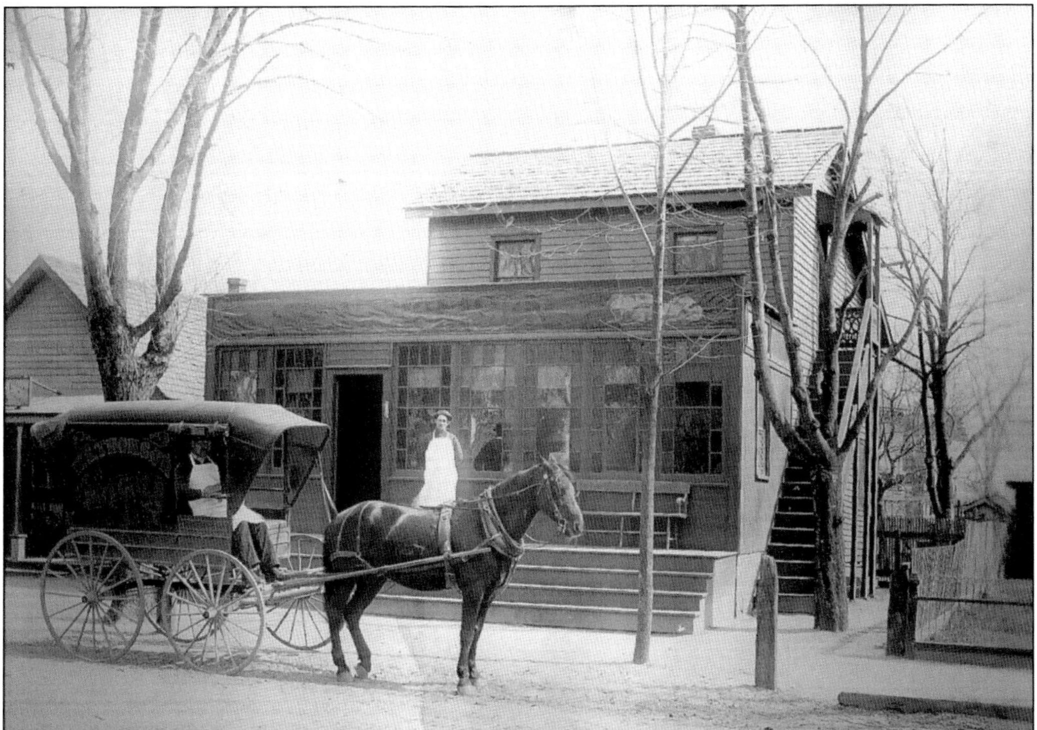

W. S. Thompson's butcher shop and horse-drawn delivery wagon are seen in this photograph.

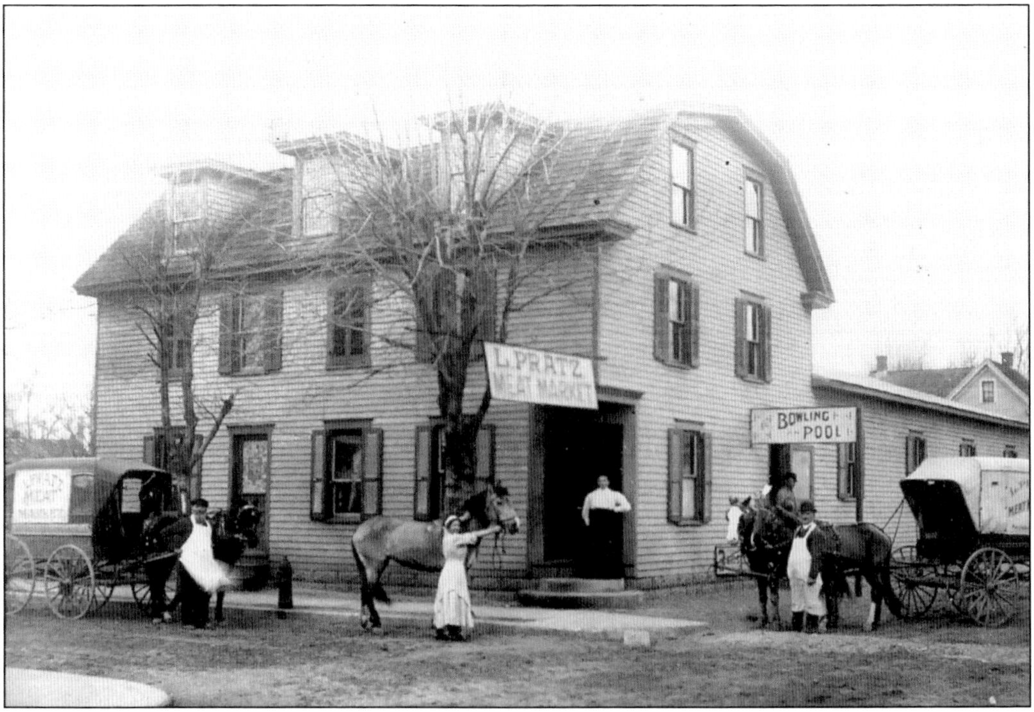

The meat market of Leonard Pratz was located on the corner of Washington and Chestnut Streets next to a bowling alley and pool hall. Leonard Pratz drove one of the wagons, and his son Fred, who later became a local taxi driver, drove the other.

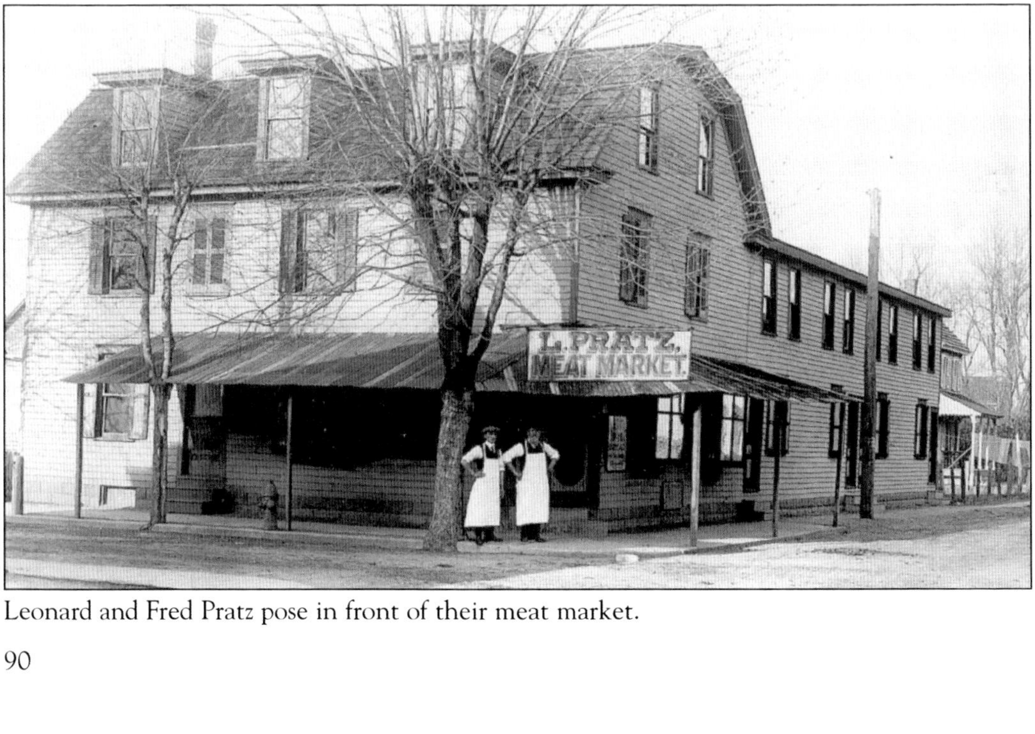

Leonard and Fred Pratz pose in front of their meat market.

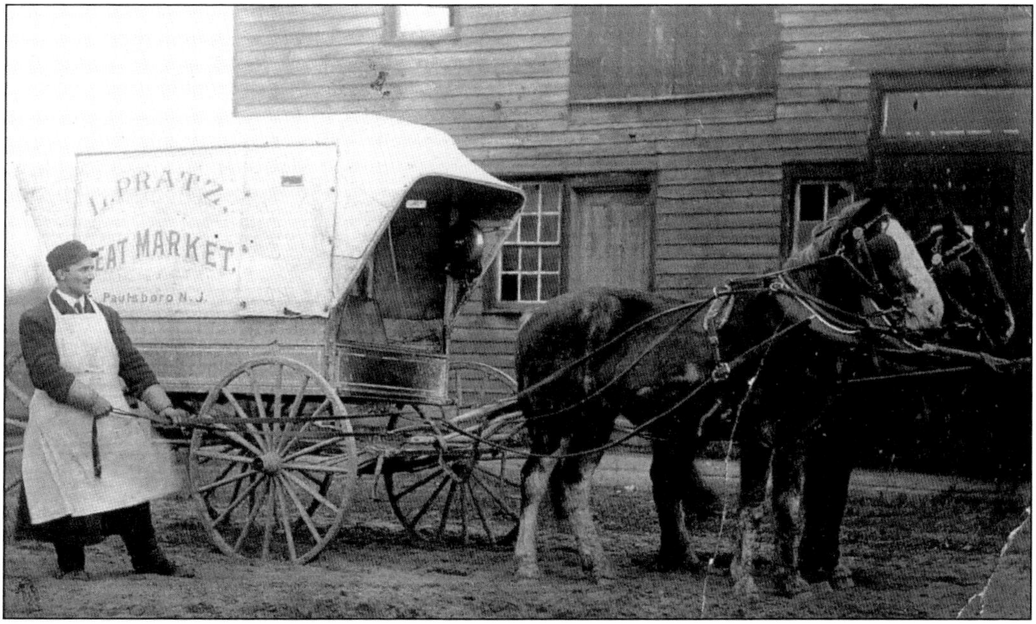

Fred Pratz poses with his delivery wagon for this photograph.

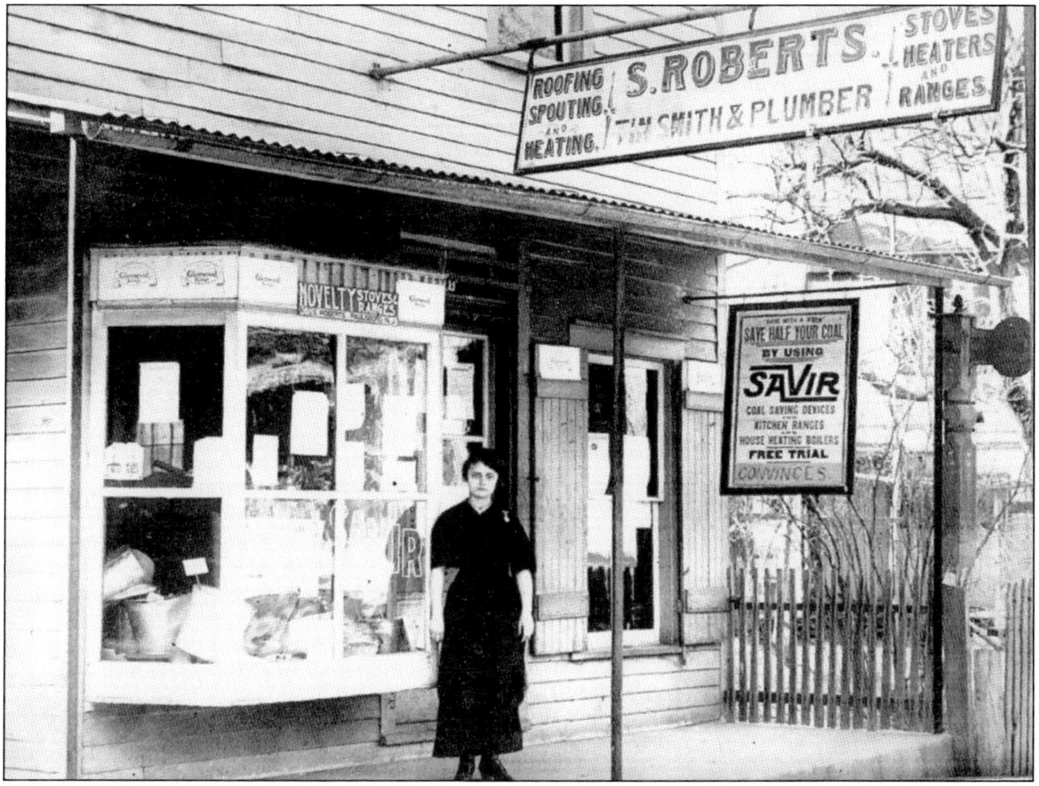

Daisy M. Sharp poses for this *c.* 1914 photograph in front of tinsmith S. Roberts's shop, located at 1410 Swedesboro Avenue.

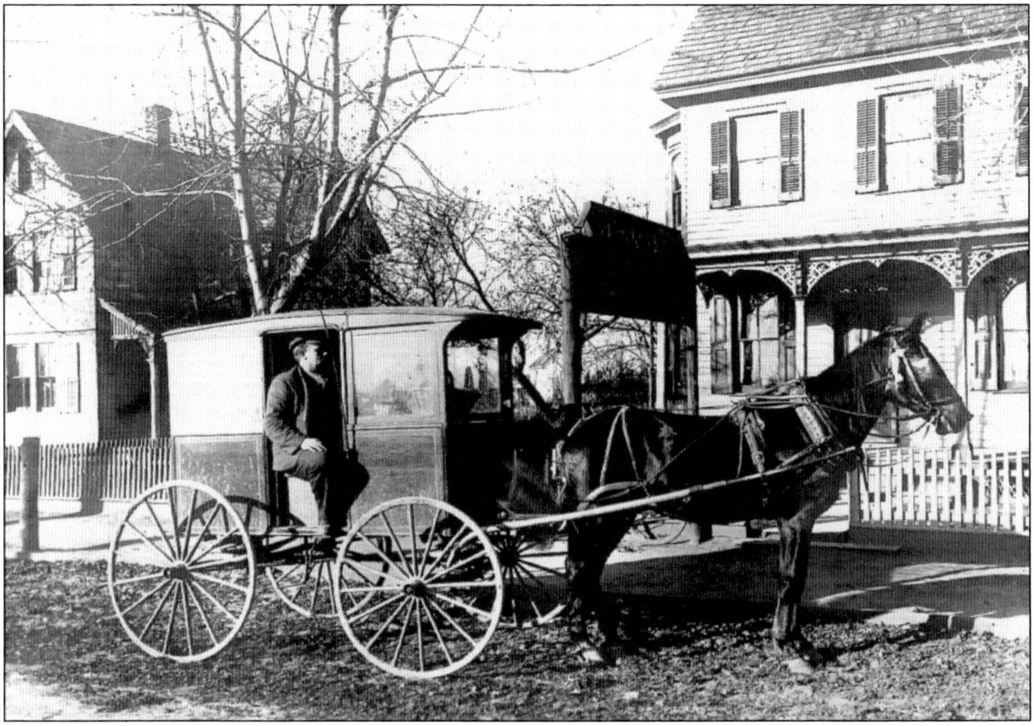

The delivery wagon of T. Schwebel's bakery is stopped in front of the Davis Cottage Boarding House.

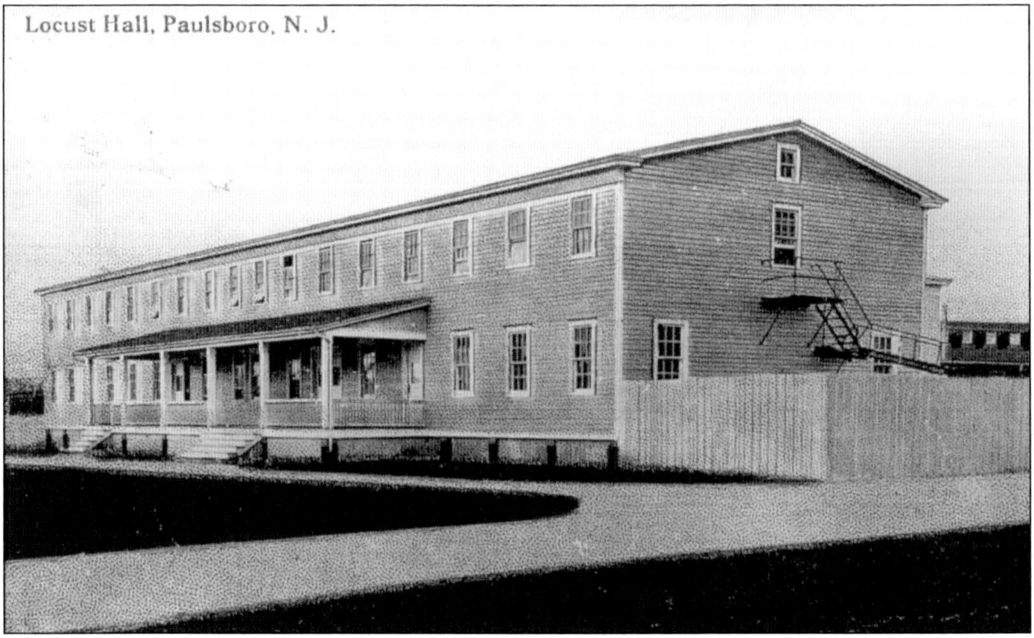

The Locust Hall Boarding House of Standard Fuse Company was located on Mantua Avenue. This later became the Sandura Rug Company, which burned down on February 4, 1934.

Six

Fire Departments

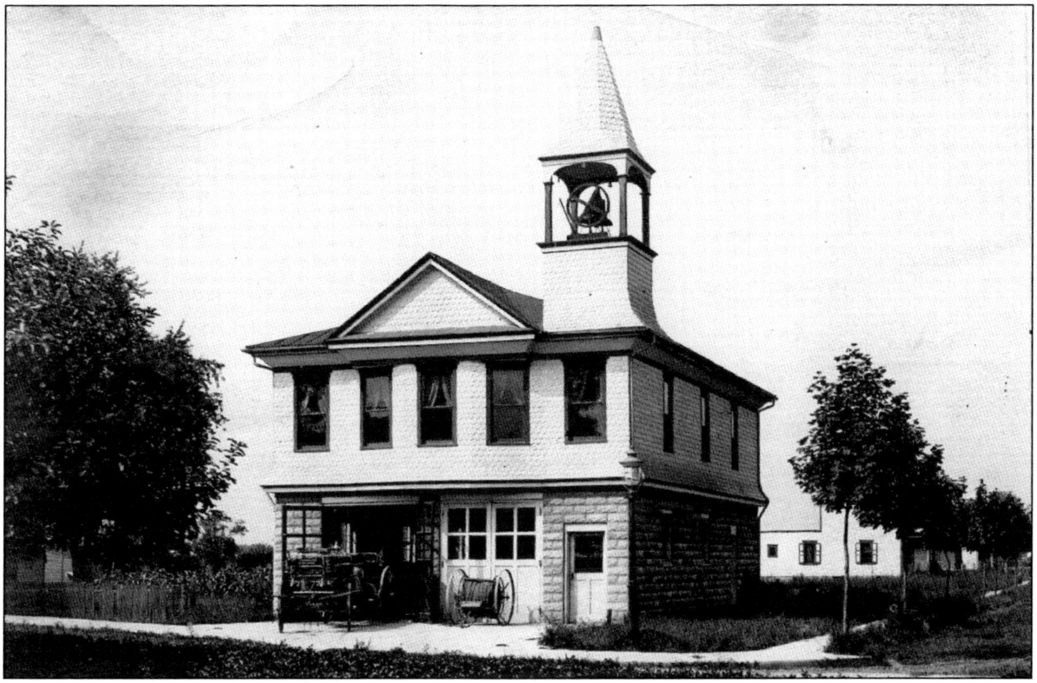

The Paulsboro Volunteer Fire Company was established in 1899. This building first opened on February 8, 1908. Notice the old fire apparatus in front of the doors.

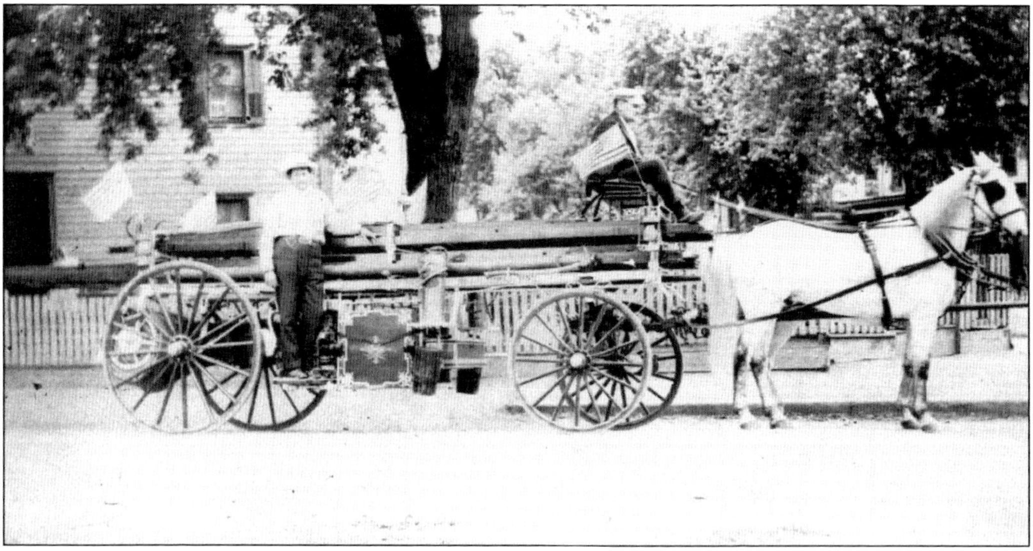

The Paulsboro Volunteer Fire Company poses with a horse-drawn fire apparatus for this photograph taken in the early 1900s.

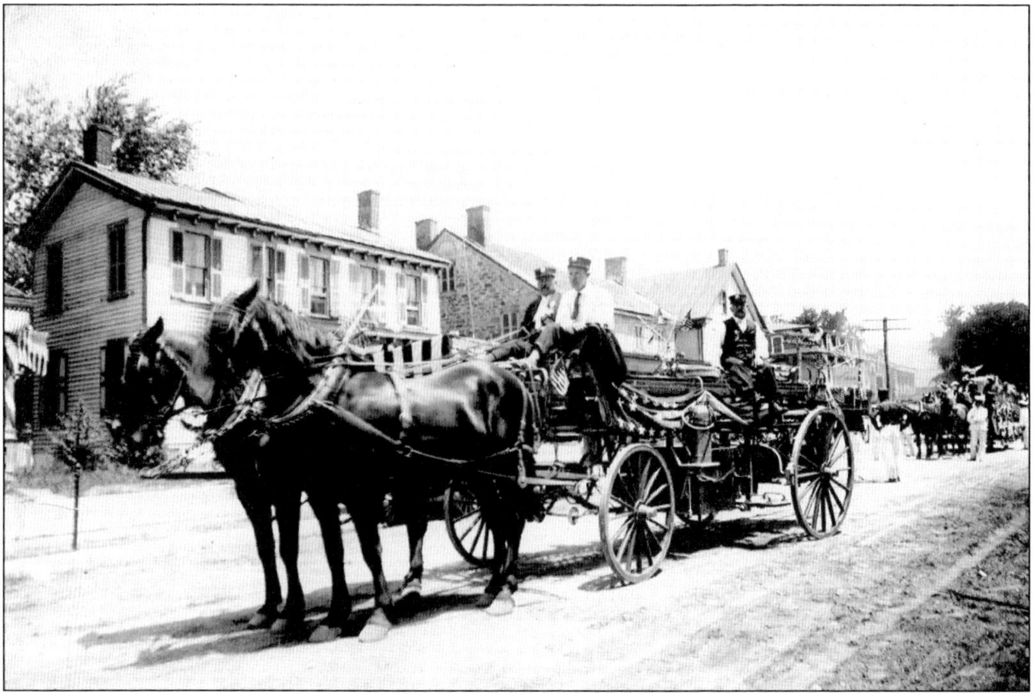

Joseph and Ben Paul pose with an unidentified person on the horse-drawn fire apparatus for the Fourth of July parade.

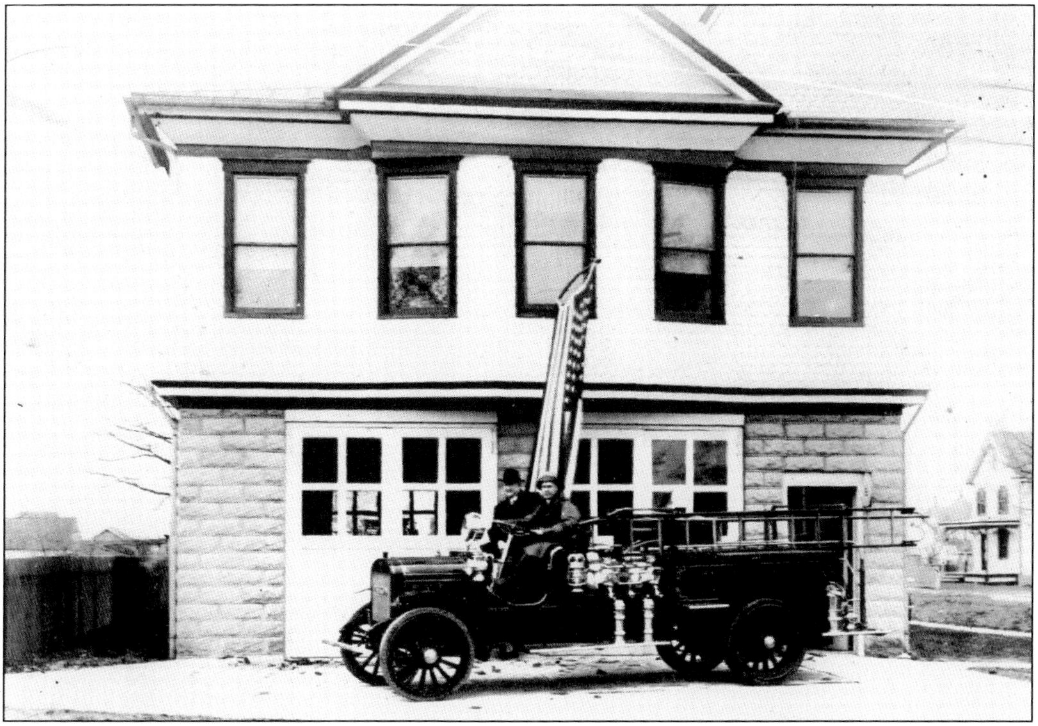

The front of the old firehouse is the backdrop for Paulsboro's first motor-driven apparatus, a 1915 Brockway.

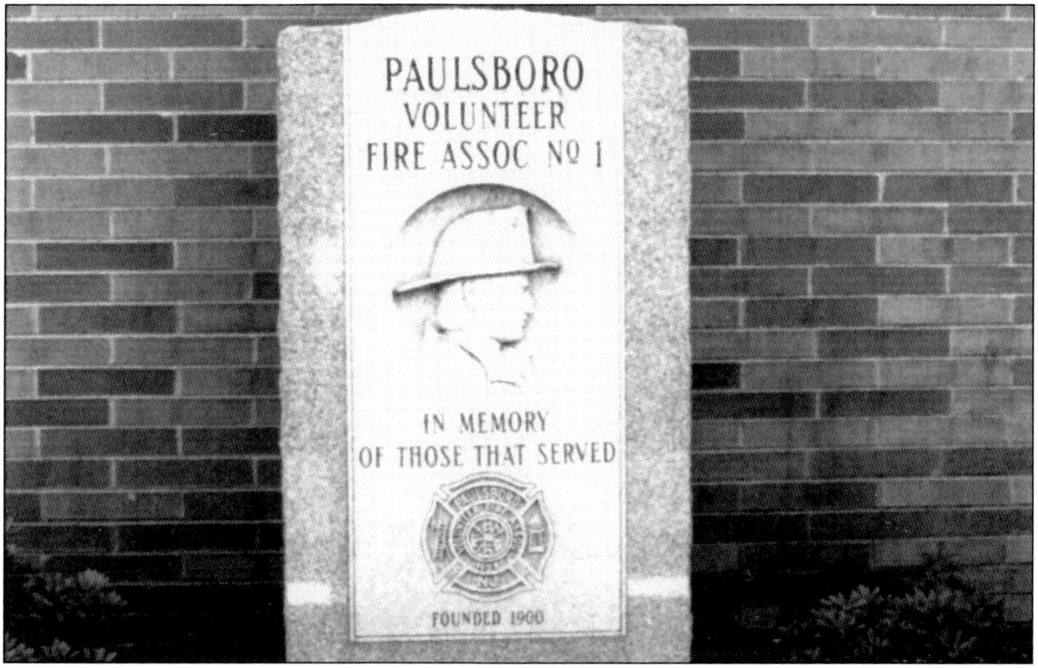

The Paulsboro Volunteer Fire Association No. 1 monument reads, "In memory of those that served."

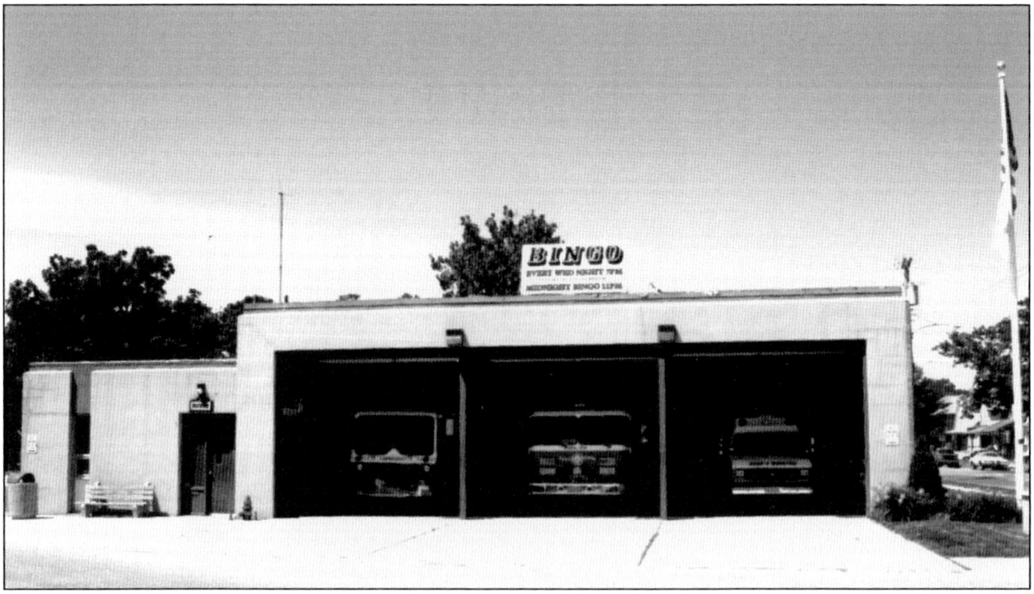

The Paulsboro Volunteer Firehouse, built in 1962, is shown in a present-day view.

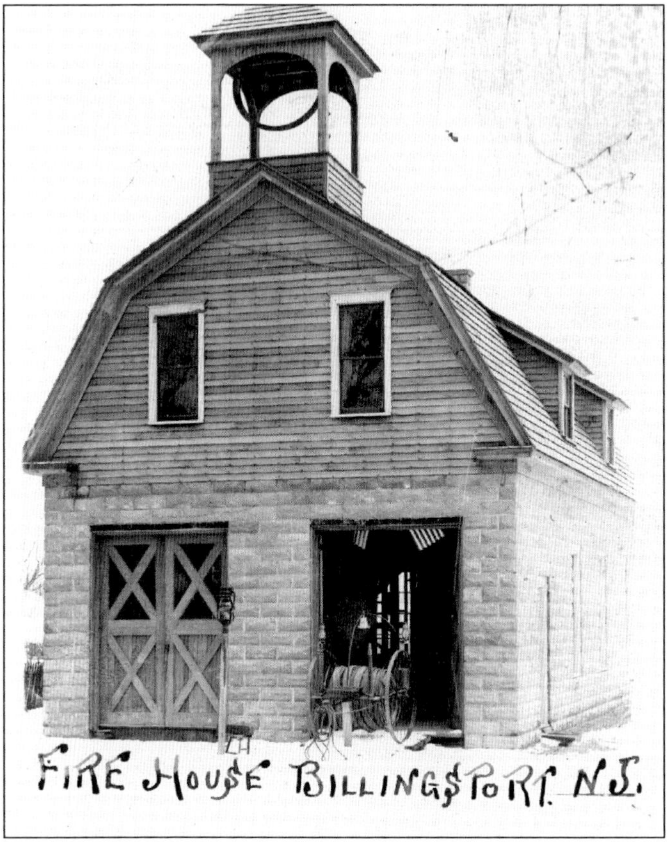

The Billingsport Volunteer Fire Company was formed on October 8, 1904, and incorporated on May 14, 1905. (Donated by Clara Wilkerson Jones.)

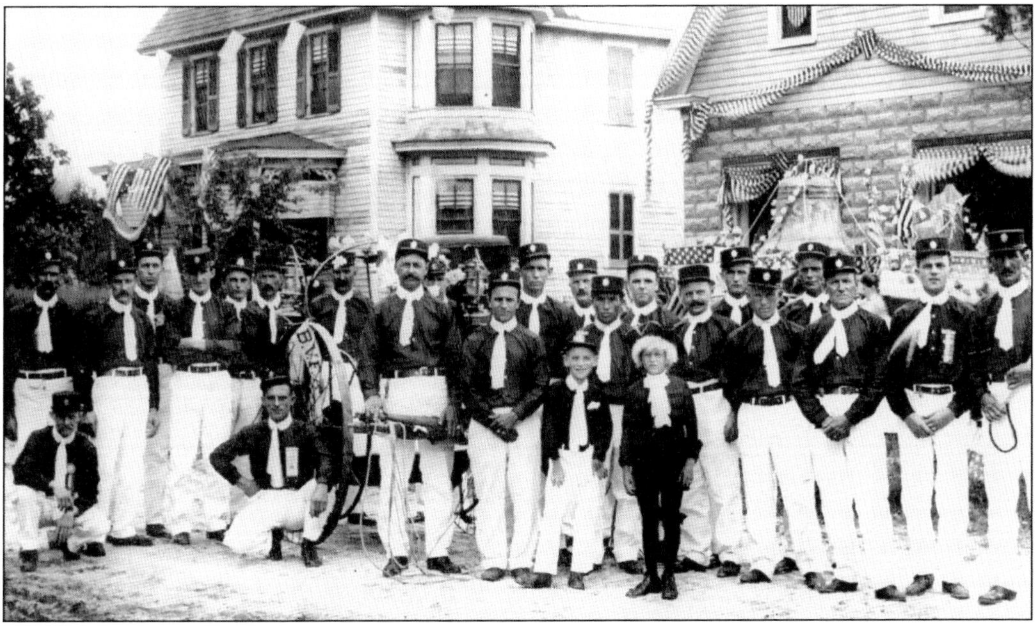

The Billingsport Fire Company is ready for its first parade. Members, from left to right, are as follows: (first row) H. Smedley, D. Pote, R. Springer (holding hose reel), J. Banks, and two unidentified boys; (second row) S. Davis, G. Schroeder, A. Heppard, H. Lowrie, W. Davis, G. Rivell, E. Schuck, J. Hofmann, J. Pote, F. Pote, and Chief O. Sheets; (third row) R. Gibbs, W. Hunter, J. DeVault, B. Locke, J. Murray, W. Flowers Jr., E. Locke, and J. Murray.

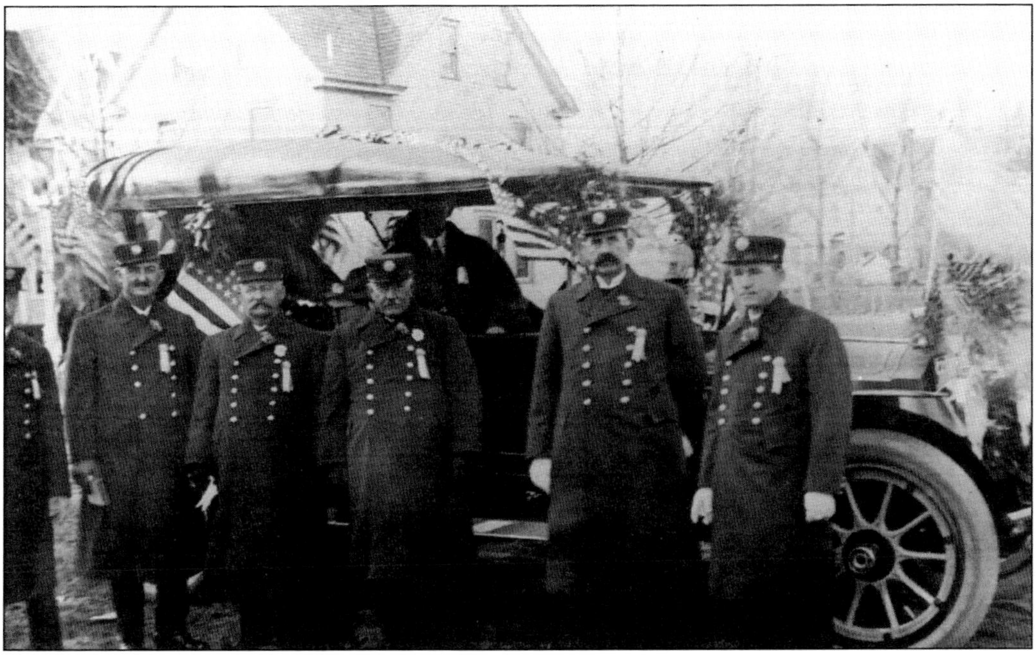

This *c.* 1915 photograph shows members of Billingsport Volunteer Fire Company. From left to right are H. Sinexon, Gill Hannold, Ben Paul, Charles Saulsbury, Percy Lodge, and Charles Haussman.

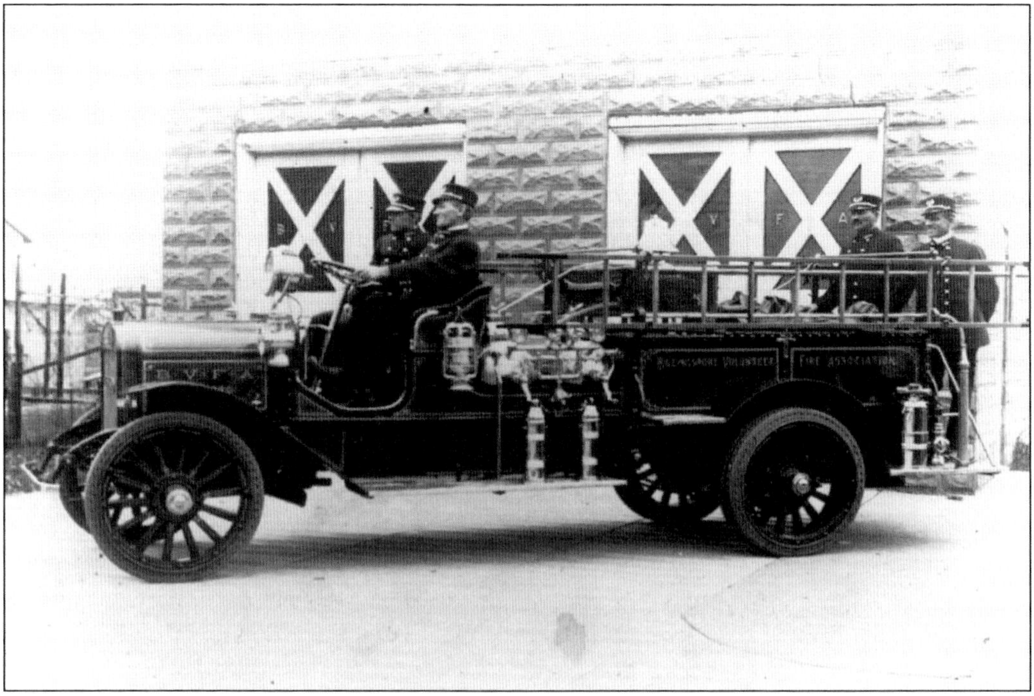

Firefighters pose with an old fire truck in front of Billingsport Firehouse.

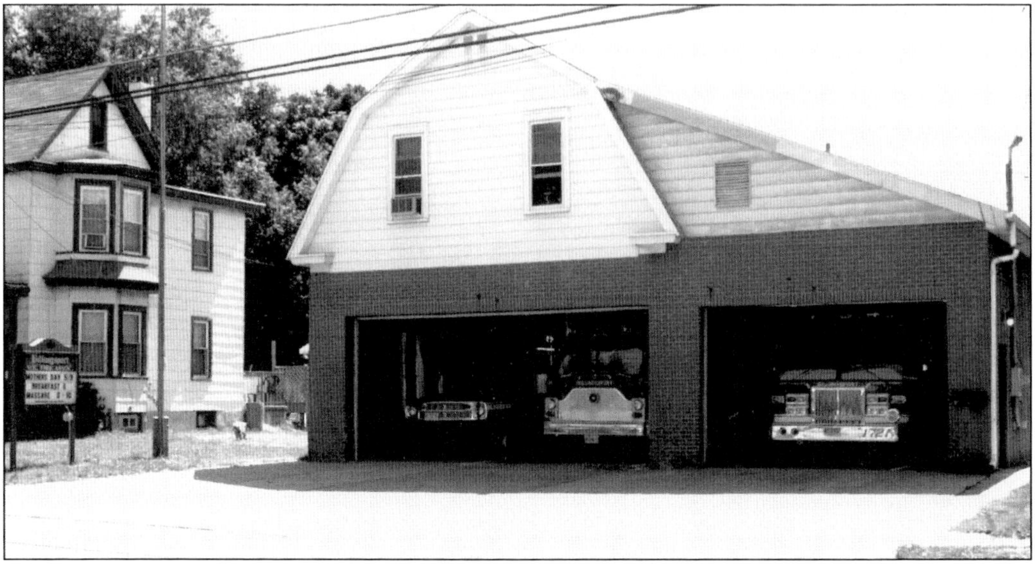

This present-day photograph shows the Billingsport Firehouse with the fire trucks ready to go out on a call.

Seven

Bridges and Lighthouses

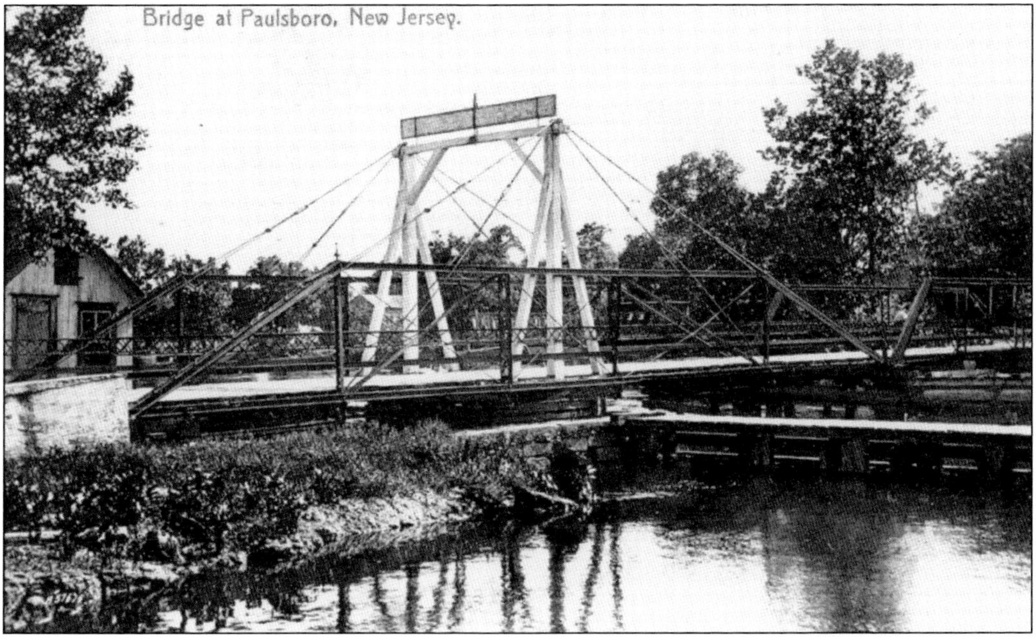

This image features the wooden bridge crossing Mantua Creek, as well as the bridge keeper's house. (Postcard by E. W. Humphreys.)

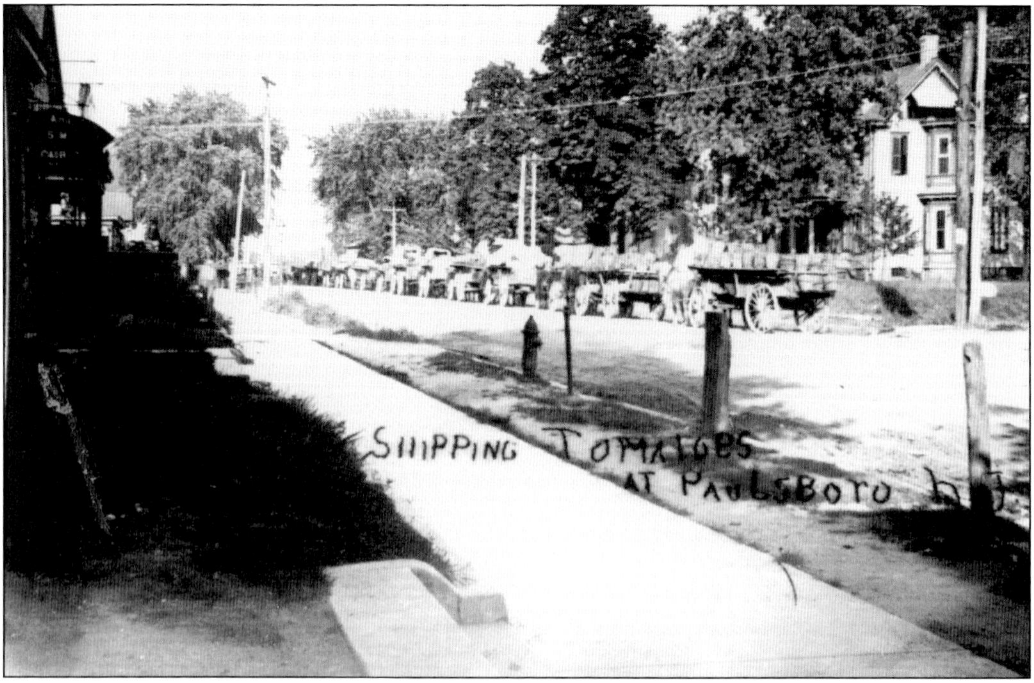

Wagons are lined up on Broad Street to ship local produce to Philadelphia from the wharf next to the Mantua Creek Bridge *c.* 1917.

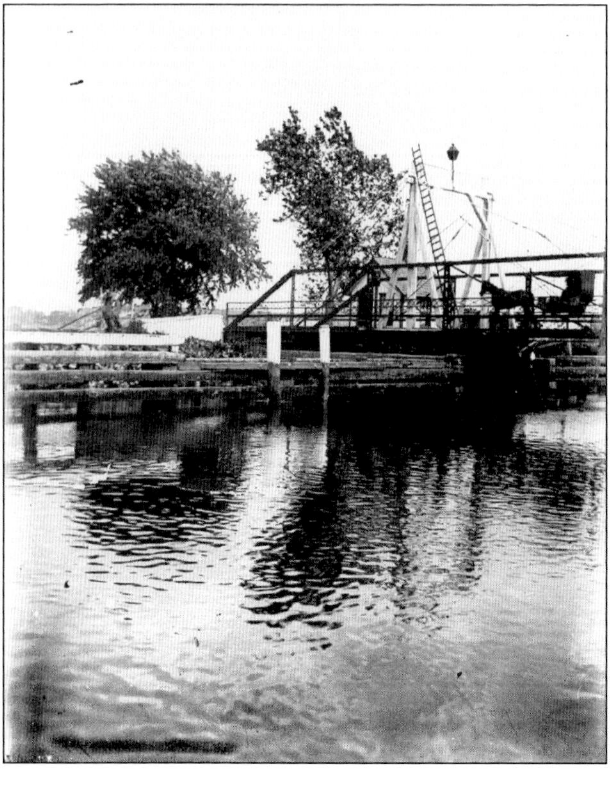

A horse-drawn buggy heads out of Paulsboro over the wooden bridge *c.* 1903. The sign over the bridge reads, "Ten dollar fine for traveling over this bridge faster than a walk."

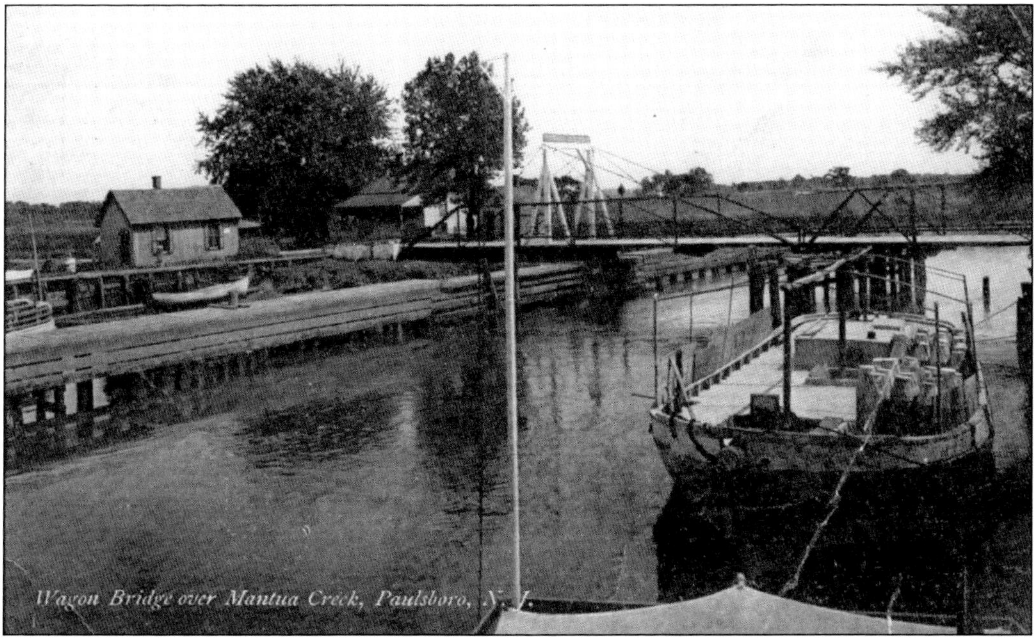

Looking south, this *c.* 1914 view shows the wagon bridge over Mantua Creek. In the foreground, flatboats can be seen being loaded for market.

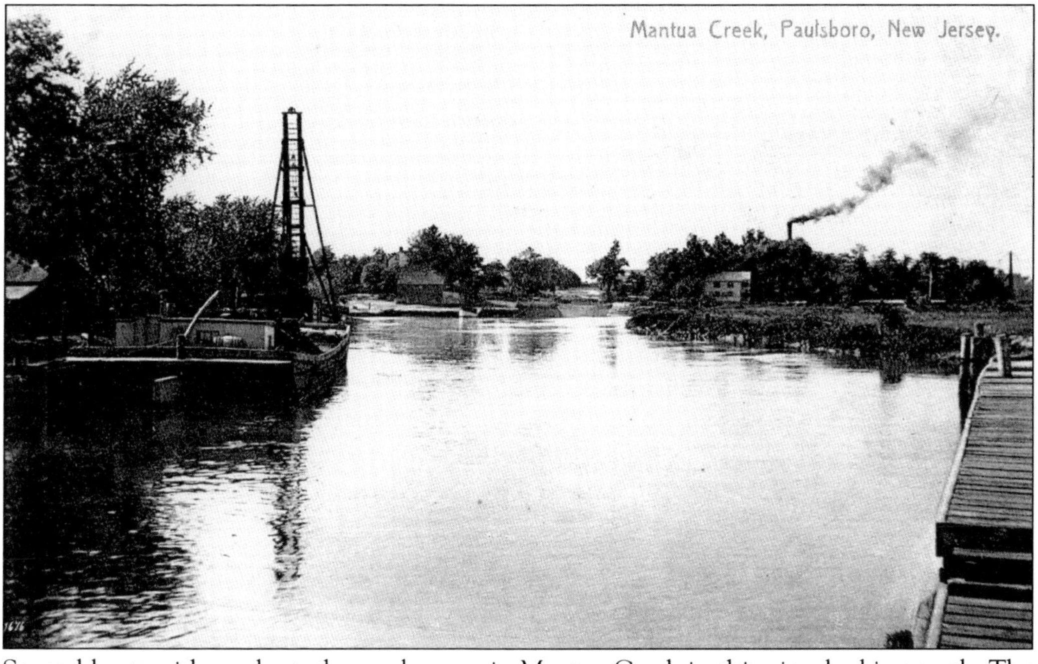

Several boats with smokestacks can be seen in Mantua Creek in this view looking north. The train bridge is in the distance on the right. (Postcard by E. W. Humphreys.)

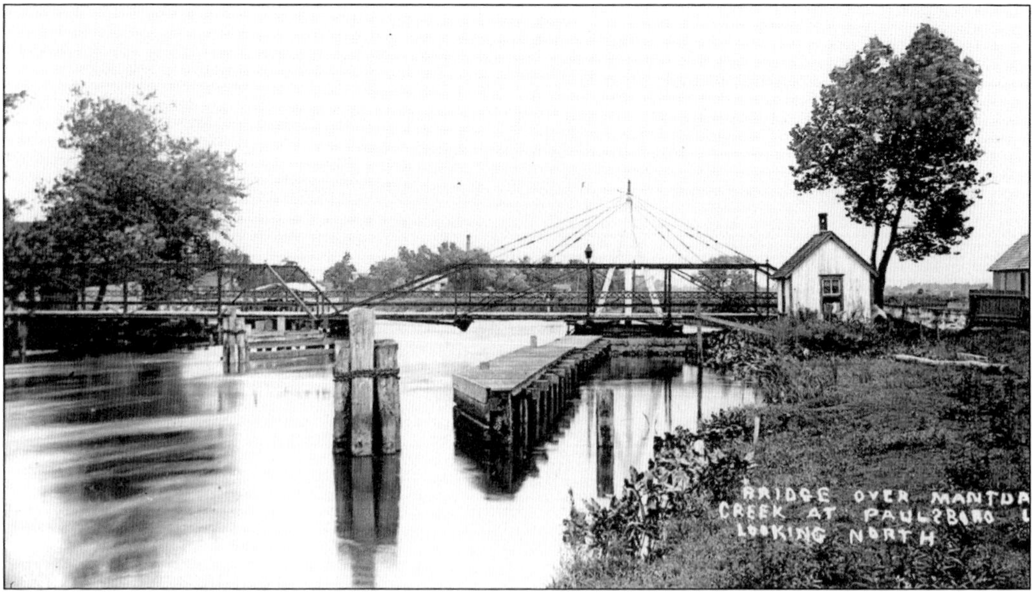

This c. 1903 view of the bridge over Mantua Creek looks north.

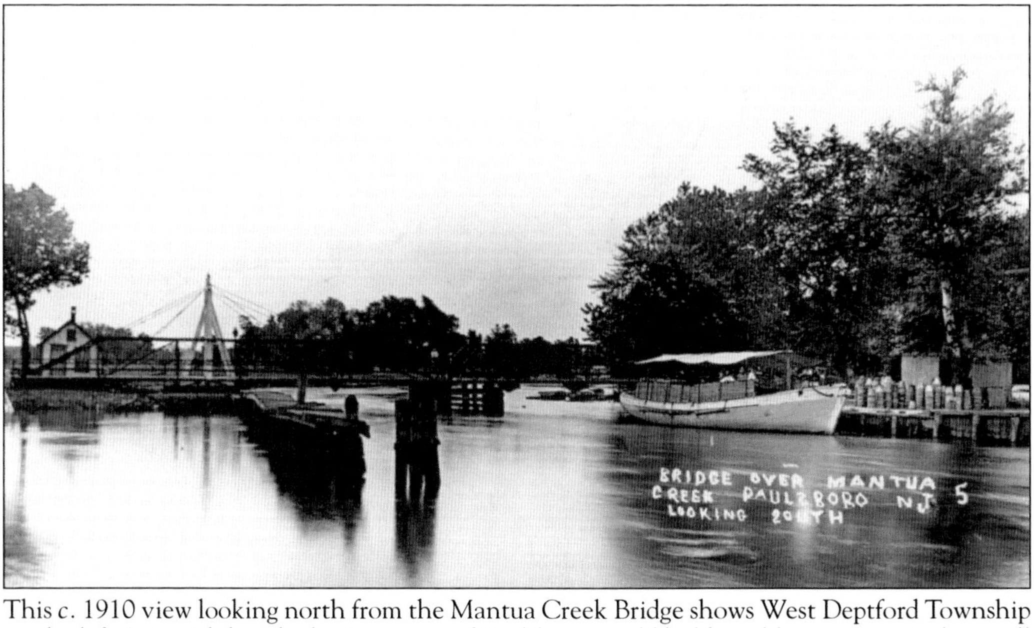

This c. 1910 view looking north from the Mantua Creek Bridge shows West Deptford Township on the left. It is said that the businessmen of Paulsboro would hold weekly meetings in the small buildings to the left. Notice the truck boat in the right foreground with the baskets stacked neatly on deck.

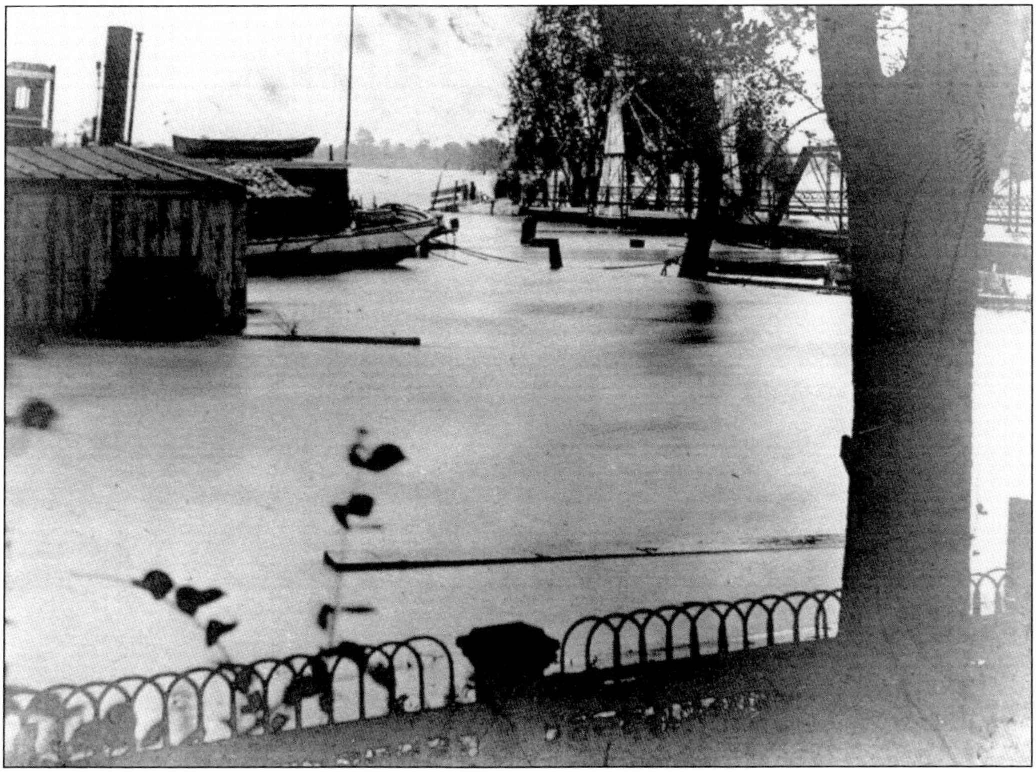

The Mantua Creek is seen overflowing its banks with the bridge flooded out *c.* 1903.

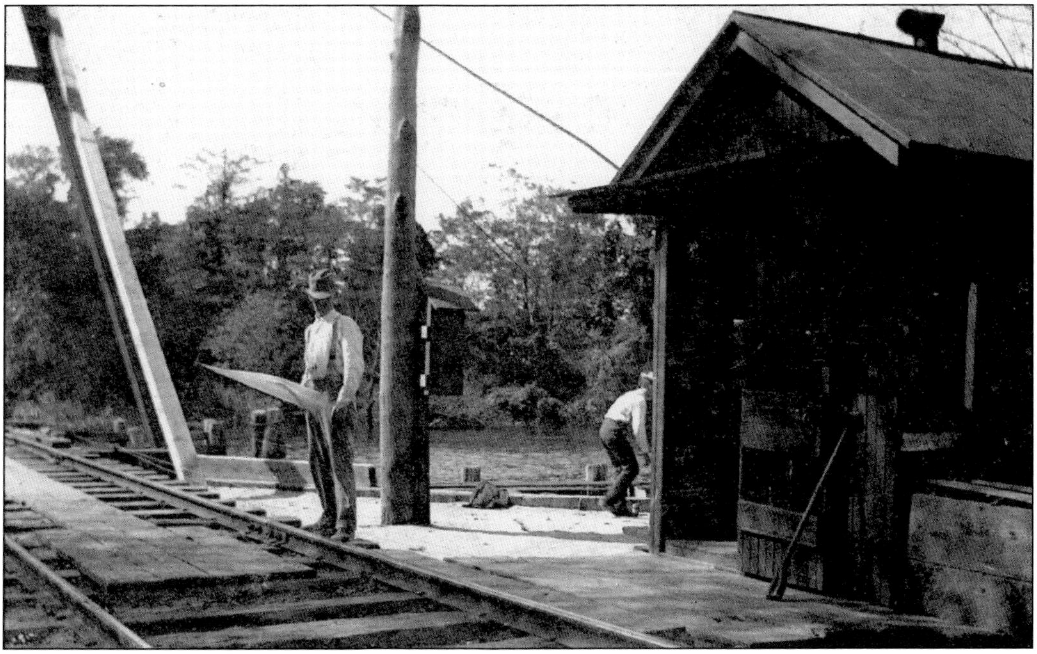

Men pose for a photograph while working at a railroad bridge over Mantua Creek.

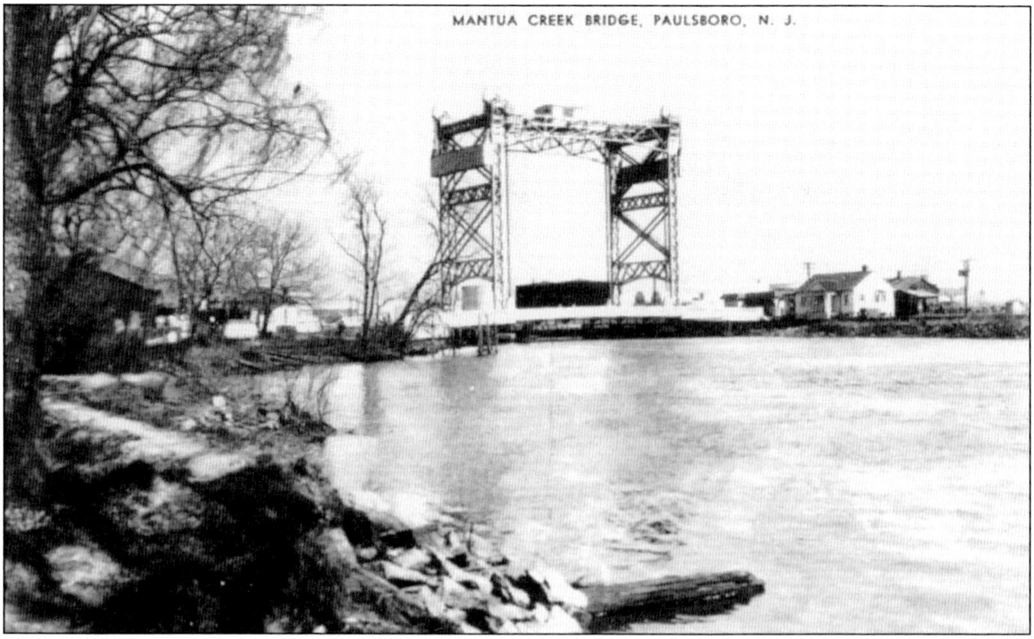

This photograph shows the Mantua Creek Bridge and houses along the east side of the creek bank. The houses are no longer there.

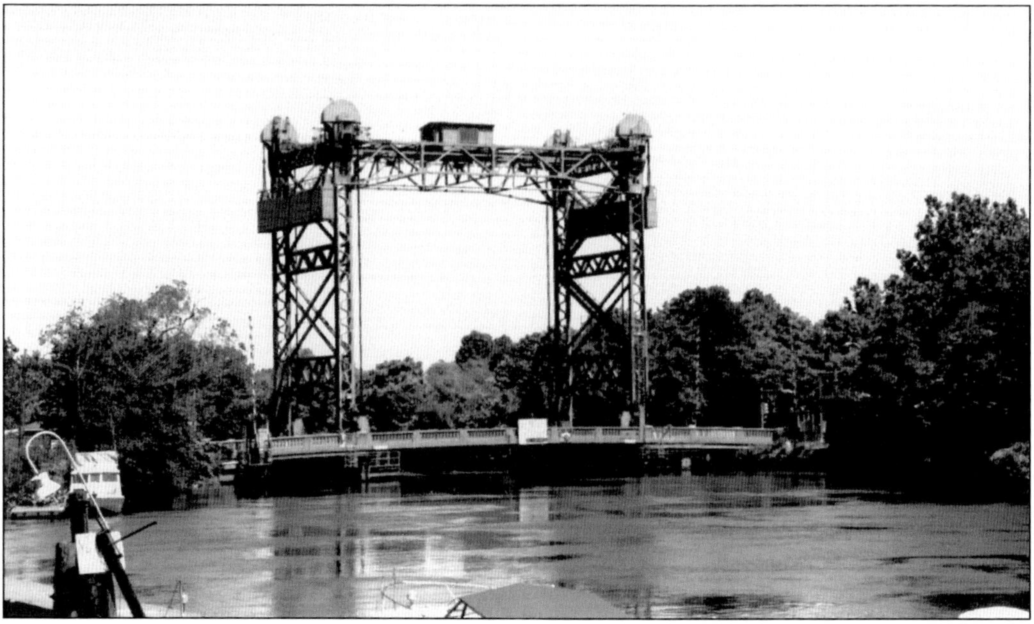

This photograph shows how the Mantua Creek Bridge looks today.

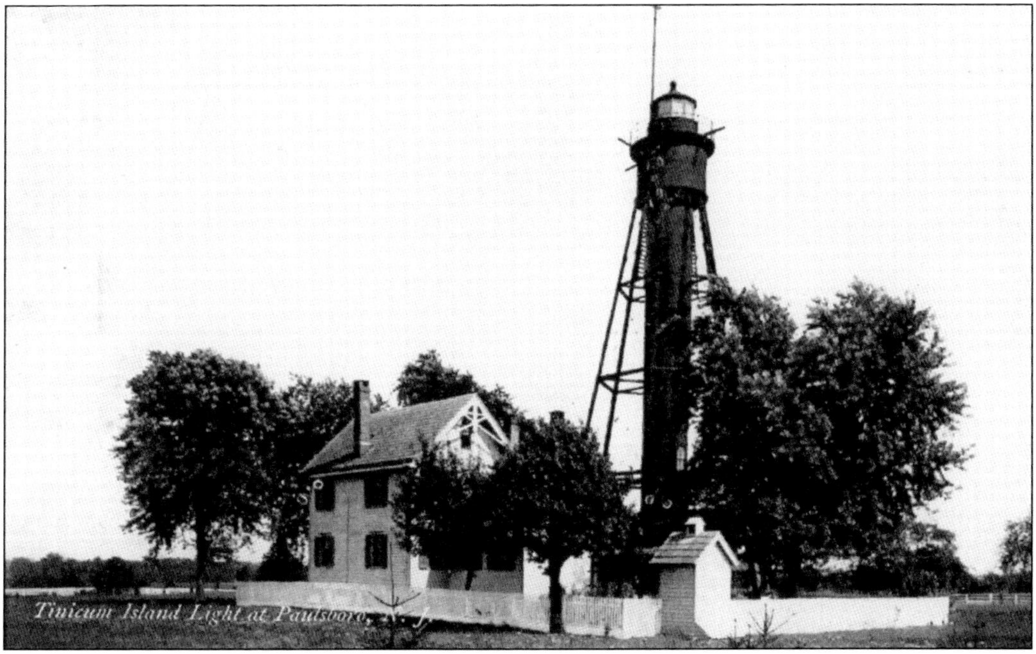

The Tinicum Rear Range Lighthouse, located at Second Street and Mantua Avenue, was built in 1880, and its first lighting took place on night of December 31, 1880. This lighthouse is still active and is equipped with a fixed red light with a 1,000-watt lamp exhibiting 500,000 candlepower. The light keeper's house is no longer there.

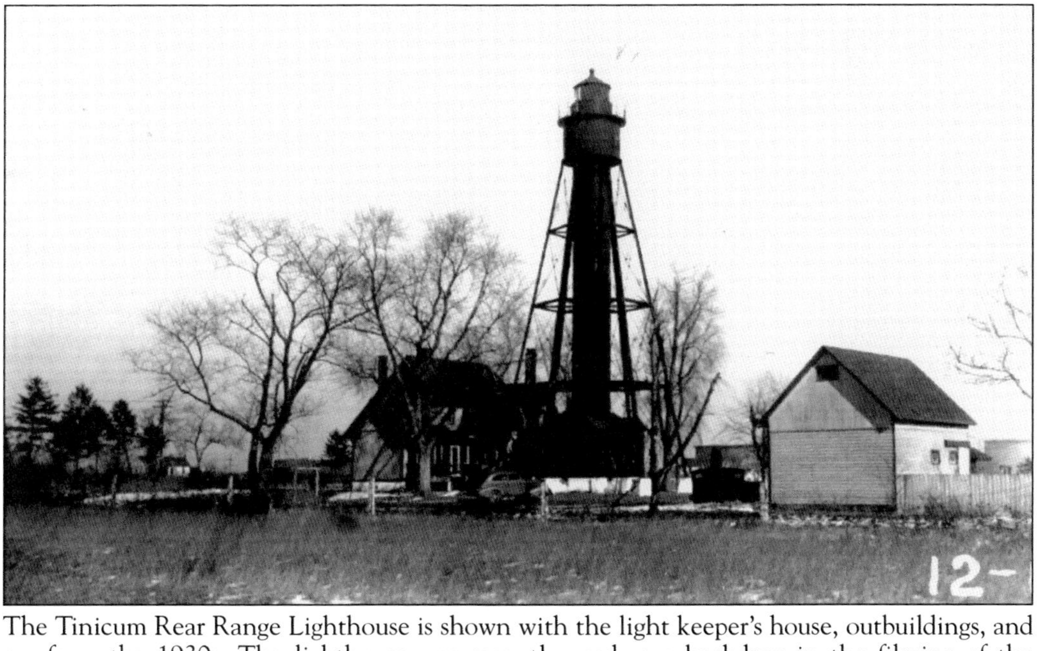

The Tinicum Rear Range Lighthouse is shown with the light keeper's house, outbuildings, and car from the 1930s. The lighthouse was recently used as a backdrop in the filming of the movie *Jersey Girl*.

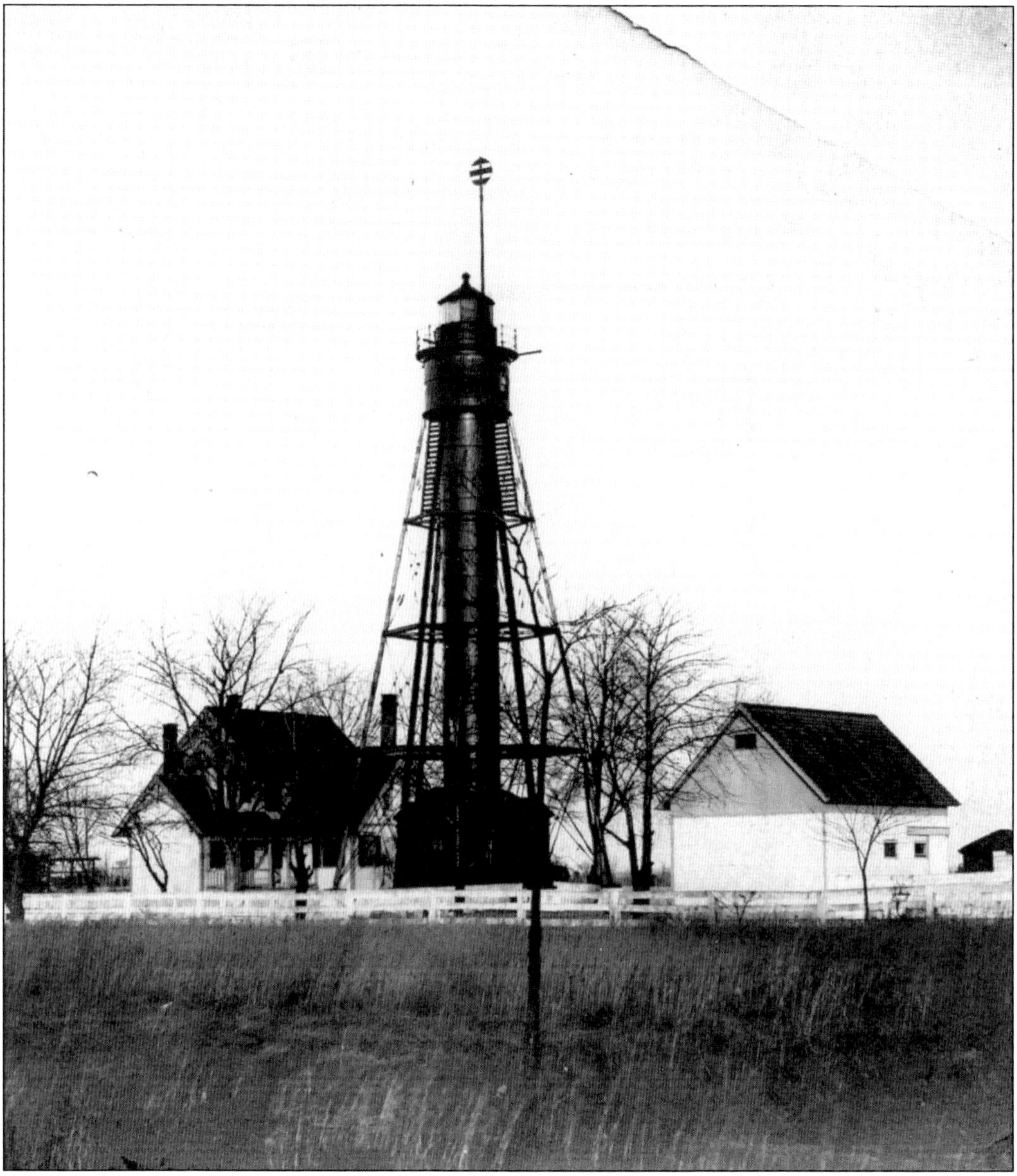

The Tinicum Rear Range Lighthouse is shown with the keeper's house to the left and a barn to the right. The house and barn were torn down in the 1940s or 1950s. All that remains today is the cast-iron lighthouse with a masonry foundation. The lighthouse continues service today as an important navigation aid for the Delaware River shipping traffic.

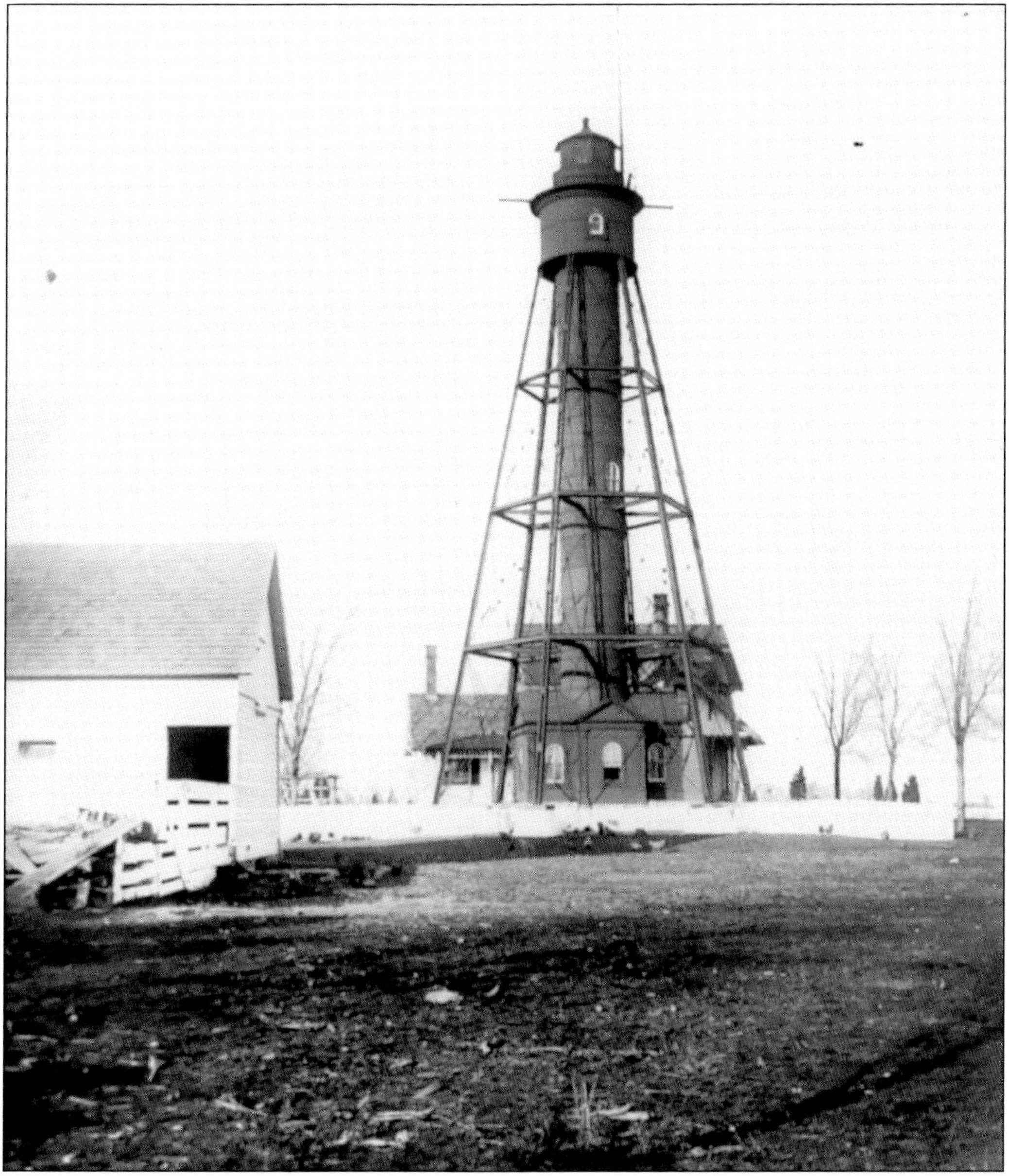

This photograph of the Tinicum Rear Range Lighthouse shows the keeper's house behind the lighthouse with the barn to the left. John Birch was the lighthouse's last keeper, retiring in 1933. Today, the house has an automated fixed red light and is maintained by the U.S. Coast Guard.

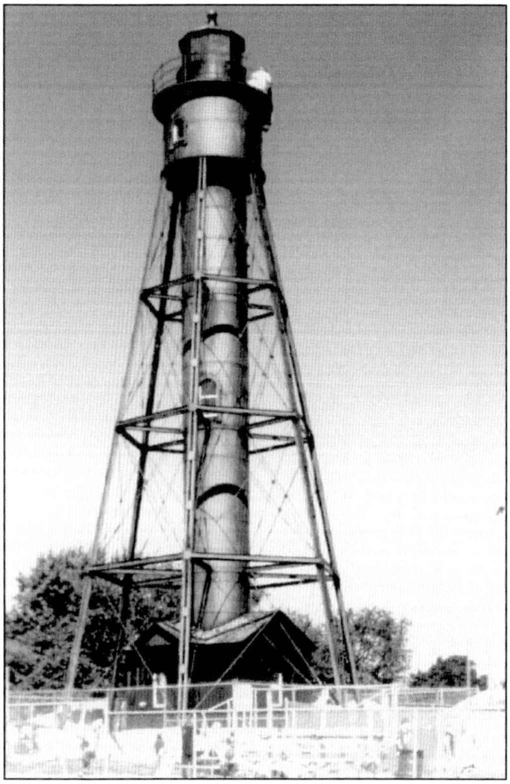

Tinicum Rear Range Lighthouse has scheduled openings from April to October on the third weekend of each month. It also has a special holiday opening in December.

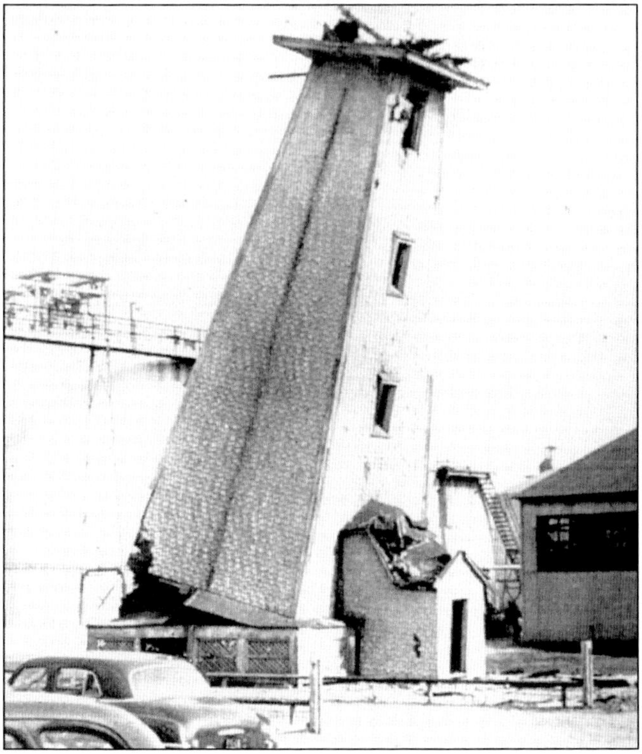

This photograph shows the Fort Mifflin Bar, Rear Lighthouse being torn down in 1953.

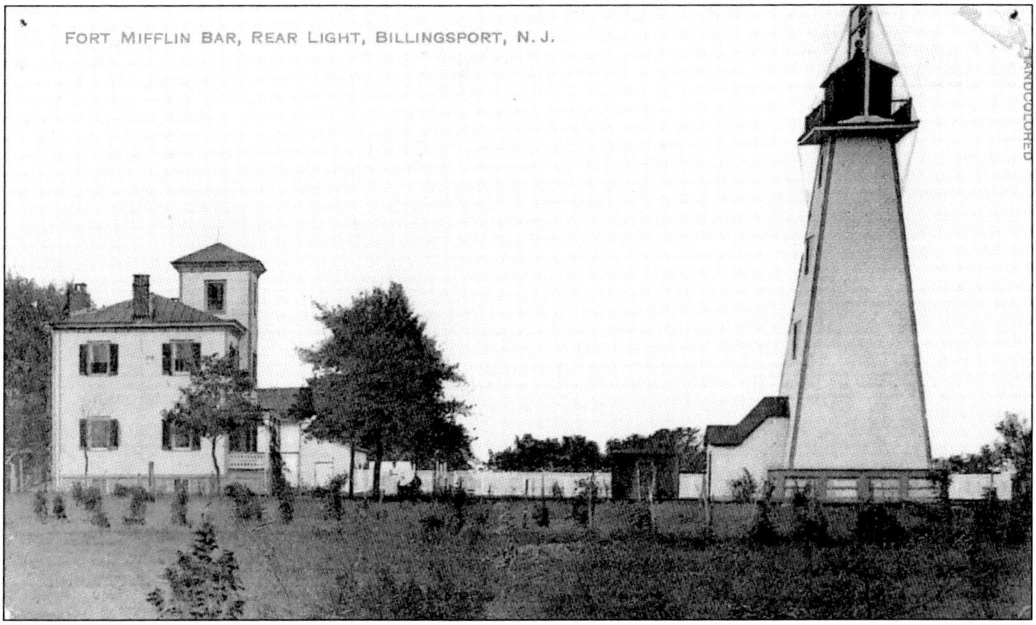

This view of the Fort Mifflin Bar, Rear Lighthouse shows the light keeper's house, located to the left of the lighthouse. (Postcard by W. J. Moore.)

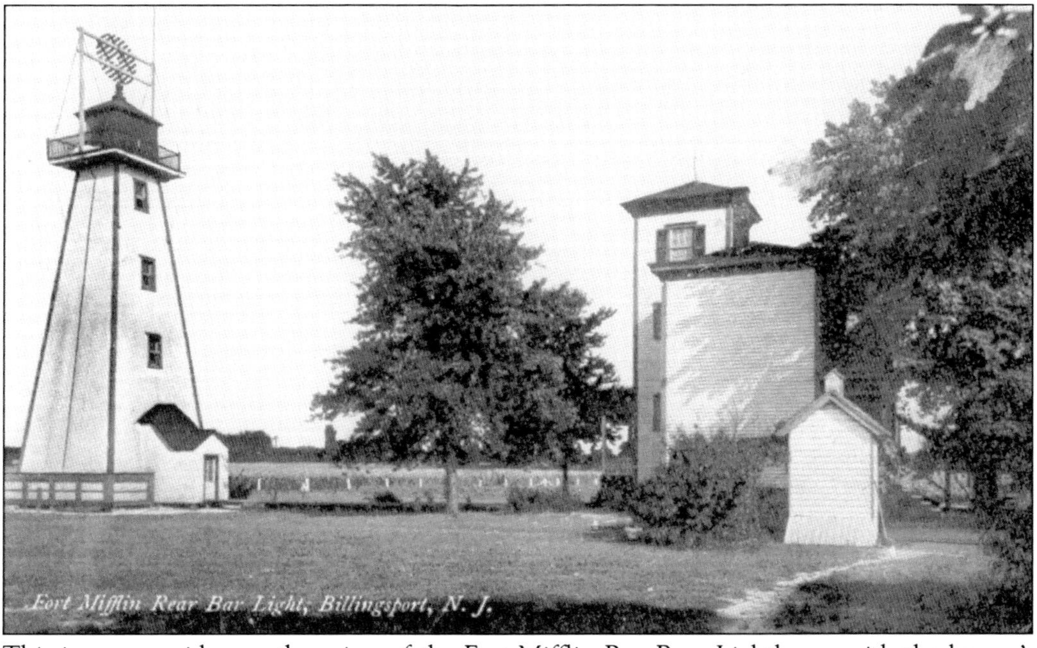

This image provides another view of the Fort Mifflin Bar, Rear Lighthouse with the keeper's house on the right. This lighthouse was torn down in 1953, but the light is still operational today. Mobil owned this land for many years until the company sold the industrial plant to Valero.

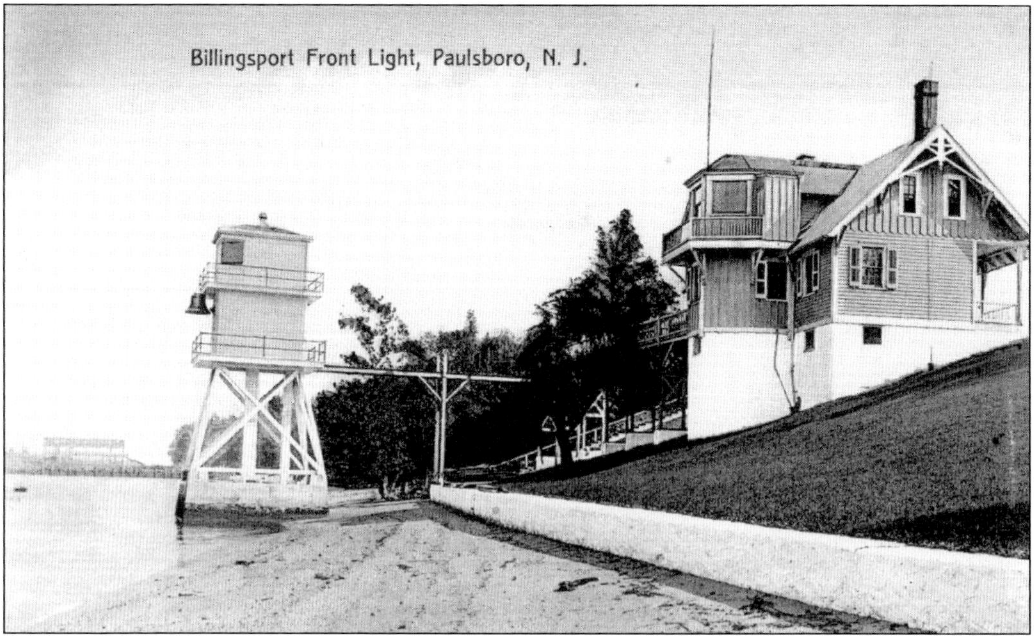

The Billingsport Front Range Lighthouse is shown in this *c.* 1920 photograph with the connecting walkway to the light keeper's house, which was torn down in the early 1950s. The old Billingsport Ferry slip can be seen in the distance at the top left. (Postcard by B. F. Furry.)

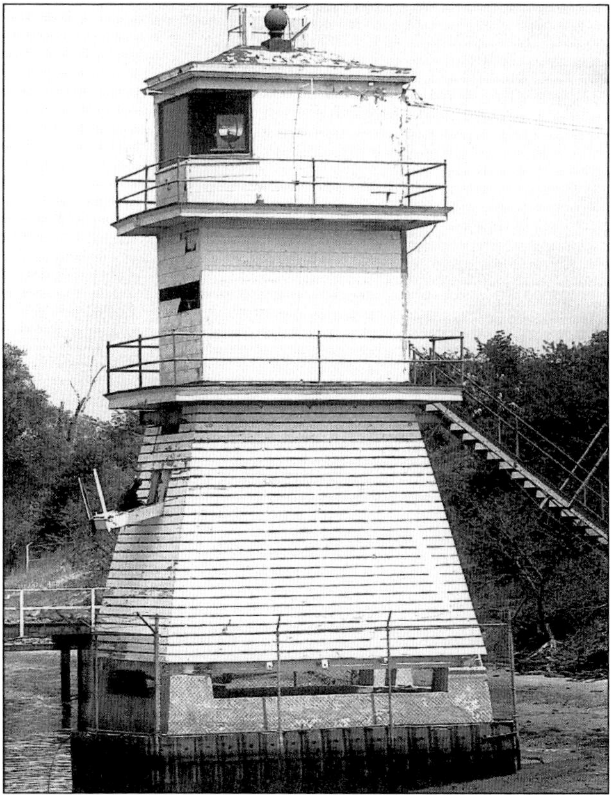

The Billingsport Front Range Lighthouse is shown in this photograph from the early 1970s. All that remains today is the light.

Eight

LINCOLN PARK

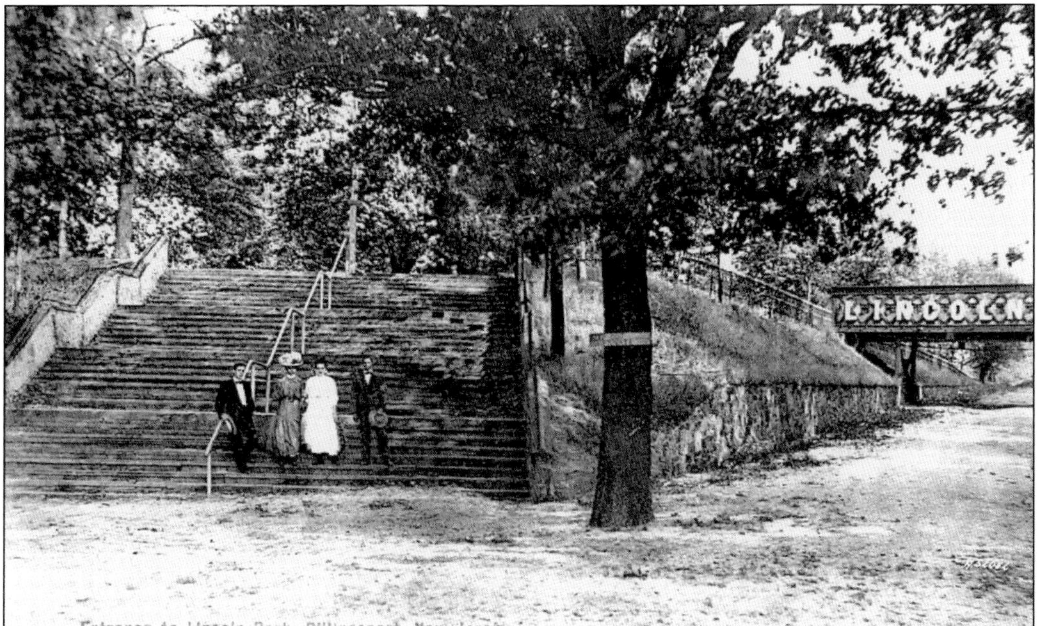

The step entrance to Lincoln Park that went down to the pavilion and Billingsport Ferry slip is shown here *c.* 1900. Shown, from left to right, are Ralph Hammitt, Jennie English, Linda M. Cowgill, and C. Paul Cowgill. (Postcard by E. W. Humphreys.)

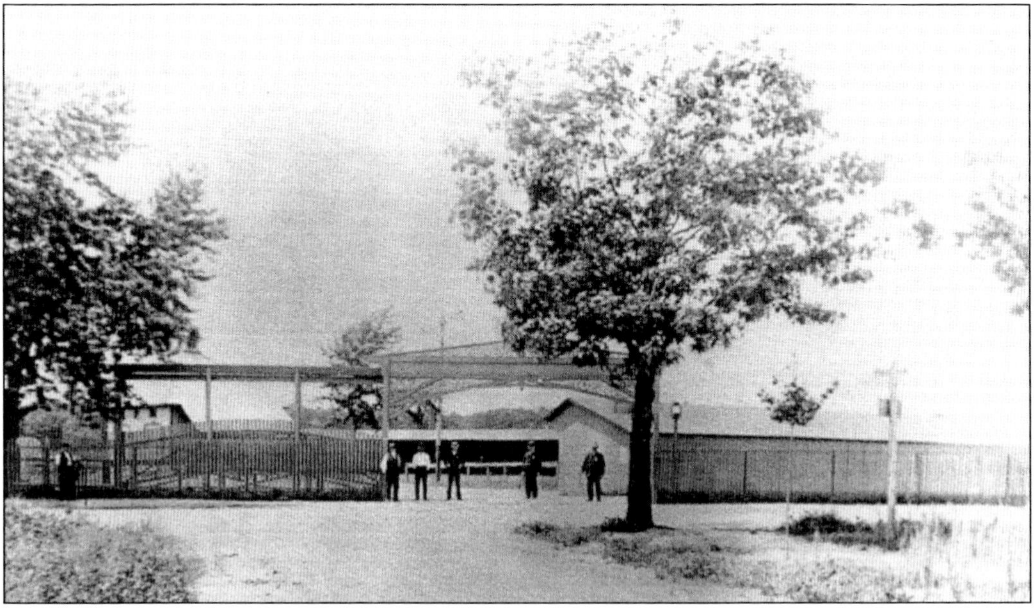

Lincoln Park's stable entrance is featured in this *c.* 1900 photograph. Folks would leave their horses and carriages here and continue on foot into Lincoln Park for a day of fun. Third Street can be seen in the foreground, and Billingsport Road can be seen beyond that running from left to right. The original home of the Billingsport Fire Company was located in the right corner of this picture.

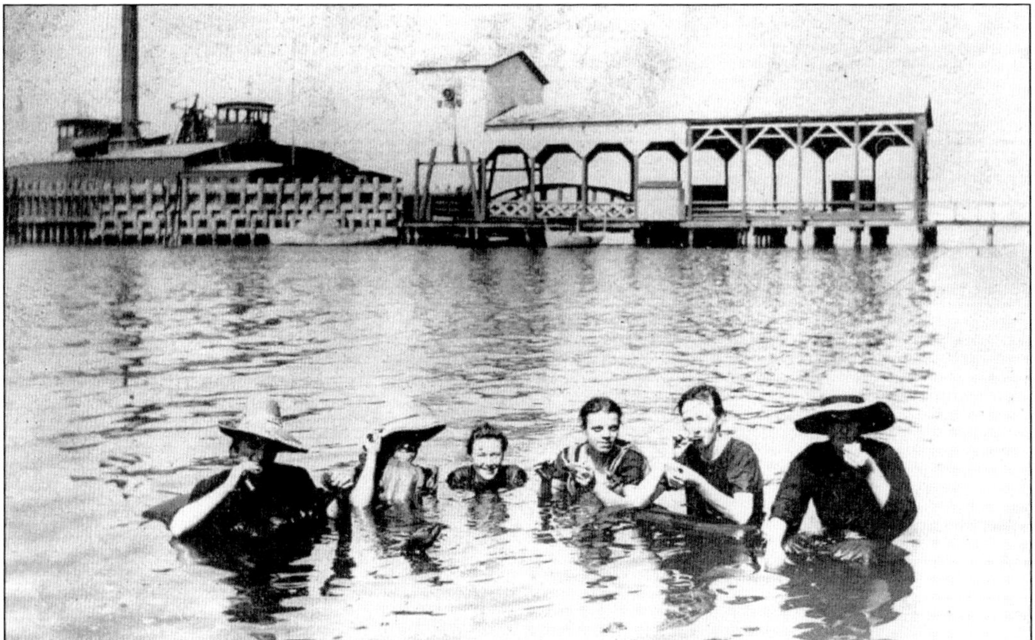

This photograph of the Billingsport Ferry slip at Lincoln Park shows bathing beauties in the foreground. Round trips costing 25¢ were made daily to bring visitors from Philadelphia to Lincoln Park to enjoy a day of fun.

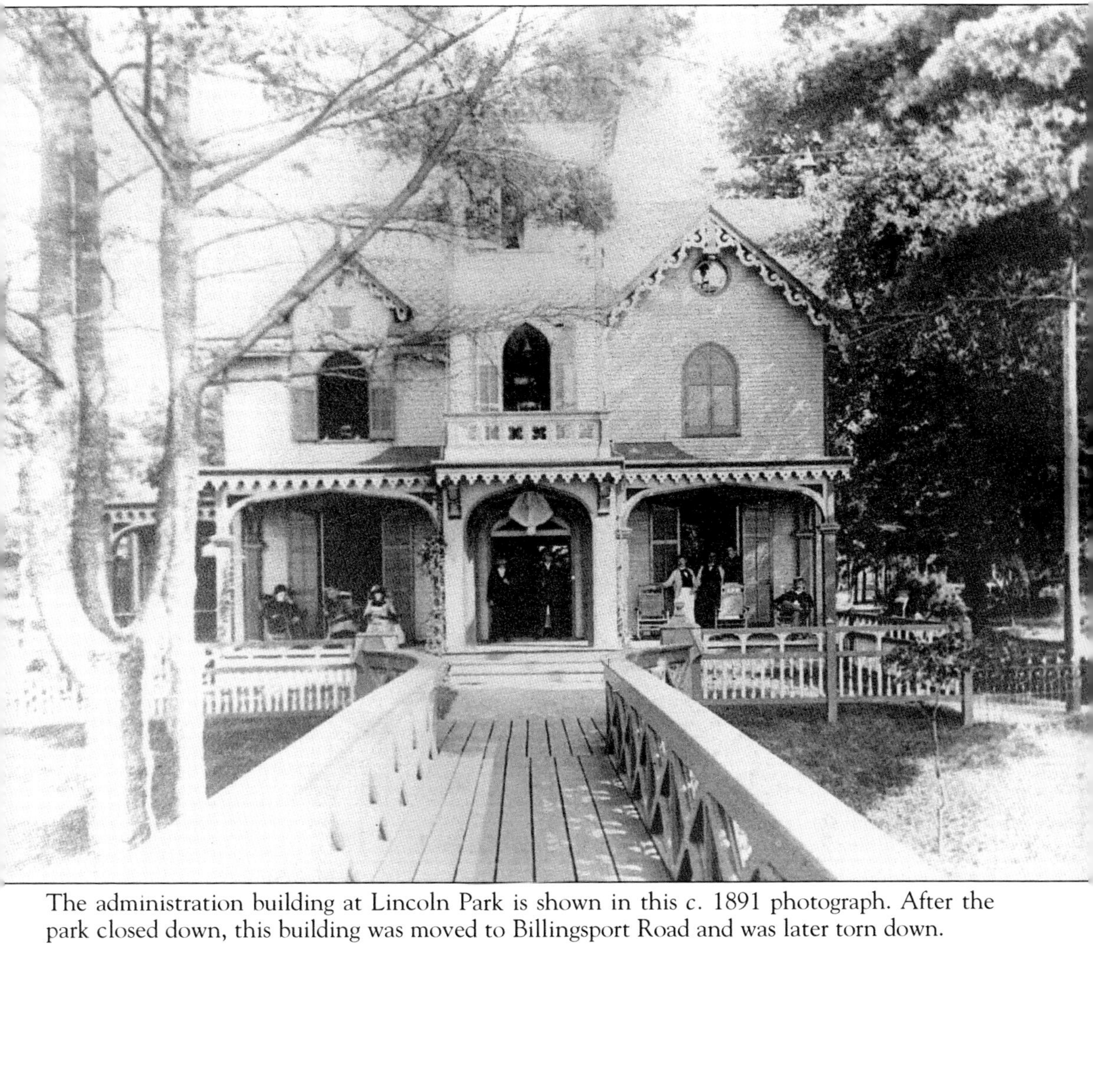

The administration building at Lincoln Park is shown in this *c.* 1891 photograph. After the park closed down, this building was moved to Billingsport Road and was later torn down.

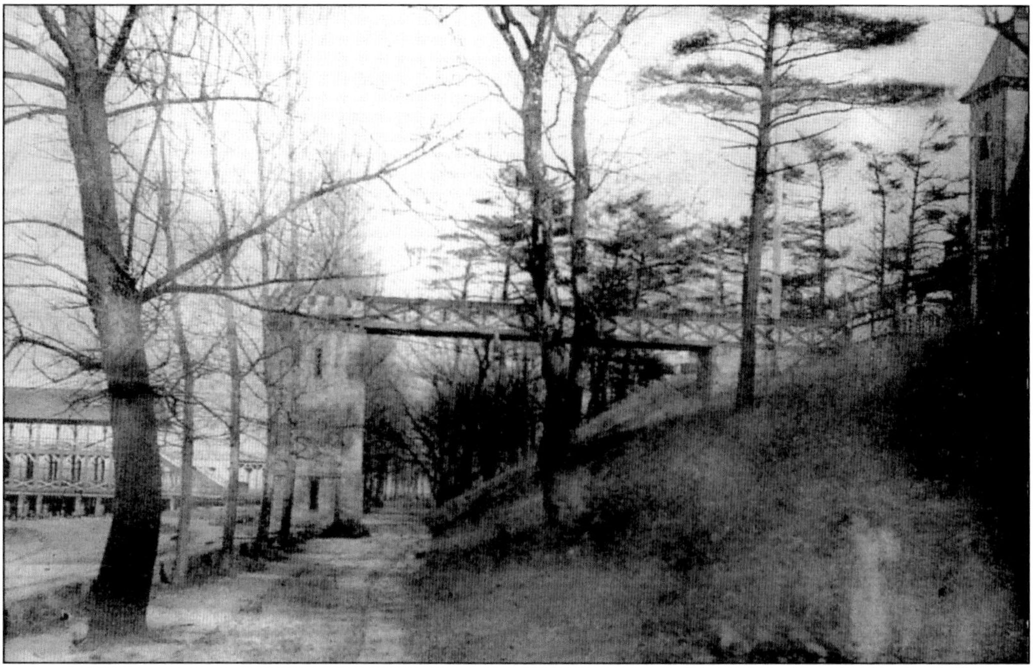

This *c.* 1900 photograph shows the connecting walkway that ran from the administration building to the observation tower. The old Billingsport Ferry slip can be seen to the left.

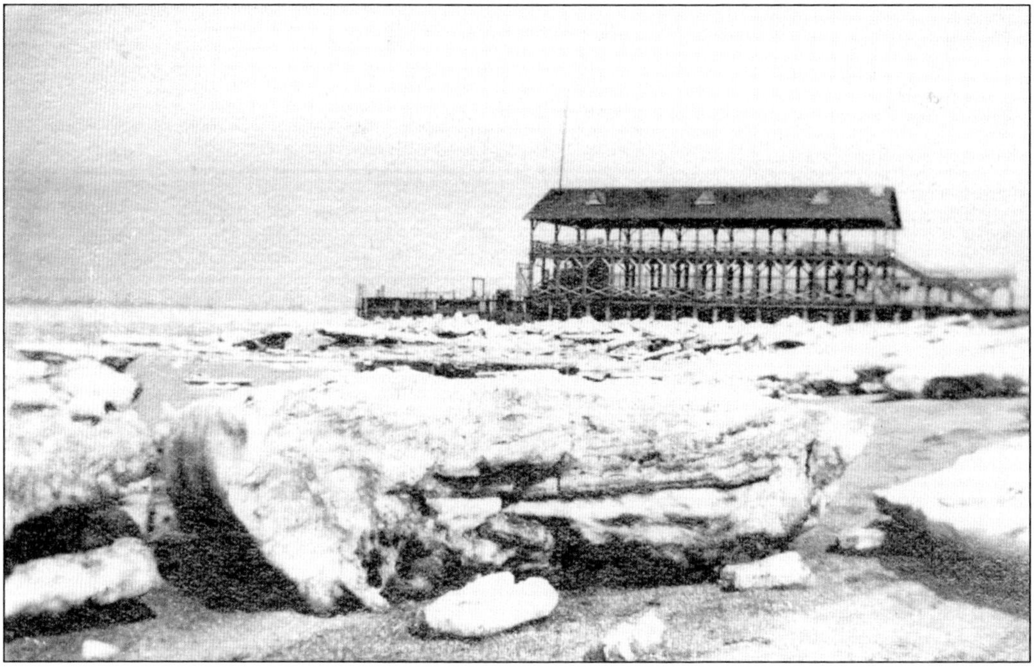

Shown is the Billingsport Ferry slip at Lincoln Park during the big freeze in 1912. In the foreground are the large chunks of ice washed up on the beach from the river freezing. This ferry was the major transportation used by visitors from Philadelphia. It departed from Race Street Wharf in Philadelphia for a round-trip fee of 25¢.

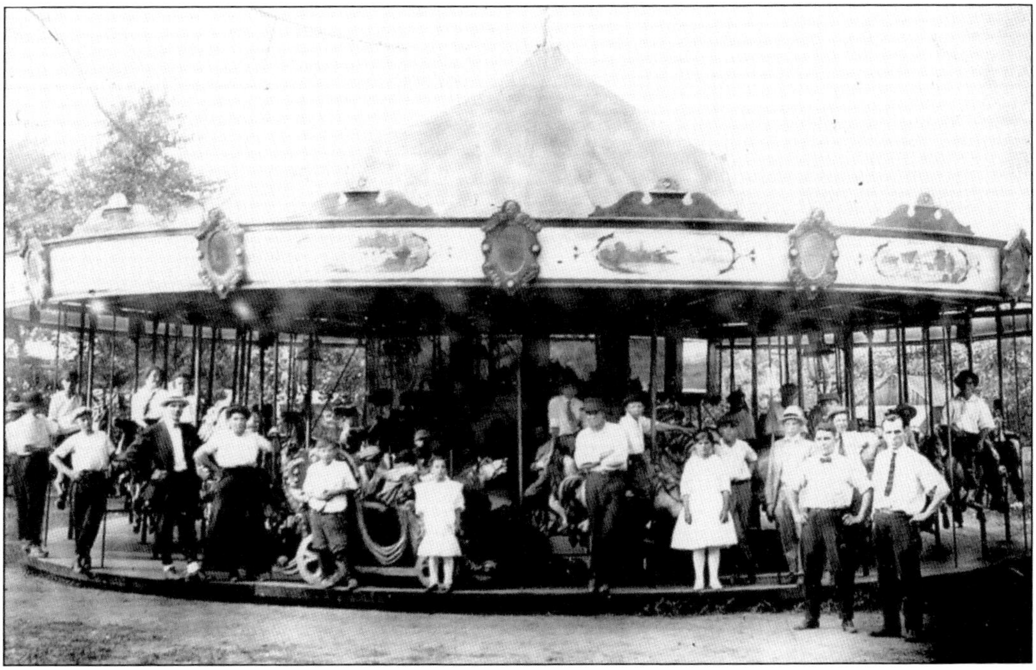

This photograph captures the faces of visitors enjoying the carousel at Lincoln Park.

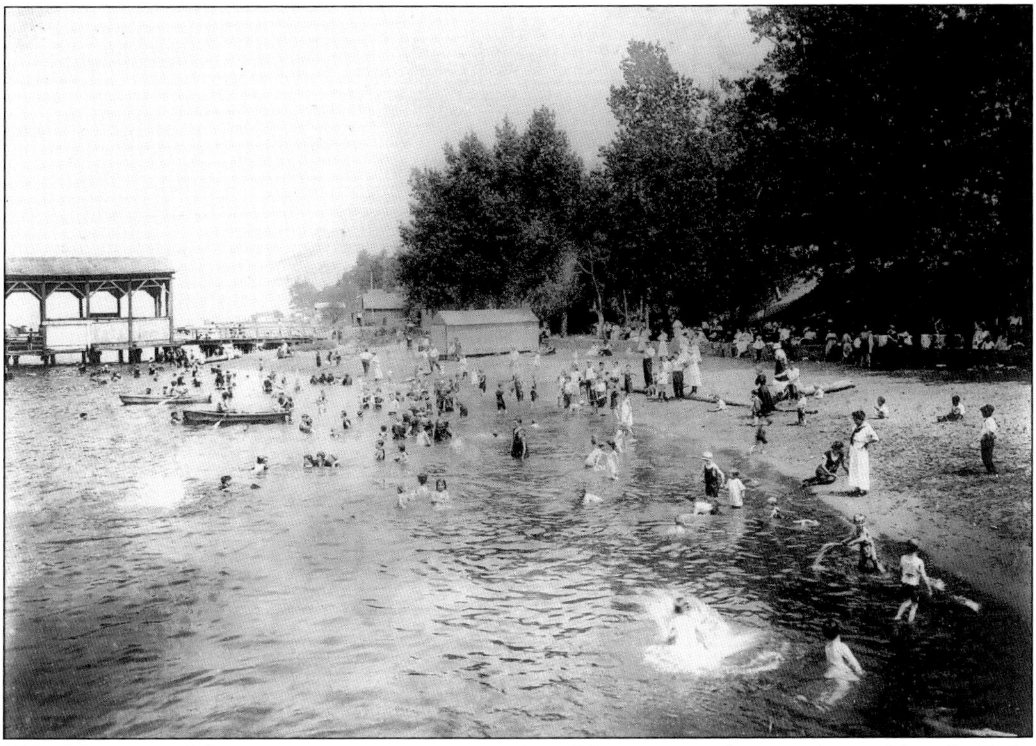

Here are some of the many visitors enjoying a day of fun, sun, and swimming at Lincoln Park. In this photograph you can also see the old Billingsport Ferry slip to the left.

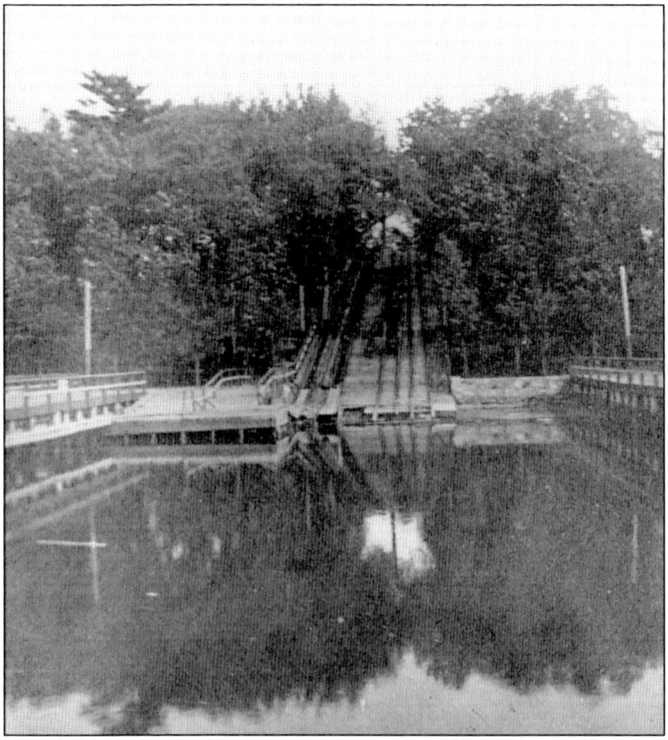

Pictured here is the Shoot-the-Shoot, one of the water amusements that visitors enjoyed at Lincoln Park.

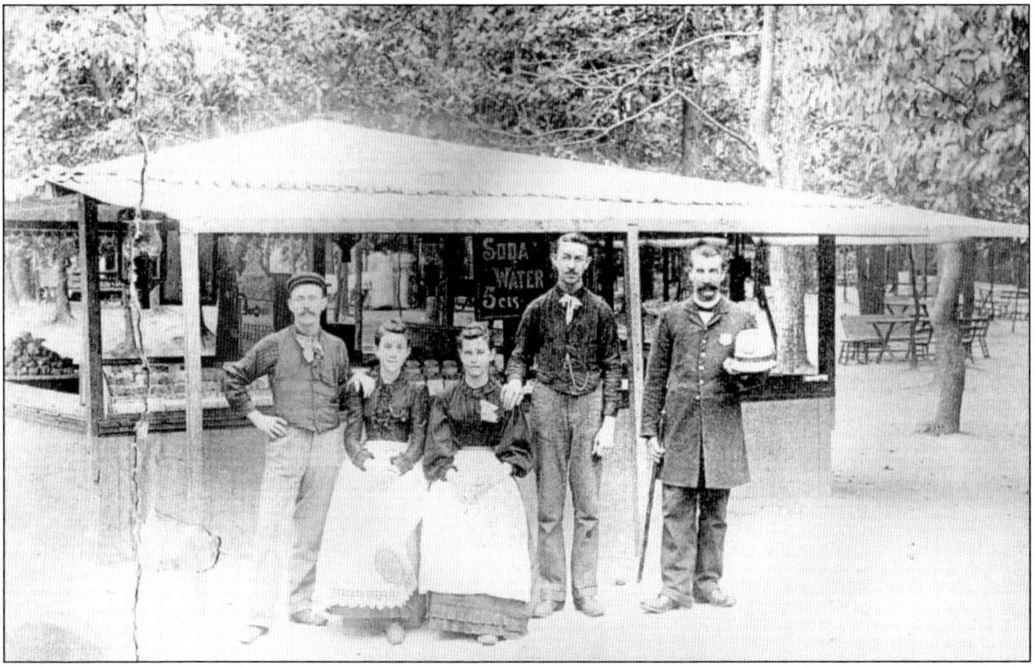

This 1890 photograph was taken the year Lincoln Park opened for business and is one of the oldest photographs of Lincoln Park in the library's collection. Shown, from left to right, are Samuel Locke, Ada (Davis) Gibbs, Mary (Murray) Beckett, George A. Adamson, and George DeVault.

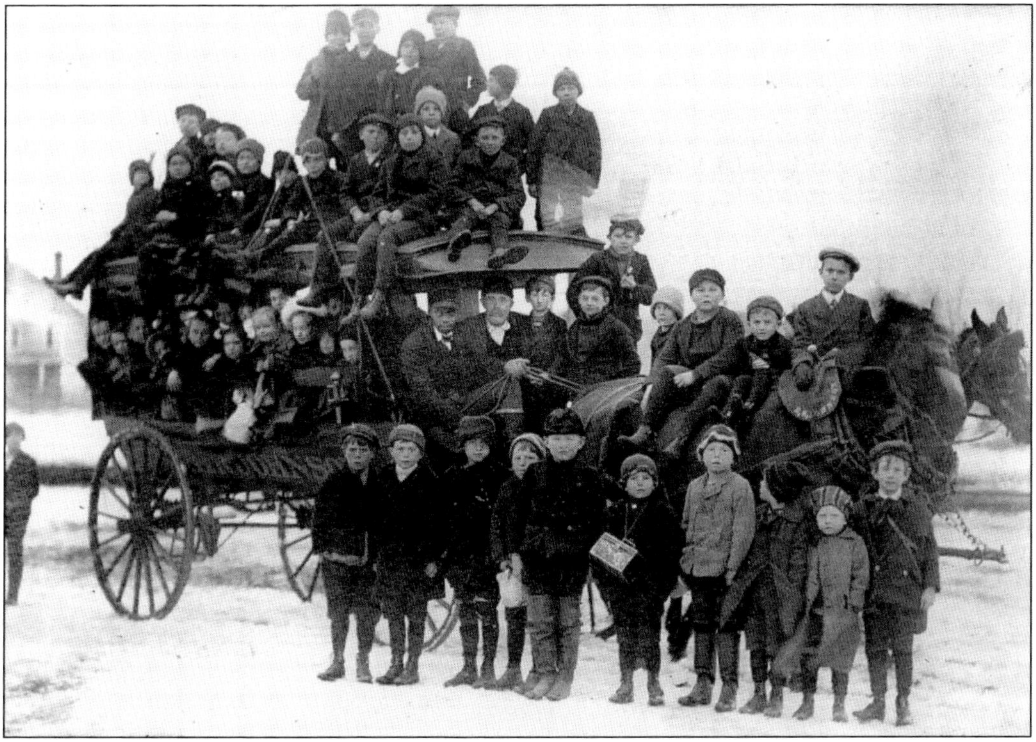

Ben Johnson poses in one of the coaches used to haul folks from the train station to Lincoln Park. The ride from the train to the riverfront cost 10¢.

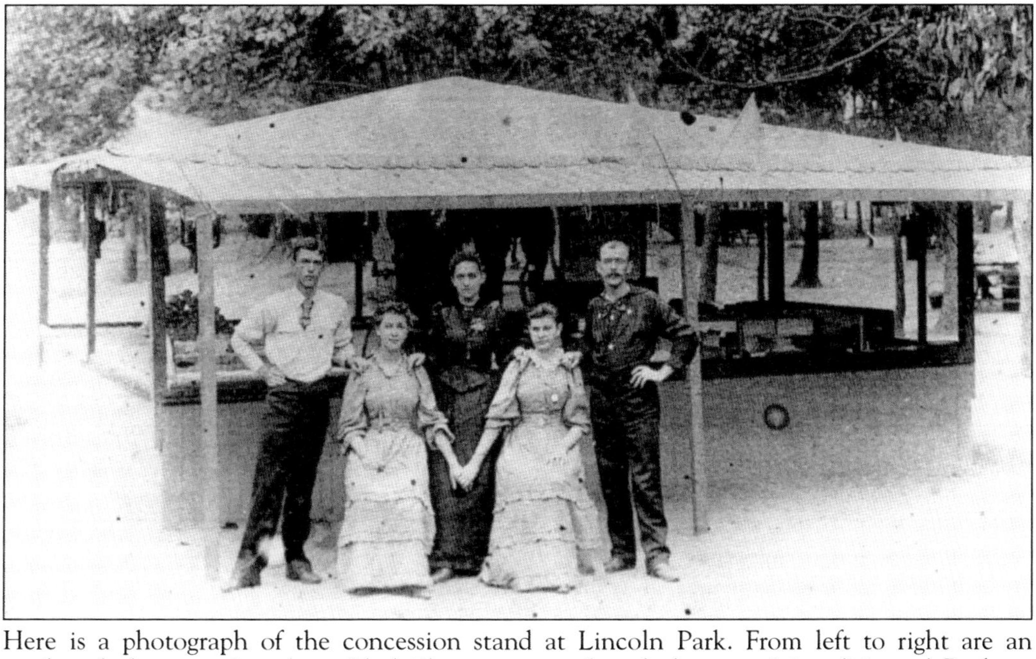

Here is a photograph of the concession stand at Lincoln Park. From left to right are an unidentified person, Josephine Clark Flowers, an unidentified person, Mary (Murray) Beckett, and Samuel Locke.

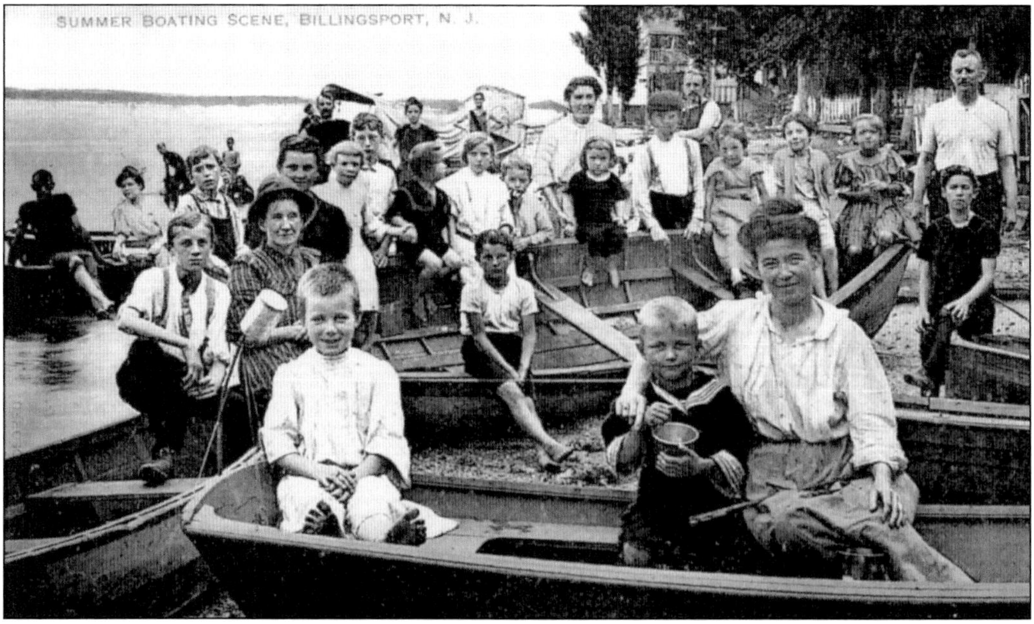

This photograph of a summer boating scene along the Delaware River in Billingsport shows summer cottages at the top right. (Postcard by W. J. Moore.)

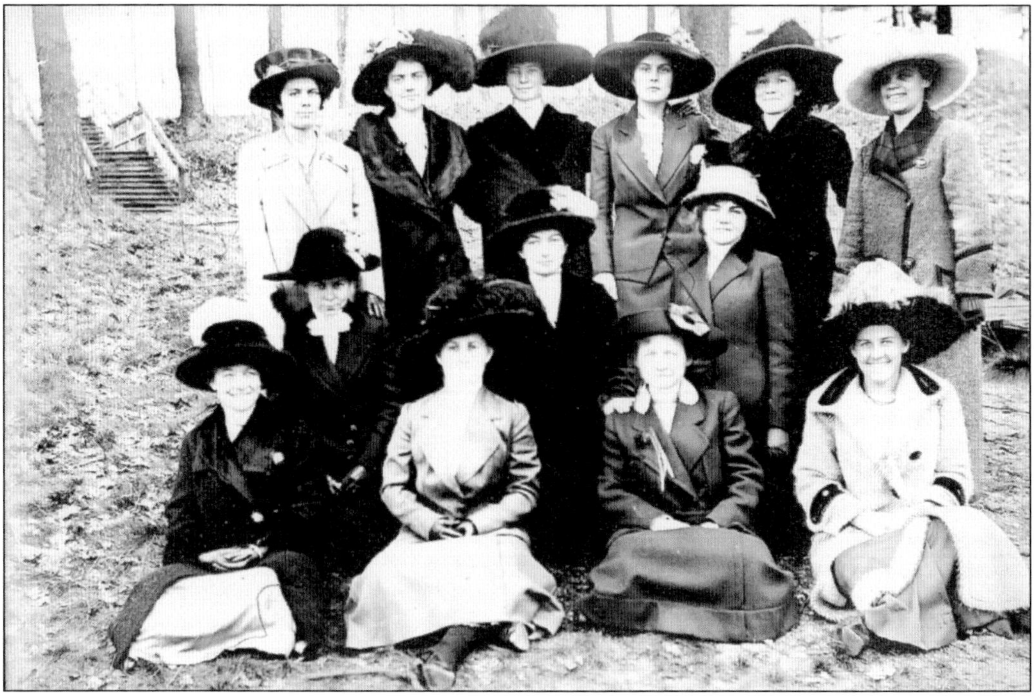

The Ladies B.T.S. Club poses on the Lincoln Park steps *c.* 1910. Members, from left to right, are as follows: (first row) Violet (Bonsack) Thompson, Myrtle (DeVault) Gill, Julie Rowe, and Claire (Chesney) Murray; (second row) Bertha Stetser, Edna (Beebe) Thompson, and Ester Stetser; (third row) Emma Adamson, Linda Cowgill, Annie Chesney, May (Titus) Dubrink, Margaret Chesney, and Bessie Murray.

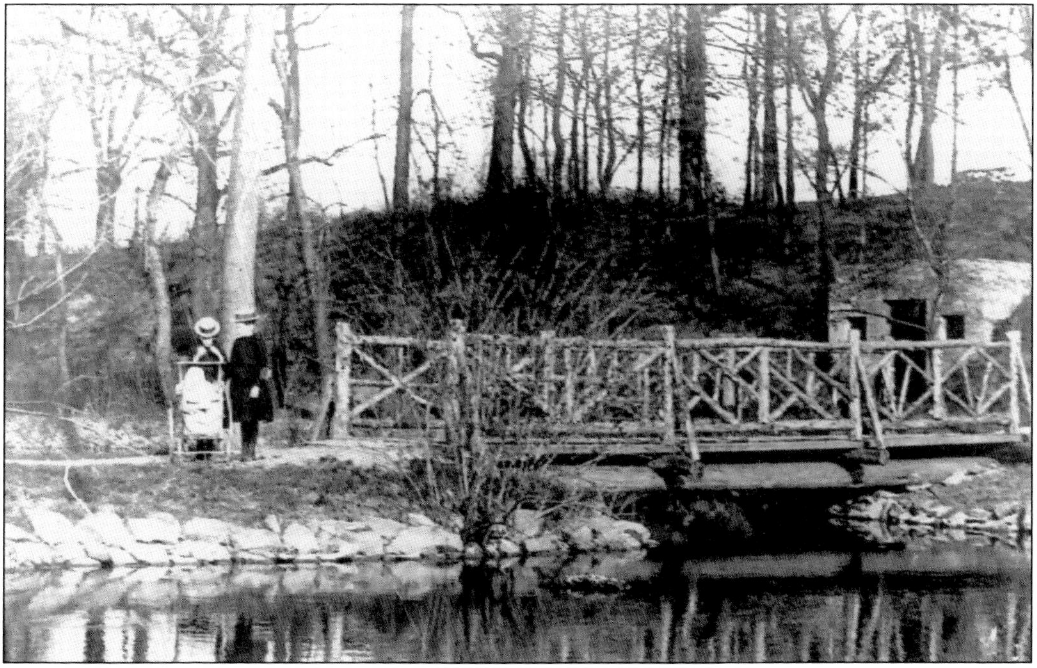

Two young ladies take a stroll around Moores Pond, located near Lincoln Park. They are Mary Bramell McCorkell (left) and Gertrude Bramell. Helen Bramell is in the carriage. The icehouse can be seen in the background.

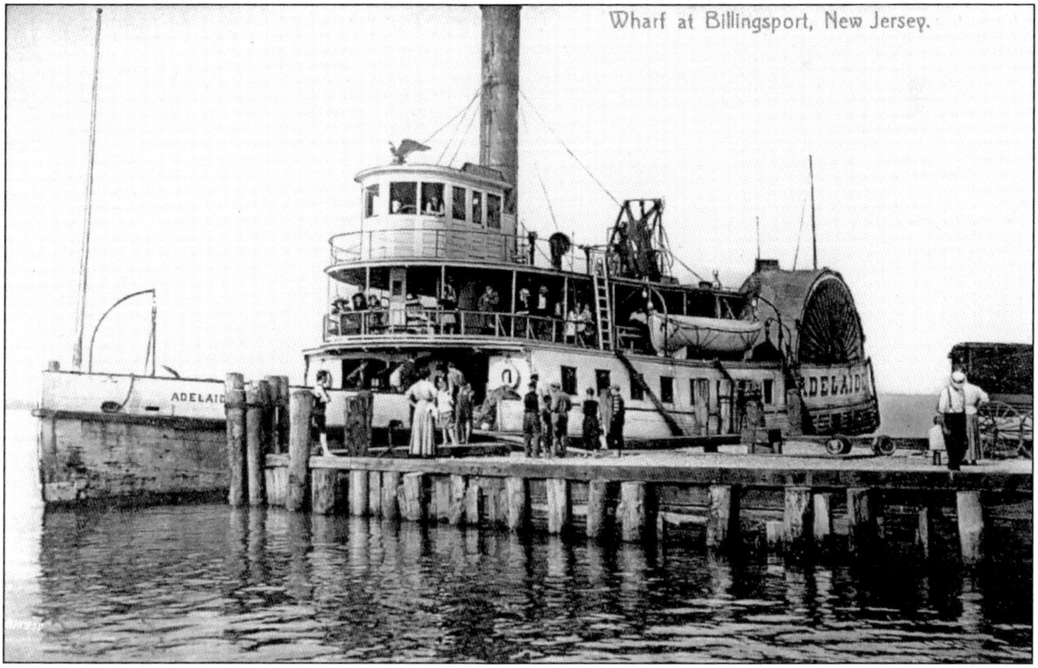

This view shows the *Adelaida* docking to drop off visitors to enjoy a day at Lincoln Park. During the park's heyday (between 1890 and 1900), thousands of visitors arrived by way of Billingsport Ferry and excursion boats daily through the summer months (Postcard by E. W. Humphreys.)

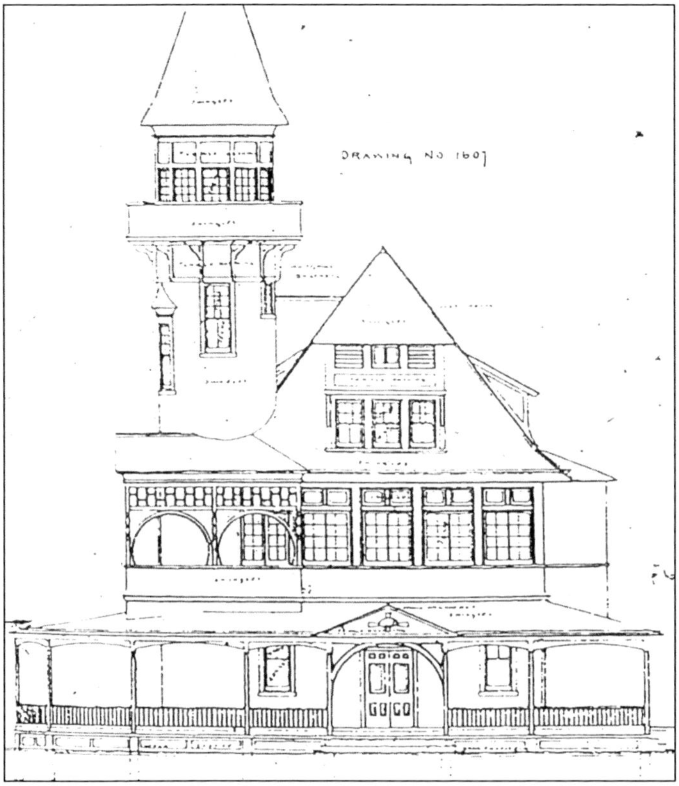

This is an architect drawing, No. 1607, of the exterior details of the main building in Lincoln Park. The drawing was created by architect and engineers Rowe and Dagit.

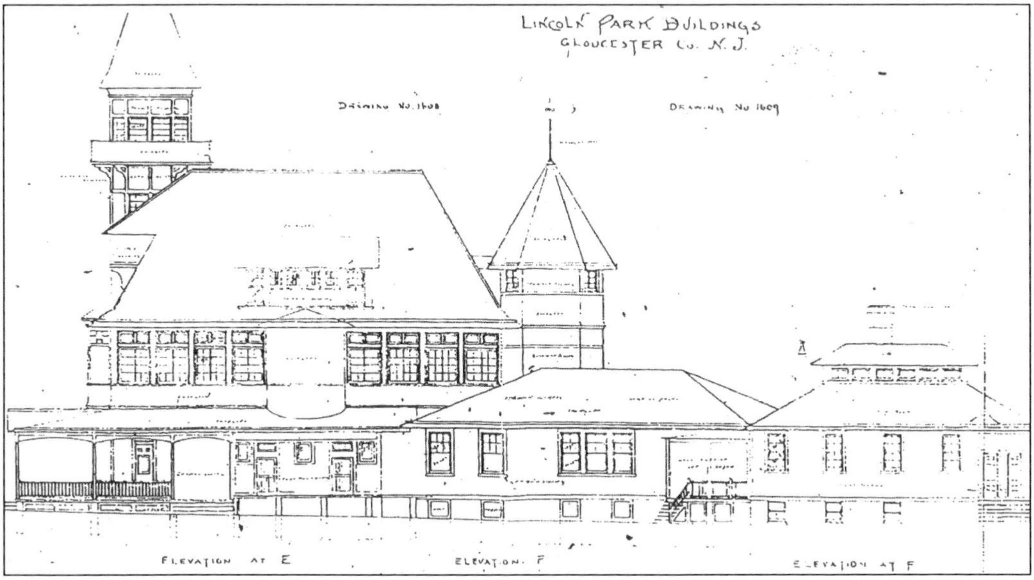

These 1880 architect drawings, Nos. 1608 and 1609, are side views of the main building at Lincoln Park.

Nine

People, Places, and Memorabilia

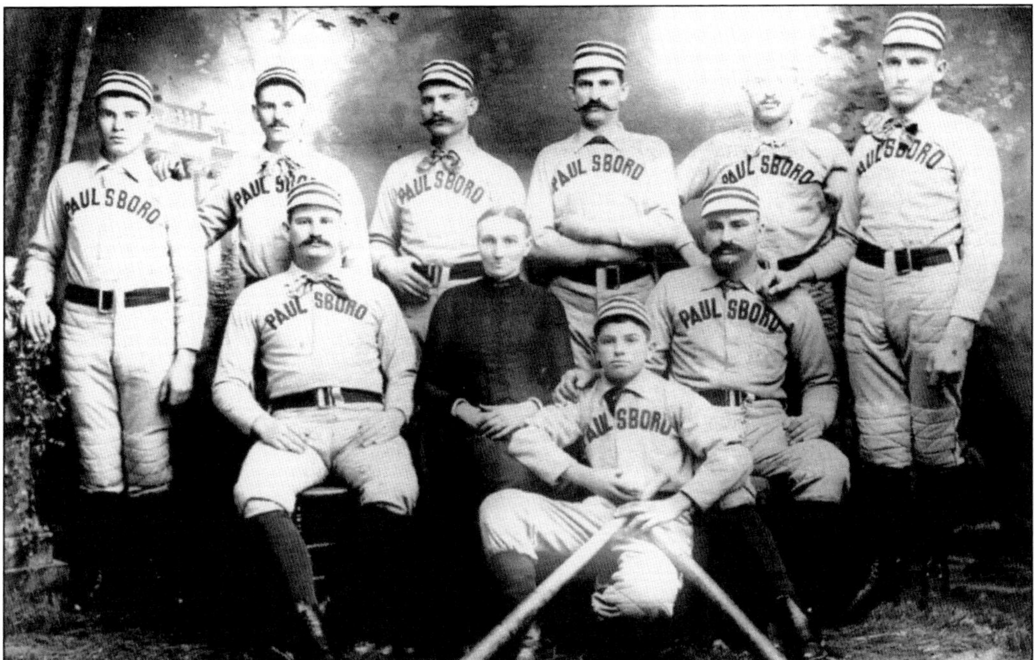

The first All-Thompson Brothers baseball team was composed of nine Thompson brothers in the 1890s. They were considered champions in their day, though they never made more than \$3 or \$4 a day. They even played exhibition games at the Chicago World's Fair in 1933. Members are, from left to right, as follows: (first row) Jesse M., Anna M. (mother), George A., and Joseph G; (second row) William G., Frank M., James T., Harry S., Cooper C., and Elwood R. Thompson.

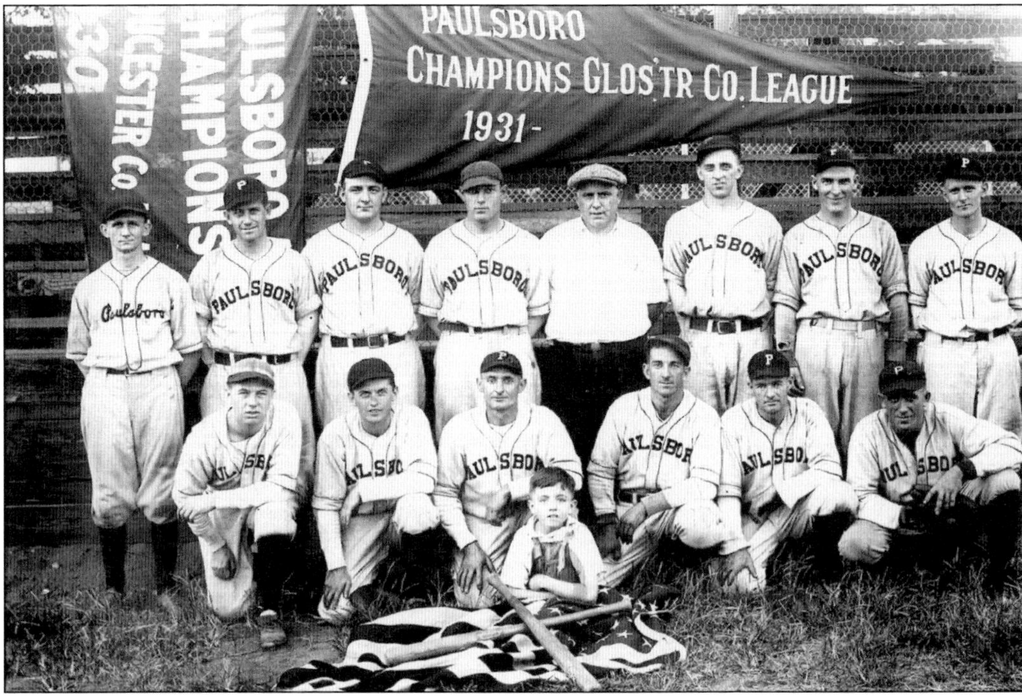

The Paulsboro champions of the Gloucester County league for the second year are shown here in 1931. The only two people identified in the photograph are Joseph Kazer (the third person in the first row) and Doc Meyers (the fourth person in the first row).

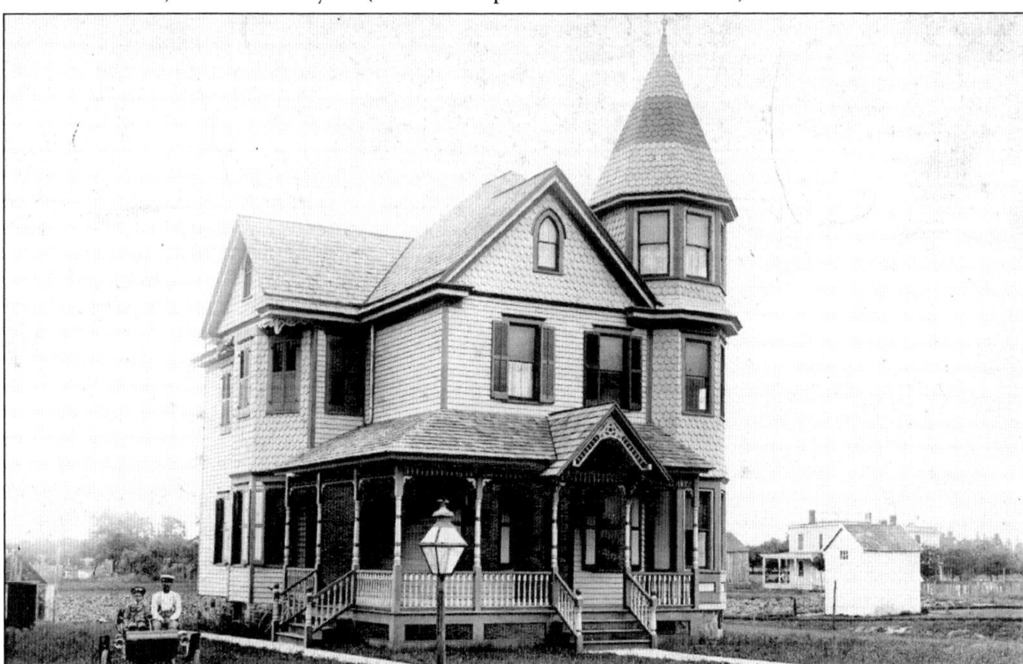

This *c.* 1909 photograph features a house on West Broad Street. In the bottom left of the photograph is one of the first automobiles in Paulsboro.

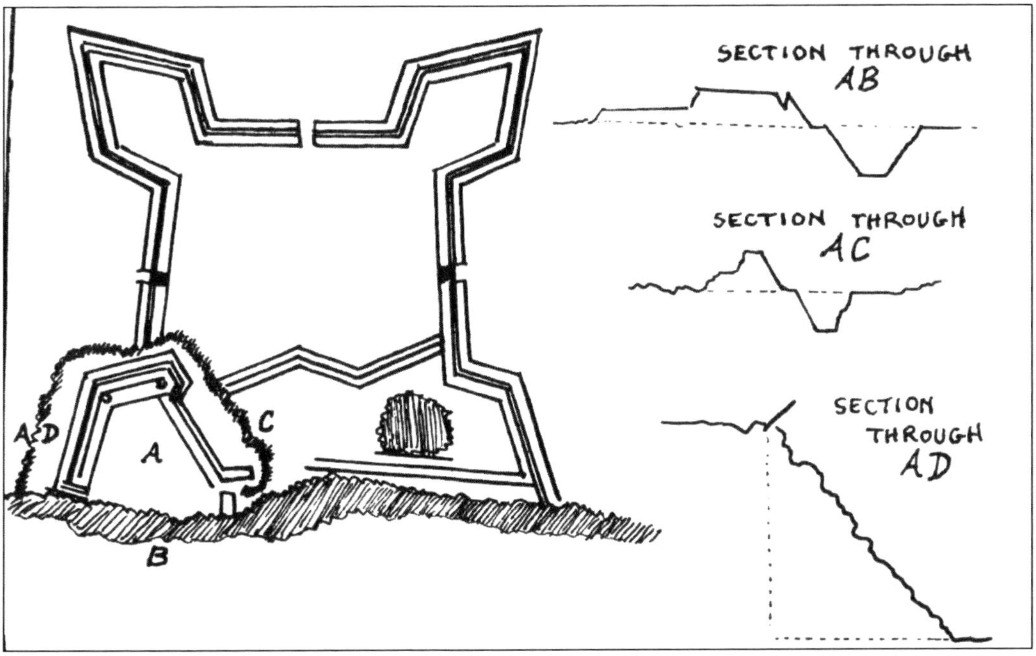

This drawing depicts the layout and elevations of Fort Billings.

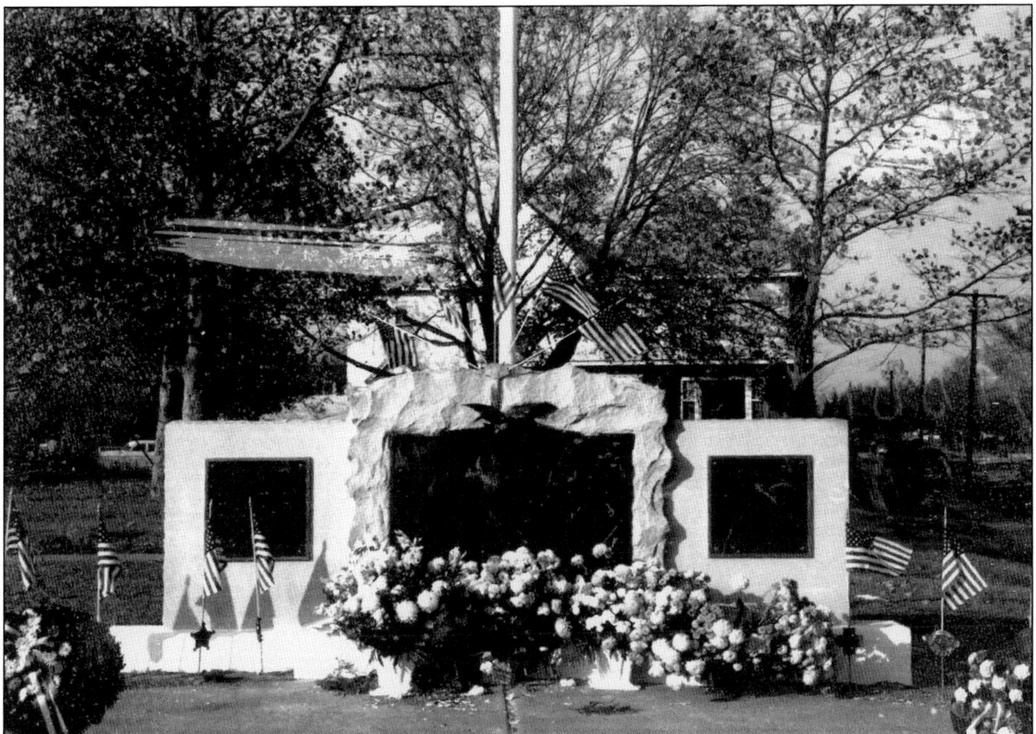
This photograph shows the dedication of the additions of the Paulsboro War Memorial, which commemorates those soldiers who lost their lives in Korean War and World War II.

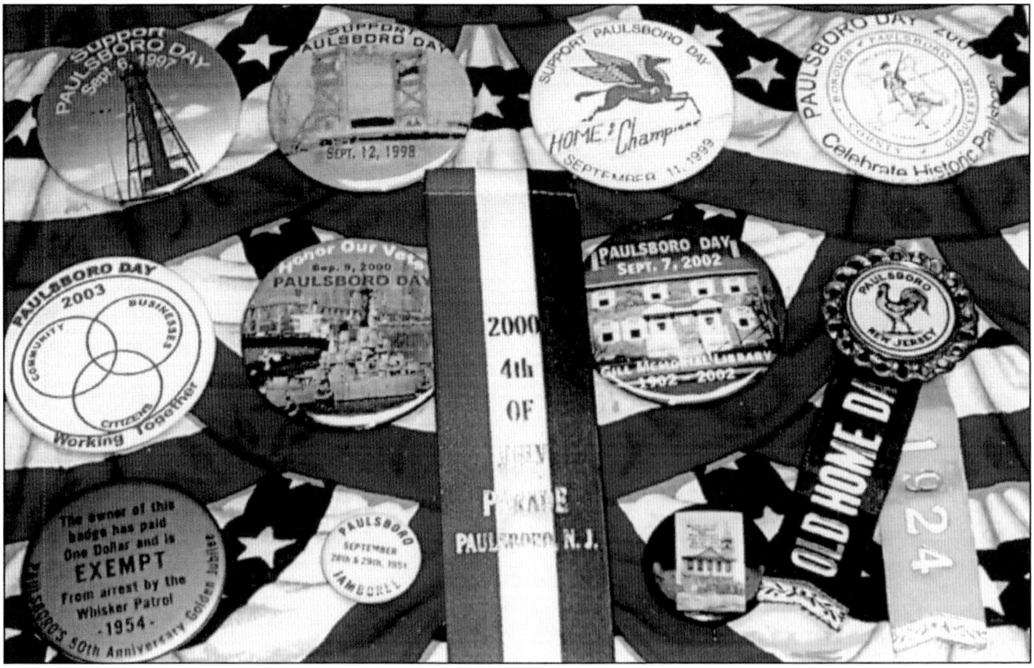

Here is a collection of buttons from the Paulsboro Day celebrations, Paulsboro's 50th anniversary, parades, and the firehouse dedication.

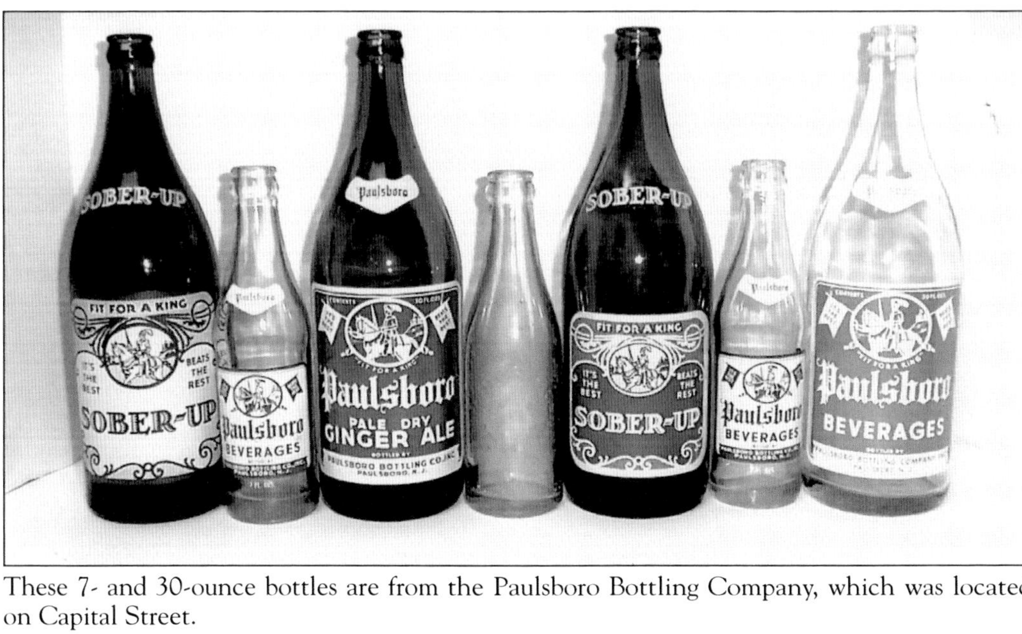

These 7- and 30-ounce bottles are from the Paulsboro Bottling Company, which was located on Capital Street.

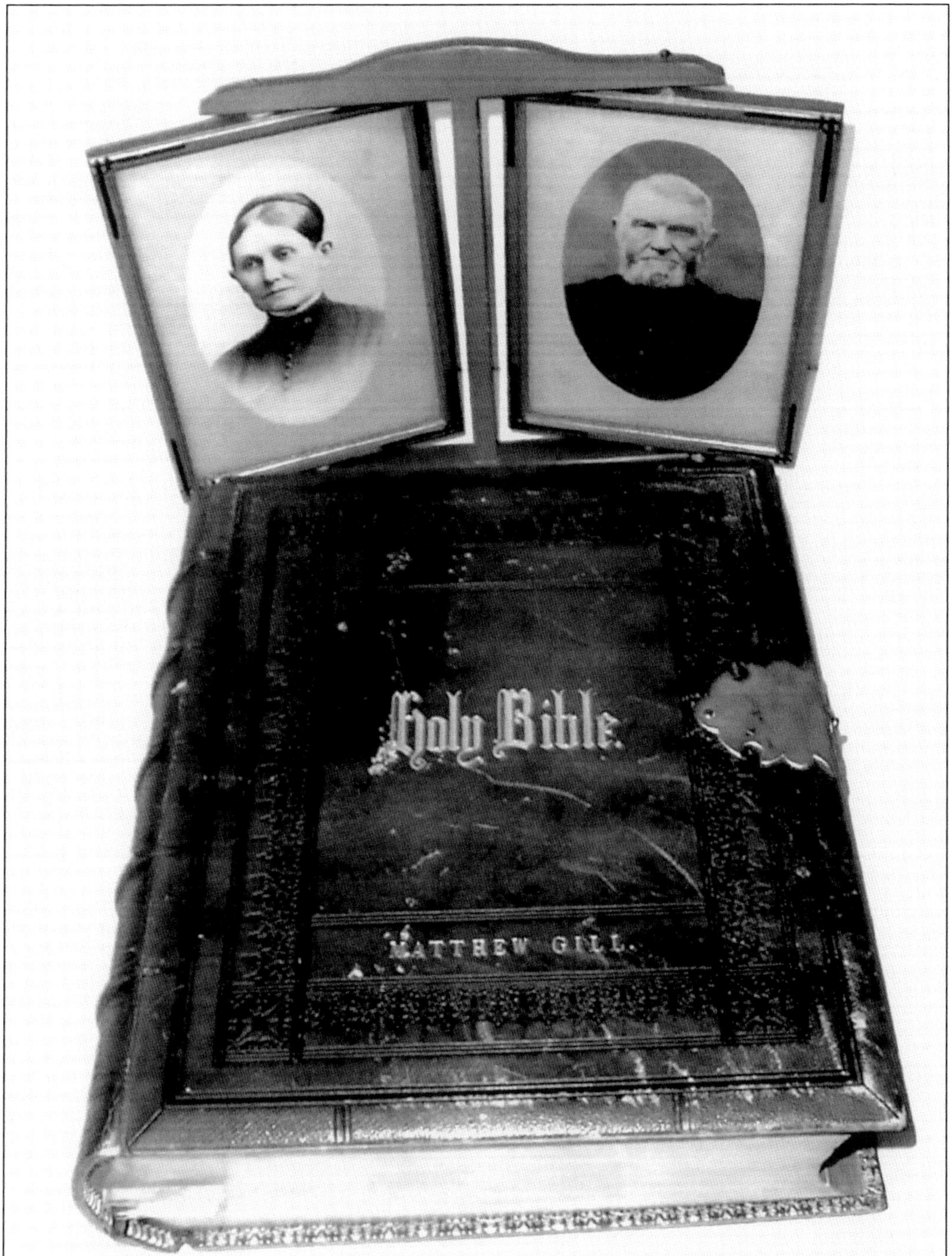

This photograph shows Mary Jessup Gill, Matthew Gill, and their family Bible, which recorded all births and marriages in the family. Some of the records found in this Bible include the birth of Matthew, son of Joseph and Dessia Gill, on October 22, 1822; the birth of Mary, daughter of James and Abigail Jessup, on April 18, 1827; and the marriage of Mary and Matthew, on December 24, 1846.

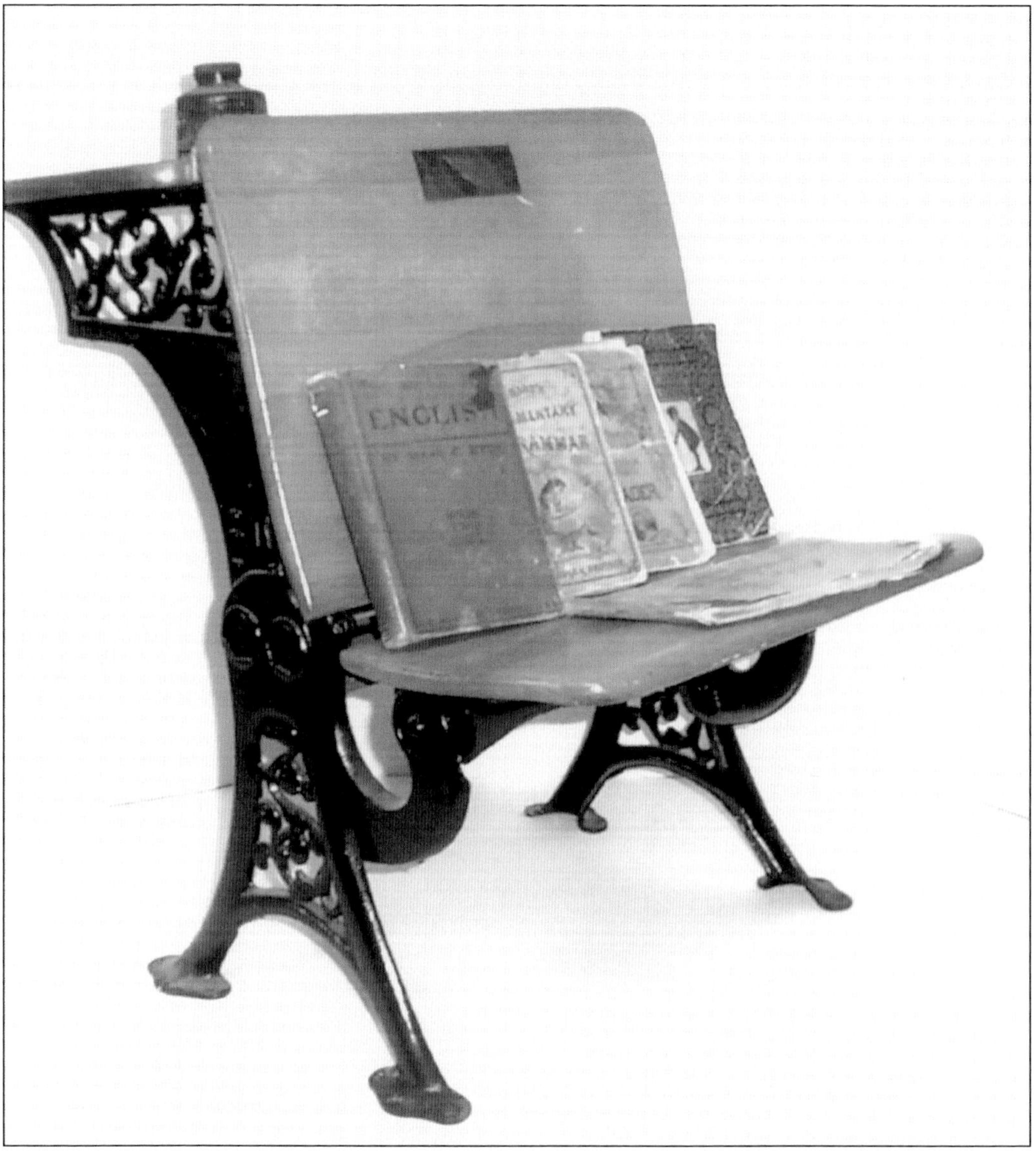

This desk, donated by Clara Wilkerson Jones, was one of the original student desks from Buck Street School. Also shown are an inkwell and old primers.

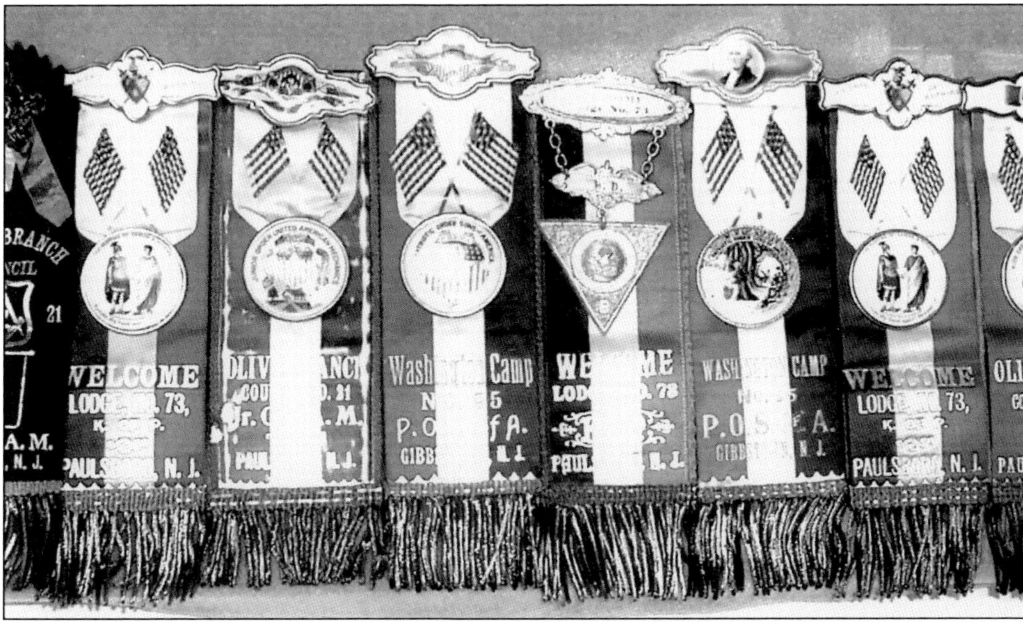

This collection of ribbons from the Olive Branch Council No. 21, the Welcome Lodge Local No. 73, and the Washington Camp No. 95 were used in ceremonies, while the reversed black side was used for funerals.

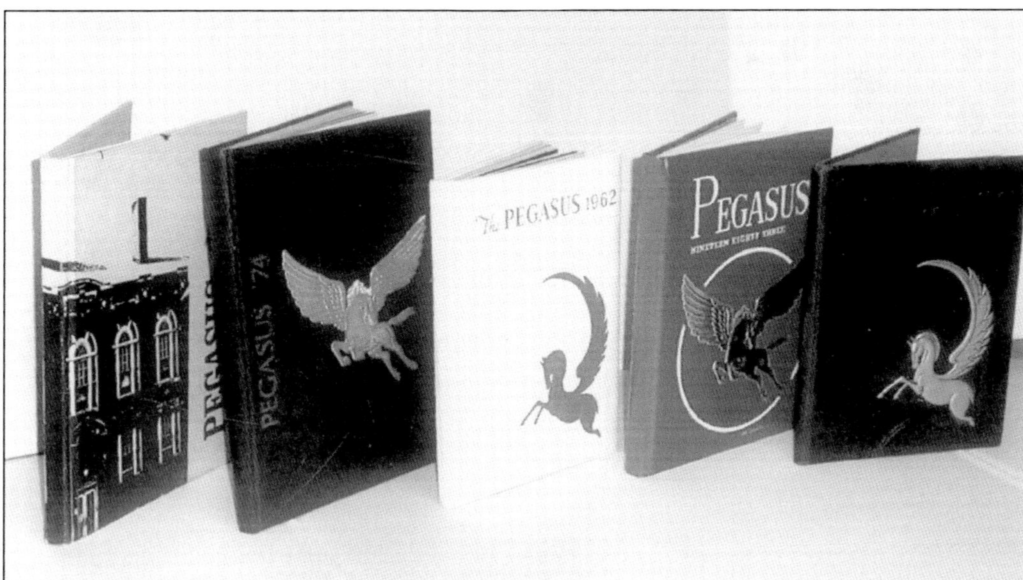

Here are just a few of the Paulsboro High School yearbooks in the Gill Memorial Library collection. The bound yearbooks date back as far as 1938. The collection also includes the 1936 and 1937 yearbooks, which were paper and were made at the school. The library is always looking for new items—such as class pictures, yearbooks, and Paulsboro memorabilia—to add to the extensive collection.

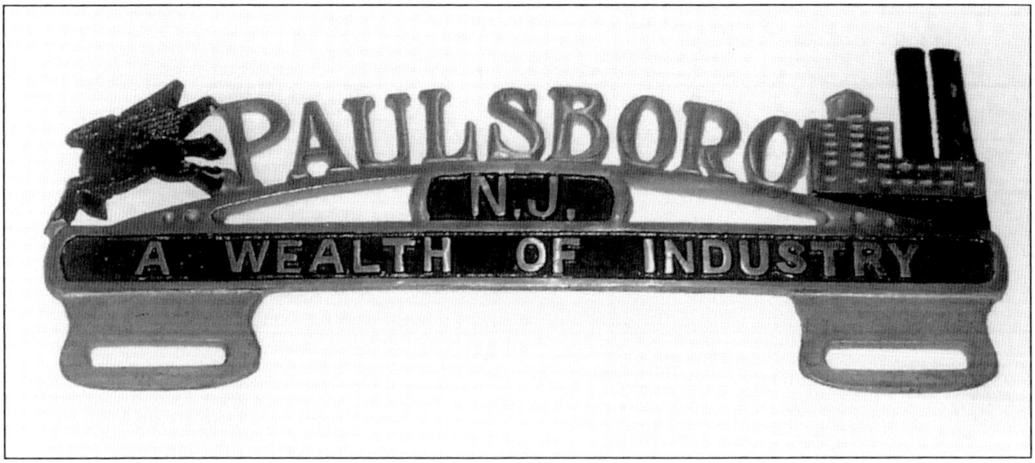

This license plate holder reads, "Paulsboro, N.J. A Wealth of Industry." It also features the symbols of Pegasus and a refinery with stacks. (Photograph courtesy of Mike Valentin.)

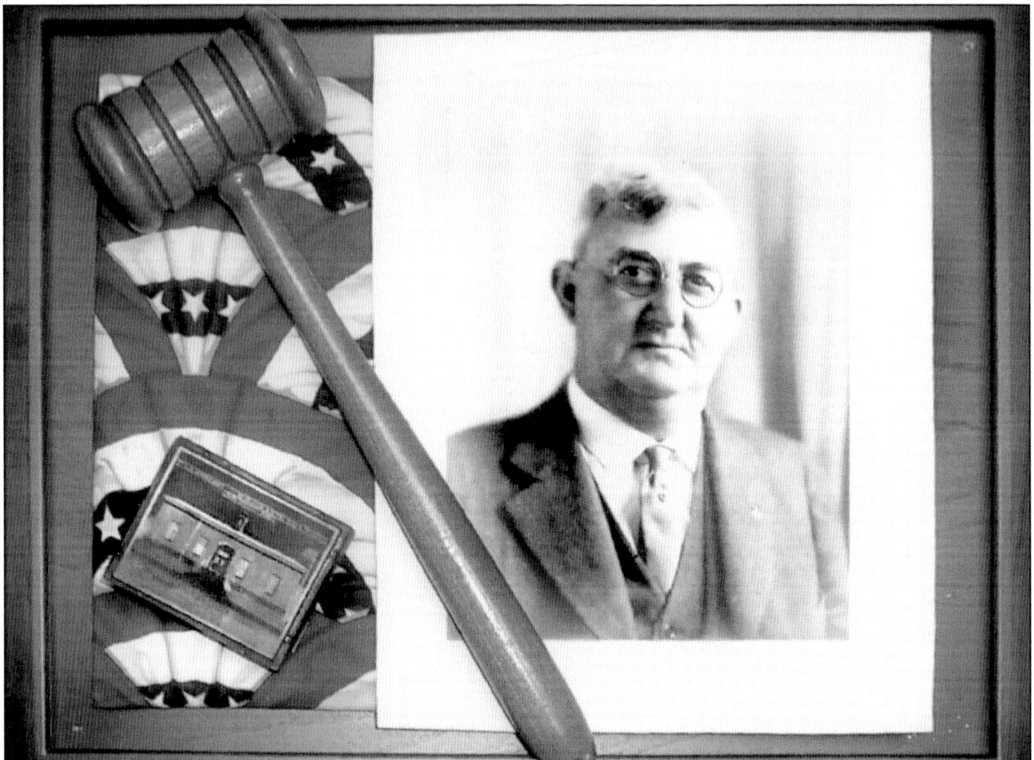

Gill Hannold, the first mayor of Paulsboro, served from 1904 to 1905. He used the gavel shown here in the first official meeting of the borough in 1904. One hundred years have passed since that first meeting, and Paulsboro pride is still very strong in the town we call home.